DECONSTRUCTING ANXIETY

Praise for *Deconstructing Anxiety*

"Fear distorts our perceptions, imprisoning us in views of ourselves and the world that limit our lives and rob us of joy. In this remarkably comprehensive exploration, Dr. Pressman helps us look clearly at our fears and learn not only to face but to transcend them. Integrating insights from diverse psychological traditions, ancient wisdom teachings, and years of clinical practice, he outlines a step-by-step process by which we can unravel our fears, reexamine our assumptions, and find lasting fulfillment. This book can help clinicians and lay people alike free their hearts and minds to live a happier, freer, richer life."—**Ronald D. Siegel, assistant clinical professor of psychology at Harvard Medical School and author of** *The Mindfulness Solution: Everyday Practices for Everyday Problems*

"Fear is the basic cause of anxiety, depression, anger and guilt . . . indeed, the stress reactions that are the cause of virtually all illness. Deconstructing anxiety is the key to health and happiness. This book gives you that key."—**C. Norman Shealy, founding president of the American Holistic Medical Association**

"I have a personal appreciation for the tremendous impact of anxiety, fear and phobia, so I welcome this 'workbook' approach written by my wonderful friend Todd Pressman. I know Todd to be a comforting and calming person, very forthright and refreshing. It is delightful that he is sharing his personal, clinical, and spiritual wisdom with us in this book. This is an important resource that must get out to people!"—**Raymond Moody, author of** *Life After Life*

"This book explores a truly profound and important area and does so in a wonderfully readable, enjoyable fashion. Its central point is well expressed by the Upanishads: 'Where there is other, there is fear.' This notion is greatly expanded upon and creatively explored in the book, with the purpose of helping the reader overcome fear altogether, replacing it with the original, ultimate, and ever-present Oneness . . . whole, coherent, and unified." —**Ken Wilbur, author of** *Integral Meditation*

"Todd Pressman posits that there is a Universal Oneness, a transcendent experience of fulfillment we all share. With the rise of fear and anxiety, this original state was shattered, separating us from it and one another. In *Deconstructing Anxiety*, Pressman takes us on an archeological dig down through the many strata of our fears and defenses to unearth the one core fear at work below all others. More importantly, he helps us find the courage to face it head on, that we may find our way back."—**Sharon Salzberg, Buddhist meditation teacher and author of** *Lovingkindness and Real Happiness*

"A really fascinating book. I've never encountered a deeper analysis of fear than what Todd Pressman offers in *Deconstructing Anxiety*. As he weaves together many strands of psychology and other disciplines, he exposes the lies of fear that shatter our connection with fundamental wholeness. In doing so, Pressman offers a detailed plan to turn the tables and discover lasting peace."—**Seth J. Gillihan, PhD, psychologist and author of** *The CBT Deck* **and** *A Mindful Year*

"Kudos! A truly excellent book. . . . A great book for clients and therapists. Dr. Pressman provides insight and clarity for working through the root causes of crippling anxiety/fear that block a more fulfilling life."—**Peter Gariti, former clinical associate professor of psychiatry in social work, University of Pennsylvania**

"An extraordinary work of love, insight and wisdom. This book weaves together various psychological models, neurophysiology, philosophical perspectives, and historical references to create a thorough and intimate approach to dealing with the fear that limits our ability to be our best. What is unique and refreshing about this work are the concrete exercises, practices, and interventions, with case examples, illustrating the unique process Dr. Pressman offers us from his heart."—**Bernardo Merizalde, MD, psychiatrist and assistant clinical professor at Thomas Jefferson University**

"Todd Pressman is visionary in creating groundbreaking strategies to dismantle the stronghold of anxiety. His work has the potential to promote an 'evolutionary shift.' . . . In distilling human conflict to its fundamentals of fear versus fulfillment, he provides practical strategies to embrace emotional freedom and curate productive ways of relating to the world. From a personal and professional perspective, the tools in *Deconstructing Anxiety* provide lasting outcomes with numerous emotional dividends."—**Christine Batra, licensed associate counselor**

"Dr. Todd Pressman provides a book that this troubled world longs to have. With unique integration, he maps a path for the future understanding of the human condition we are all destined to experience. This book will serve those dedicated to the healing fields as well as those seeking deeper spiritual expression."—**Rabbi Richard Simon, spiritual director and rabbi emeritus, Temple Har Zion**

"Dr. Pressman's latest book provides us with life-changing tools to break the cycle of fear and defense. With wisdom and humanity, he challenges us to free ourselves from the shackles of anxiety and reach our true potential . . . a sense of oneness with the world. Through case studies and step-by-step examples, the reader can easily put into practice the theories and principles in this life-enhancing book. As a fellow clinician, enthusiastic participant of Todd Pressman's seminars, and fellow human searching for fulfillment, I wholeheartedly recommend this book."—**Patricia F. Cooke, licensed professional counselor**

"This captivating book is for anyone fascinated with the workings of the human mind. It is also for anyone working with anxiety. Pressman brings a brilliant mind, warm heart, and keen insight to the subject. He shows us how to live through what we had feared and proves that fear has no substance. He suggests addressing the correct fear in the most accessible way and leads us to solutions through practical, simple, and profound exercises. Reality is re-described and perception illuminated. With examples culled from the great philosophies, religions, literature, science, and stories, along with actual case histories, Pressman encourages our ability to leave behind the fears of separation, emphasizing wholeness, freedom, and fulfillment."—**Ruth Dalphin, licensed acupuncturist and meditation and yoga teacher**

"Truly a breakthrough! An extraordinary analysis that transforms worry and anxiety into fulfillment. Integrative and complete, this book allows for a new view and experience of one's world!"—**Leonard Grossman, philosopher**

"This book offers clinicians and lay people alike an unprecedented guide to understanding the origins of anxiety and an effective strategy for living free of it. A unique perspective that draws from psychology, religion, philosophy, common sense, and years of clinical experience, it deconstructs anxiety and demystifies what can often feel nebulous to even the most seasoned clinician or self-aware individual. This book is an important tool for anyone dealing with anxiety."—**Kelly L. Bassett Buono, MEd, licensed psychoanalyst**

"A truly awesome book . . . a graduate level text for training psychotherapists . . . a lifetime accomplishment. [Appropriate for] students and clinicians, as well as lay people who [seek] enhanced insight into their own or a loved one's anxiety. [It should] become 'state of the art' for practitioners and scholars. Congratulations on this fine work."— **Bonita Blazer, PhD, educational specialist and consultant**

"Compelling! [This book] is not only a formula for individual freedom; it is a compendium of wisdom for . . . liberation."—**Jonathan Cohen, licensed psychologist and leader emeritus of The Mankind Project**

"Dr. Todd Pressman has taken on one of the most important questions in psychology today. Why are so many people, especially teenagers and young adults, having such psychological difficulty? Why so much fear, anxiety, disquiet, and angst? [In this book,] Dr. Pressman helps us to look at the deeper levels of fear, for only there can real change be made. Positive affirmations, exposure therapy, and insight therapy are all potentially helpful, but they don't take us to the bedrock of fear, so no real cure is possible. What is required is that we acknowledge we are responsible for what we see and we choose the feelings we experience. As Dr. Pressman expresses it, 'We must be willing to follow fear to its most subterranean hideout.' Only then can we be free."—**Jon Mundy, author of** *Living a Course in Miracles*

"A valuable therapeutic resource for either clinicians or the general public . . . [with] far-reaching implications for personal well-being and the wellness of society as a whole. The book presents a concise, systematic set of methods for discovering the central fear underlying most psychological difficulties. . . . As a psychologist with thirty years of clinical experience, I can most enthusiastically recommend *Deconstructing Anxiety: The Journey from Fear to Fulfillment*."—**John Monopoli, PhD, clinical psychologist**

"This is fascinating! *Deconstructing Anxiety* . . . is a guide to recognizing and addressing the underlying fears we all carry . . . the exercises will help readers learn to confront and remove barriers that prevent them from . . . living their best lives. [It has] substantially improved my life, helping me see my fears for the illusion they are and allowing me to move more fully into my potential."—**Gail Tishman, Jewish spiritual leader**

"*Deconstructing Anxiety* is an empowering book. It tells us that we are not the victims of our upbringing, our environment, or our biochemistry. By cultivating penetrating insight and making courageous choices, we have the power to change. Part one shines a light into the dark recesses of fear and anxiety and exposes their deceits. Part two is a step-by-step practical guide for breaking their hypnotic spell over our lives and finding fulfillment in living our greater purpose. This is a book for all who deal with fear and anxiety in themselves or others. In other words, it is a work for everyone."—**Richard Katz, founder and codirector of the Flower Essence Society**

"Dr. Todd Pressman does the impressive job of explaining why we have anxiety, how it's a natural phenomenon, and how to work *with* it as opposed to working against it! *Deconstructing Anxiety* is essential reading for professionals and nonprofessionals looking to understand and work with anxiety, resulting in a better and more self-aware tomorrow."—**Rita Sousa, PhD, ACS, CCC, registered psychotherapist**

"An exceptional book on familiar and challenging topics that we all deal with. It points out how we have become accustomed to our fear and that our investment in anxiety is costly. We learn from these pages that fear has no backbone and therefore is approachable with sincere inquiry. This book is unpretentious in its delivery and forthcoming with strategies to achieve results. I recommend suspending doubt and leveraging the exercises to conduct your own examination into the illusions of fear. This book takes what we normally process in our heads and blends it in a way to soothe our hearts."—**James Maskery, MS, program management professional**

"Very insightful! Dr. Pressman draws from his knowledge and experience in psychology and spirituality to guide us in a step-by-step approach to lessening our suffering by

identifying and working through our fears. A great book for layman and professionals."—
Leah Brecher-Cohn, LMFT

"This book can help you learn to live your life without the all-consuming fear that controls our daily existence. Rising above our child-based anxiety, we can see clearly what is real and true, giving us a choice in how to act and enjoy our life, be fulfilled, and most importantly to be happy. It has helped me personally to understand who I am, to rest and relax and not always be on guard, and has made a drastic improvement in my life."—
Ralph Dauito, MD

More Praise for *Deconstructing Anxiety*: Workshops, Lectures, and Continuing Education Seminars

"Outstanding presentation. . . . Ingenious. . . . This is worth the world's attention."—
Stanley Krippner, PhD, psychologist and author

"One of the most exciting things I've come across in a long time."—**G.S., program director**

"Hands down the best hour and a half of the conference for me."—**Y.R., licensed psychologist**

"I loved, loved, loved your training—for me it was life-changing."—**S.C., licensed professional counselor**

"That short presentation of yours that I attended . . . has breathed new life into the anxiety work I do."—**E.G., licensed clinical social worker**

"Awesome. Transformative training."—**P.B., educator**

"Great and enthusiastic presentation . . . inspiring."—**P.R., psychologist**

"Extremely enlightening."—**J.S., social worker**

"Rare wisdom."—**F.D., executive**

"One of the best seminars I've attended!"—**S.H., education specialist**

"Excellent. Interesting, passionate, empathic presenter."—**F.F., licensed clinical social worker**

"Extremely worthwhile."—**J.P., licensed professional counselor**

"The exercises were so powerful for me and so timely. I had just received a very alarming e-mail from my family of origin in crisis. I was filled with anxiety, but since doing the exercises it is gone."—**S.B., licensed clinical social worker**

"A whole new perspective on anxiety."—**J.B., psychologist**

"Fascinating."—**S.K., social worker**

"I highly recommend [this seminar for] mental health professionals, allied health professionals, and lay people interested in learning about an effective technique for addressing anxiety, depression, and irrational fears. I will definitely be incorporating it into my training and practice."—**L.M.W., licensed psychologist**

"One of the best teachers I ever had for a professional training conference."—**I.F., masters in social work**

"The information and techniques are relevant to many of the patients I see and will be of great value to me in assisting them. It gave me very clearly defined methods for helping patients resolve fear."—**W.M., licensed clinical social worker**

"Enlightened, passionate teacher."—**G.M., licensed clinical social worker**

"Extraordinarily important."—**P.D., psychologist**

"This is absolutely masterful."—**S.W., psychologist**

"A significant contribution."—**J.D., licensed clinical social worker**

"Favorite course I have ever taken!"—**B.R., graduate student**

"Best professional development course I've attended"—**A.M., psychologist**

"What an excellent and useful program! I thoroughly enjoyed the . . . exposure to new ideas, theory, and techniques."—**B.C., psychiatrist**

"This training is one of the best trainings that I have ever done. . . . It will absolutely enable me to better help my clients and enhance my career."—**R.T., licensed clinical social worker**

"Powerful and very useful."—**N.E., executive**

"It was an extremely interesting and helpful seminar. One of the very best I have attended."—**G.S., nurse practitioner**

"It was a superb lecture."—**B.N., licensed professional counselor**

"This was an excellent talk—by far one of the most clinically relevant talks I have attended."—**J.W., psychologist**

"Amazing."—**B.P., special education teacher**

"This was an excellent presentation that gave me the opportunity to experience the transformational power of Dr. Pressman's work."—**A.R., psychoanalyst**

"A *very* effective way to have the therapist address their own fears in order to help others."—**M.R., psychiatrist**

"I got a lot out of this training, which is high praise for me."—**C.S., clinical director**

"Outstanding. Probably the most helpful course I've ever taken."—**T.J., licensed professional counselor**

DECONSTRUCTING ANXIETY

The Journey from Fear to Fulfillment

Todd E. Pressman

ROWMAN & LITTLEFIELD
Lanham • Boulder • New York • London

Published by Rowman & Littlefield
An imprint of The Rowman & Littlefield Publishing Group, Inc.
4501 Forbes Boulevard, Suite 200, Lanham, Maryland 20706
www.rowman.com

6 Tinworth Street, London SE11 5AL

British Library Cataloguing in Publication Information Available

Library of Congress Cataloging-in-Publication Data

Name: Pressman, Todd Evan, author.
Title: Deconstructing anxiety : the journey from fear to fulfillment / Todd E. Pressman.
Description: Lanham : Rowman & Littlefield Publishing Group, Inc., [2019] | Includes biblio-
     graphical references and index.
Identifiers: LCCN 2019011270 (print) | LCCN 2019012654 (ebook) | ISBN 9781538125410 (elec-
     tronic) | ISBN 9781538125397 (cloth : alk. paper) | ISBN 9781538125403 (pbk. : alk. paper)
Subjects: LCSH: Anxiety. | Fear. | Mindfulness (Psychology)
Classification: LCC BF575.A6 (ebook) | LCC BF575.A6 P734 2019 (print) | DDC 152.4/6—dc23
LC record available at https://lccn.loc.gov/2019011270

♾ ™ The paper used in this publication meets the minimum requirements of
American National Standard for Information Sciences Permanence of Paper
for Printed Library Materials, ANSI/NISO Z39.48-1992.

CONTENTS

FOREWORD

Stanley Krippner, PhD

These times are often called "The Age of Anxiety," though it seems as if fear and apprehension have always characterized the human condition. In this remarkable book, Todd Pressman gives us a new understanding of the causes of anxiety and how it can be healed at the source. He proposes not only that anxiety creates a distorted perspective but also that this can be deconstructed and resolved, paving the way to a more fulfilling life.

From the first time I met him, I was aware of Todd's curiosity about the nature of human beings and their relationship to the world. He pursued this interest with unusual zeal, always seeking to find answers for our suffering in the service of greater fulfillment. He is now sharing what he learned in this outstanding book.

In *Deconstructing Anxiety*, Pressman considers that, although dysfunctional, people become "hypnotized" by fear to the point that it becomes their overriding mood. He posits that fear is not "real" and one may discover as much with a thorough deconstruction. Even when a rational person sees that most apprehensions never materialize, it can still be difficult to avoid their influence. But Pressman proposes a "three doorways" model for addressing this problem—in mind, body, and spirit. One of the treats of the book is Pressman's application of this model to show why some of the major approaches for dealing with anxiety have yielded only moderate success.

Readers are then taken on a mythological sojourn as Pressman re-envisions the creation story, showing how anxious people have fallen away from the "state of oneness" that is their true home. Perception frames our individual and consensual realities, helping us to "see" our world in a manner that is more functional. Anxiety is described as being the root of all suffering, taking five primary forms: abandonment, identity, meaning, purpose, and death. Each of these has its own developmental pathway, one that varies from individual to individual, as well as from culture to culture.

For the Buddha, desire was the basis of suffering. For Pressman, it is anxiety, and he shows the connection between the two. It seems to me that in both cases there is a mismatch between perceptions and emotions, and therefore the reality they are supposed to represent. This creates a consensus reality based on anxiety, a worldview that the collective will try to preserve. Pressman's model is designed to move that consensus reality closer to "true" reality. The closer the alignment between the two, the more joy results. The more accurately a "map" describes a territory, the more likely people are to reach their destinations.

Pressman presents several important and new concepts within his approach, including the "deceptions and manipulations" of fear, a three-phase model of personality development, the five universal themes of loss, and a blueprint for realizing fulfillment. The approach as a whole can be considered transpersonal in its conception of an original state of "oneness"—how it was lost and how it can be regained. This hero's journey is also existential in that anxiety is rooted in concerns affecting one's daily existence. Such a "transpersonal existentialism" might provide the basis for a psychotherapy that is truly holistic.

Pressman's exercises in the book's second half are both ingenious and well-described. This is the most valuable part of *Deconstructing Anxiety*, transforming it into a viable "self-help" manual. It is here that Pressman builds a creative synthesis, joining principles from psychodynamic, cognitive-behavioral, mindfulness, and other practices to compose an entirely new approach to healing. Readers are guided to discover their "core fear" and "chief defense," presented as the true source of suffering, and then given the tools for transforming them. A section on resolving the "resistance to resistance" opens up new avenues for dismantling that which gives rise to anxiety in the first place.

The final chapter, "Vision Questing," brings readers to the end of their journey with the real possibility of fulfillment. They have deconstructed their fears in both the architectural use of the term and also the postmodernist's application. The former provides a step-by-step developmental sequence, while the latter employs a critical analysis. Both are needed for a complete approach. In this book, Pressman has combined spirituality and science, image and symbol, deconstruction and rebuilding, in a delightful yet profound adventure.

PREFACE

This book promises a revolution in thought. It offers what you will likely find to be a radically new understanding of the cause of suffering and how to relieve it. It makes the remarkable claim that fear (considered here as a generic term for "anxiety"), and fear alone, is the source of all such suffering. If, then, we were to thoroughly deconstruct the mechanics of fear—that which creates and sustains it—we might peer into the essential secrets of the human predicament and find new answers for its resolution. And without the constraints of fear, our way would then be cleared for the pursuit of a transcendent fulfillment. In the end, this book becomes a quest for just such a fulfillment, meeting the five universal needs we will discuss: love, identity, meaning, purpose, and even a peaceful acceptance of death.

The model and techniques presented here are the result of my own intensive explorations, both personally and professionally. These explorations have been the work of a lifetime, beginning at age twelve. In truth, I suppose, they began with a very happy childhood, thanks to my two greatest influences . . . my parents. My father was a psychoanalyst when it was still a new discipline in America and, as he would often say, "the only game in town." His teachers were students of Freud himself so I like to imagine I'm a fourth-generation Freudian. But he was a true explorer and his own search took him far into fields of Eastern and even mystical teachings, which he successfully integrated with his traditional training. My mother was a social worker and biofeedback therapist, but her greatest legacy to me was to exemplify the true meaning of love. No doubt, the influence of my parents gave me the inner conviction as well as the determination to pursue the kind of fulfillment promoted in this book.

At age twelve I had an overwhelming experience of what is sometimes called the "Void." Confronted with the existential truths that came with awakening adulthood, I was stunned by the emptiness of our social constructions, our fundamental aloneness, and the inevitability of death. Like all good adolescents, I was plunged into the throes of significant inner turmoil. The wonderful container of my childhood innocence had been lost. I was staring into an infinite universe, unable to avoid my apparent insignificance in the face of it.

This set me on an intense search for meaning. I spontaneously began a process of deconstructing my experience by asking a series of "Why?" questions—for example, "Why do we suffer?" and in response to whatever answer came forth, "Why is that so?" responding to each new answer with another such "Why?" in an effort to get to the bottom of things. To my surprise, I discovered that every time I did this, I would find some fear hiding at the deeper layers of this deconstruction. Every time. I sensed that I had happened on something of vital importance, a key puzzle piece in the problem of the human experience.

Around this time, my father began immersing himself in Eastern psychology and Western esoteric teachings. I remember overhearing him say, "Everything is made of consciousness" and "All is part of a Oneness." I didn't really understand what these ideas meant at the time but something about them sent my antennae up. We began having conversations, I read what he read, and together we attended conferences such as Council Grove and those of the International Transpersonal Association. Slowly I began to collate a framework for understanding the teachings of the "perennial philosophy," giving structure to my own experience.

Then in my senior year of college, I was fortunate enough to participate in a program called Semester at Sea. This was a fantastic trip around the world on a cruise ship outfitted to be a "floating campus." We would take classes while at sea—I focused on religious studies and anthropology courses—and then visit the countries and cultures we had just studied. Several experiences on this trip opened my eyes to the farther reaches of human potential. In the jungles of Sri Lanka, I witnessed authentic firewalking, a secret and sacred tradition passed down from father to son through the generations. In Kyoto, I meditated on the famous rock garden in the Zen monastery of Ryoanji and learned of the principle of "emptiness." I celebrated with fakirs in Bali who, while deep in trance, had hooks dug into their backs as a sacrifice to their deities. The fakirs quivered with ecstasy; there was no blood or evidence of pain. And I exchanged with a Zoroastrian high priest outside the Fire Temple of Mumbai while staying with a Jain family whose reverence for life had them feeding sugar to the ants in the kitchen at night. This cross-cultural sampling of so many expressions of humanity and their attempt to create meaning in the human condition was, for me, life-changing.

When I returned from this experience, I felt a great need to deepen my own path. It was at this time that I picked up my father's copy of *A Course in Miracles* (1975). This extraordinary psychological and spiritual teaching spoke to me like nothing I had encountered before. It introduced the idea, in unequivocal terms, that fear is the only source of suffering and that it is, as we will also discuss, an "illusion." More importantly, it assured me of the possibility of transcending my limitations and finding an ultimate experience of fulfillment.

After college at the University of Pennsylvania, I chose psychology as a career path. I enrolled in Saybrook University for my doctorate work, a wonderful school that supported my interest in consciousness studies while providing a broad knowledge base in traditional psychology as well. During this period, I was also highly attracted to the teachings of Zen Buddhism and spent considerable time visiting and practicing as a lay student at the Zen Mountain Monastery in upstate New York.

All of this came out of an inexhaustible drive to solve the question of suffering and recapture a fulfillment I had once known. But if I were to integrate everything I had learned in an authentic way, I would have to make it "work" in my own life. And so, over the years, I developed the techniques presented in this book. As I discovered what these techniques could do for me personally, I would apply them to the clients I was now seeing in private practice. Learning from each person I worked with, I refined this evolving model into my first book, *Radical Joy: Awakening Your Potential for True Fulfillment* (1999). Over the past twenty years, significant new developments and refinements have occurred, resulting in the need for another book . . . the one you are now reading.

As you read this book, you will be, in a sense, recapitulating my own journey. Together, we will explore the deep recesses of the unconscious, encountering the twin drives of fear and fulfillment. We will then revisit the creation story to witness the birth of fear, discovering how the psyche organizes itself around anxiety. Next, we will investigate the mysteries of perception, learning that when we put on fear-colored lenses, a world of suffering appears before our eyes. Understanding that we get lost in this world by virtue of taking it as real, we begin to find a viable path to resolving our problems. We realize that what we were so upset by is only a projection of fear, casting dark and grotesque images before our eyes. Next, we will deconstruct the architecture of anxiety, introducing the dynamics of the "core fear" (our basic interpretation of danger) and "chief defense" (our primary strategy for protecting ourselves from it). We will then uncover the progression by which our entire personality gets built upon the foundation of these dynamics.

With our hands on the controls of perception and insight into the constructs of our experience, we are ready for the second stage of our journey. Here we enter into a training program that will set us free from our projections and unravel our anxiety. This program involves powerful and highly effective techniques—including the Alchemist, the Witness, and the Warrior's Stance—that are unique in their approach to the release from suffering. Because they are derived from a fully deconstructed analysis, they offer the potential for resolving anxiety in a deep and lasting way. And with this, at last, the path to fulfillment opens before us. In the final chapter, we will embark on a "vision quest" to translate our newfound freedom into actions that create meaningful change, in pursuit of the transcendent fulfillment we seek.

Research is currently underway demonstrating the effectiveness of this model. It is being offered as a six- to ten-week program for resolving not just anxiety but depression, loneliness, "stress," relationship struggles, and more, each understood as having anxiety at their root. Jason, a forty-four-year-old man with extreme social anxiety, went through the program and concluded, "At one point during the exercise, my anxiety just floated away; I can see it so clearly . . . it's simply not real. It lost its ability to fool me." Carol, a seventy-two-year-old woman who had suffered from a lifetime of depression and loneliness, ended up saying, "I guess there isn't anything we can't become peaceful with" when discovering a calm in the midst of her greatest fear of being isolated. Debbie described her unyielding anger at a neglectful mother as being "absorbed by a higher purpose" while she let go of a painful identity as someone who had to be dutiful and compliant. And Jenny had a profound experience of the "death" of her consuming obsessions as she then watched herself being "reborn from a blob of potential" that she could shape and develop as she wished, free from the obsessions that had plagued her.

Therapists, too, are reporting great success in using these strategies. One described uncovering an early trauma that was clearly at the root of her client's difficulties. The client was at first confused and then surprised by the discovery, saying, "I could never have imagined the answer would be so simple. I guess, if it's that simple, there's nothing keeping me tied to my pain." Other clinicians have described the techniques as "life changing" for their clients, with "breakthroughs in the first session." Many have stated the program has given them "a whole new perspective on anxiety" and have found it to be "deeply moving and extremely effective."

A note to psychotherapists: This book is certainly intended to be a manual for clinicians to use in their treatment of clients, anxious or otherwise. But it is also written in a way that can benefit anyone interested in healing and growth. You will notice that I have chosen the terms "you" and "we" throughout this book to adequately address both groups. This language is appropriate for several reasons. First, I believe it's important to acknowledge that we, psychotherapists and clients, are "in it" together. As clinicians, we are assigned a role of authority, guide or mentor. This can make it tempting to appear as though we are "above it all," hiding behind a fear of acknowledging our fears. Not only does this impede our own path, it deprives our clients of the chance to learn by our example. Next, I firmly believe the optimal way to learn a new theory and technique is by going through the program yourself. And finally, resolving our own anxieties evokes our deeper potential in general, including enabling us, as therapists, to better help our clients. For all these reasons, I encourage you to consider undertaking the program yourself before applying it to your clients.

And a note to non-professionals: If you are reading this book, it is likely because you want to find relief from your own suffering. Or perhaps you are simply in hot pursuit of a greater fulfillment. If you are eager to dive right into the exercises in the second half of the book, by all means, feel free. You'll want to come back later to the theory of the first half that, I believe, is necessary for completing the shift into a worldview that can transform your understanding of who you are and the nature of reality.

Whether professional or layperson, anxiety sufferer or purpose seeker, you will find in this book an entirely new theory and practice for resolving anxiety and all that blocks our fulfillment. The clarity of this model makes it possible to see that fear is truly the only barrier in our way. With this, we may reliably transmute habitual response into free choice, anxiety into empowerment, and the obstacles of our frustration into opportunities for a deep and lasting fulfillment.

PROLOGUE
The Three Postulates

1. There is an absolute truth that can be realized. It brings a transcendent experience of fulfillment and is characterized by wholeness, completion, and freedom from limitation. It is our original and natural state.

    This is the premise of the book.

2. Fear (anxiety) distorts this truth, fracturing it into partial, relative "truths." It breaks up the wholeness, leaving us feeling incomplete and vulnerable to suffering. It separates us from our natural state.

    This is the theory of the book.

3. Deconstructing anxiety resolves fear's distortions, opening the way back to absolute truth and returning us to our natural state of fulfillment.

    This is the practice of the book.

INTRODUCTION

All of us suffer from anxiety. Not necessarily the clinical type, but anxiety nonetheless. Philosophers, psychologists, and spiritual adepts have always pointed to fear in some form as the fundamental problem of the human condition.[1] Our vulnerability in the face of an unfathomable universe can leave us feeling helpless, exposed, and profoundly overwhelmed. When asking the inevitable existential questions—"Who am I?" "Why am I here?" "Is there meaning to life?" "What is to be done about suffering?" and "How can I be happy?"—we hear our questions echoing in a seemingly endless void. But these questions, the essence of our human predicament, beg for answers. We are compelled to rise above our unknowingness, to find some mastery over our circumstances, no matter how daunting the task. We cannot quit in this; our need for answers will not relent. It is a task worthy of our greatest devotion. In the end, what else really matters?

And that is our purpose in coming together here. With the understanding that fear is the fundamental problem in being human, we have our starting point. To pursue this quest, we must fully deconstruct anxiety, reveal its origins and mechanism, and find its resolution. While this book can serve as a manual for those working with identified anxiety, anyone who seeks to resolve suffering in general and discover a true fulfillment in life will find a path here.

The three postulates prepare us for this path (see the prologue). Despite the anxiety that seems inherent in our state of affairs, there is something in the human spirit that yearns for an absolute truth, a transcendent experience beyond fear's reach.[2] It is a yearning to be whole and fulfilled, to find a unified and harmonious way of being beyond all relative, shifting states. We long to know who we truly are, with a constant and certain sense of self. Exhausted from the ever-fluctuating moods and changing identities of our usual experience, we seek a solid place to stand. We want a satisfaction that does not continually give way to disappointment, to know that we live in more than a random, chaotic universe. We are called to find something greater, something that is, indeed, absolute.

Too often, though, this seems an impossible challenge. We arrive in the world ready to be afraid. Helpless and vulnerable, we are completely dependent on others. Bit by bit, we become caught in a web of defensive postures and self-protective maneuvers to ensure our needs will be met. Fear becomes our chief advisor in this effort. We learn to seek its counsel first in every situation. Its strategies are supposed to provide security but inevitably lock us into ever-more-fearful ways of being. Like a hermit crab peering out of its shell, we move through life anxiously looking for signs of danger, ready at an instant to jump back inside and hide behind our door.

This fearful approach to life exacts an extraordinary toll. Its walls of security place blinders on our experience and boundaries on our potential. Like looking into a broken mirror, they fracture the unified truth we seek into many partial views, vacillating perspectives that can leave us hopelessly lost about who we are and how to be happy. We try valiantly to accept that this is the best we can expect—a sort of truce with our suffering—buying into the social conditioning that this is what it means to be "well adjusted." Still, the need for something greater, for a deep and true fulfillment, will not leave us. And so we live in a constant state of restlessness, complying with fear yet yearning for wholeness.

It has become "fashionable" to accept the inevitability of our human condition, to believe that transcendence and an absolute truth are not possible. We are, as a culture, cynical and suspicious of anything that suggests this transcendent view. Many will vehemently defend their cynicism, but their vehemence gives us cause to question their objectivity. The stance that says we must "accept reality" (while certainly an advance beyond Pollyanna-type thinking) will always leave us unsatisfied, even dejected. And what is the value of accepting a "truth" that does not promote well-being? No matter how convinced we are that there is no absolute truth, we simply cannot rest until we pursue the question further. When negating the possibility of transcendence we must instead ask, Why do I need to defend this position? What is the fear if I at least consider the alternative?

Furthermore, what if the idea that there is no absolute truth is *itself* a relative truth, the result (as in our second postulate) of hidden fears not fully examined? What if the only reason we have not experienced an ultimate state is that we have not yet fully deconstructed and resolved our fear, seeing it all the way through to its other side (the third postulate)? We cannot afford to predetermine that this goal is out of reach before finding out for ourselves whether this is so.

AN IRREFUTABLE ANSWER!

The second postulate—Fear distorts truth—and the third postulate—Working through fear paves the way to truth—provide the great key to answering these questions. And the answer is irrefutable. For it *must* be so that fear distorts truth because by definition, fear makes us too afraid to see the truth of things calmly and objectively. Fear causes us to invest ourselves in seeing the truth we wish to see, not the truth that is. This is perhaps the single most important principle we can rely on to find a path to freedom. Simply put, fear makes us afraid to see reality as it is— we *need* to see it in a way that makes us feel safe. Freeing ourselves from fear, therefore, necessarily reveals the truth behind the distortion. This, then, becomes our task: to let go of any investment in seeing things as we wish to see them, becoming willing to see them as they are, whatever we may discover.

And this applies to how we approach the question of an absolute truth. If we reject the possibility out of hand before adopting such a willingness to consider it, it can only be because there is a hidden investment—a secret need based on fear—making this decision for us. Similarly, if we insist on any particular point of view at all before being willing to be wrong, we may be sure there is an unexamined fear driving the insistence. Our exploration begins with the decision to follow the trail of this fear, deconstructing it all the way to completion so that we may then make a clear assessment of whether the transcendent view we seek is possible.

This point cannot be overstated. If we reject an idea (such as the possibility of an absolute truth), if we cling to a point of view, we must be willing to look at whether we have fully and honestly examined our reasons for doing so. We must always consider whether a hidden fear has us invested in a need to reject a thing, with a secret agenda to preserve our convictions. The *only* guiding principle we can rely on is that fear obliges us to see what we wish to see, not what is. This becomes our test of truth in every situation. If we want to know whether an absolute truth is possible, we must make certain we are unafraid to consider it. We cannot afford to sell ourselves short in this endeavor. The stakes are no less than our chance for freedom from fear and the discovery of our fulfillment.

And yet the resistance to doing so can be enormous. Wars and crusades have been engaged because of just such an investment in beliefs. It is the source of political partisanship, cultish behavior, and the wide variety of relationship struggles. All of these and more are built on fear's strategy of self-protection and security. If we seek a true fulfillment, free from the anxiety behind such an approach, we must find our way to resolving the fear that has been distorting our view.[3]

Of course, it can be challenging, to say the least, to break from the consensus. Our enculturation conditions us to buy into the strategy of fear. Seeing everyone around us doing the same, we become afraid of not playing the game of fear! In fact, we are socialized into this from the first moments of our life, as we will see. Nevertheless, we are left exhausted and depressed by this worldview and long for a different approach to life, one that offers the chance to breathe freely once again.

Our postulates propose this alternate approach. Without fear imposing its blinders and distortions, there is nothing to limit our infinite view, a view that explains all relative truths in a sort of unified field theory and shows us the way back to freedom. As with the fractals of chaos theory, when we rise above our fear, we see the tangled web of differences around us resolve into an elegant whole, a whole that is coherent, purposeful, and beautiful. But to attain this view, we must not let a worn-out conviction in fear stop us from even attempting the climb.

Deep within each of us is still the sense of wonder and awe, the love for life, that was natural to us as children. It was then that, as Emily Dickinson (2005) says, we dwelt "in Possibility," a place where we could spread "wide our narrow Hands / To gather Paradise." Deconstructing anxiety is how we reawaken this potential. Whether it is an actual memory, perhaps faded into unawareness, or merely a longing waiting to be fulfilled, we will discover that this sense lives within us still. This is not meant as a platitude and is certainly beyond wishful thinking (for it will take courage and honesty to direct our attention to fear). The postulates propose that before the learned repressions of fear, before we became jaded by the heaviness of life and its apparent disappointments, we knew this truth. Again, as I will show, it was completely natural to us. And this, precisely this, is what gives rise to the urge for transcendence of our sorrowful state and the call for a greater fulfillment. Somewhere inside we still know of this fulfillment, though it may be buried under layers of forgotten dreams, painful life experience, or the imposed pain of others who have lived too long under the dictates of fear.

It is my great hope that this book will serve as an instrument for helping people rediscover this potential, this truth that can be known beyond all relative truths. Yes, this book is a program for treating anxiety. But per the postulates, once anxiety is out of the way, transcendence is inevitable. No matter how indoctrinated we may have become by social conditioning, the mass hypnosis that would have us believe such thinking is a fantasy, I invite you to listen deeply to see if there isn't still a call for this kind of freedom and this kind of fulfillment. The three postulates and the principles in this book lay out the pathway. Let us not close the door on the possibility before finding out if it might just be attainable.

NOTES

1. We will be using the terms "fear" and "anxiety" interchangeably throughout this book. The *Diagnostic and Statistical Manual of Mental Disorders* of the American Psychiatric Association says that fear is a response to an imminent threat whereas anxiety is anticipation of a future threat. We will, instead, adopt the view that when we anticipate future threat, we are experiencing it internally as if it were happening now. It therefore has the same effect as a response to something imminent. Furthermore, it is only our fear of

what an imminent threat will lead to (in the future) that causes our distress. As we will show, our experience of the actual problem, when it arrives, is absent the quality of fear.

2. Our discussion of absolute truth has nothing to do with dogma or "belief." In fact, as will be seen, the absolute truth we are describing comes only when we let go of such relative belief systems. We seek something more than arbitrarily chosen beliefs; we are in search of an experience that transcends and is invulnerable to these kinds of limitations.

3. As an obvious example, the person who strives to find fulfillment by thinking positively all the time or using motivation to pump themselves up and keep negativity at bay is clearly afraid when you ask them to consider relaxing this stance for a moment. If their path were strong, they would not be afraid of the suggestion; they would simply explore the possibility in an open and confident way, trusting that their positive experience would prevail. They would have nothing to prove in advance. Some will protest that fear is necessary for survival, that it is, in fact, part and parcel of the survival instinct. Even more, people will argue that fear compels us to excel and do our best, a safeguard to make sure we don't fail in our efforts. After all, doesn't fear of failure motivate the college student to get good grades, or the Olympic athlete to push themselves further, or the corporate executive to find ways to improve the bottom line? But all of these accomplishments are just as achievable without fear. We can pursue them, as we will discover throughout this book, just as well (in fact, better) from an inherent drive for fulfillment. We can pursue them because of the joy they bring, because of the satisfaction of expressing ourselves completely. And when there is no fear behind the motivation, we liberate enormous reserves of energy that would have otherwise been spent on fueling the tension required to push against our imagined threats. These points will be examined in depth later on.

Part I

Theoretical Foundations

I

FEAR AND FULFILLMENT—
TWO DRIVES IN CONFLICT

The Human Drama

[The mind of fear] is torn with doubt, confused about itself and all it sees; afraid and angry, weak and blustering, afraid to go ahead, afraid to stay, afraid to waken or to go to sleep, afraid of every sound, yet more afraid of stillness; terrified of darkness, yet more terrified at the approach of light. . . .

[Resolving fear] is the answer to your search for peace. Here is the key to meaning in a world that seems to make no sense. Here is the way to safety in apparent dangers that appear to threaten you at every turn, and bring uncertainty to all your hopes of ever finding quietness and peace. Here are all questions answered; here the end of all uncertainty ensured at last.

—Foundation for Inner Peace, *A Course in Miracles* (1975)

Fear and fulfillment. These are the prime movers of our life, the two great forces that drive the human experience. Fear is a constant companion. It whispers in our ears of lurking dangers and impending catastrophes, making us ever hesitant, squashing our deep potential. Fulfillment is our high purpose, that which calls us from our most secret places and compels us to discover a freedom and wholeness far beyond what we had thought possible. These two forces engage in a constant battle within. If we forgo our fulfillment and succumb to fear, we are never fully satisfied. Our potential relentlessly insists that we realize its promise. But, fear warns us, if we venture forth, we risk the unknown; we are sure to encounter all sorts of perils and should, instead, play it safe.

Our solution, as a humanity, is to try to satisfy both drives. This results in a strange phenomenon: we convince ourselves that fear is the best strategy for finding and securing fulfillment. It is our safeguard against anything that can compromise our plans or threaten the integrity of who we are. We have an impulse for fulfillment—a desire to connect with someone or an urge for creative expression—and immediately consult our fear to negotiate the terms in a way we deem safe. Fear becomes our provocateur, rooting out from dark corners anything that might signal danger. Once fear tells us we are vulnerable, our purposes at risk, we embrace it as a technique. It becomes our warning device for taking the actions that will protect our fulfillment.

Unfortunately, the strategy backfires; it is impossible to be fulfilled while we are in fear. Not only does fear keep our attention on danger, but we know we can never truly prevent all potential threats. Our response to this is to dig in more deeply, devoting ourselves to an even greater control over danger. We fool ourselves into believing we are working toward the day when we will finally achieve the safety we seek, free to get about the business of fulfillment. Of course, that day never comes. As the Chinese proverb states, "We are always preparing to live."

Once again, it is impossible to manage fear and pursue fulfillment at the same time. The result of this faulty strategy is that the more we try to protect our fulfillment, the further we get from it. Bit by bit we become ensnared in the ways of fear, forgetting they were to be a means toward a different end. We magnify the problem even further, imagining we must protect ourselves not only from the threats in front of us but those we can forecast in the future. In short, we create an extraordinarily tangled knot of fear that never gives us the realization we seek. [1]

This is the human drama that has been playing out in every culture of every age. Our first and greatest drive is for fulfillment—we know this experience when we watch a newborn filled with the joy of being[2]—and we will not be satisfied until we reach it. Our soul rattles its cage not just for relief from anxiety but to actively create our good. But the seduction of fear is powerful. We can't really afford to dwell in the joy of the moment, it tells us. We must keep our eye on looming dangers or the possibility of a sneak attack. So we make the decision to take care of fear first, somehow hoping to get things under control in a complete and permanent way. This and only this, we have become convinced, will leave us free to live joyfully once again.[3]

When we look around at our current state of affairs, the tragic effects of this strategy are all too evident. Security is the overwhelming goal for most of us, with fulfillment getting postponed to the point of being almost forgotten. It has us live in ever-more-constricted ways, ever-more-confined territory. Fear's boundaries squeeze our once expansive, exuberant selves into a very tiny space. We learn to delay gratification, taking care of responsibilities, working to handle problems, before we can get around to what makes life really worthwhile. There seems to be always one more thing to handle, and then one more and one more. Again and again we tolerate the frustration of postponing our fulfillment until we become rigidified in a posture of waiting. When this goes on long enough, we can indeed forget our original goal.

The great irony of our approach to fulfillment, using fear as our guide, is that it is precisely the approach that will keep us from it. As very young children, we didn't have a "drive" for fulfillment because we were already established in it. We followed the flow[4] of wherever fulfillment would take us, whether chasing a butterfly, exploring the woods, or laying back in the grass to watch the shifting shapes of the clouds. But once we bring in concerns about preserving the experience, we step outside this flow. Over a lifetime of such concerns, we see our opportunity for fulfillment slipping by. We become stunned by how hard life can be, how much we've lost, how far we have fallen from the dreams and high expectations of our early life. This is why so many of us become disillusioned in the end. Because we have sought to get control over a fulfillment that never comes, the futility of the effort catches up with us and we are confronted with our emptiness. We find either that we never really had control or that it wasn't truly fulfilling. And yet as many times as we hear "Money can't buy you happiness," "You can't take it with you," or "He who dies with the most toys wins," we choose this illusion of control again and again. In the end, we become depleted, disheartened, frustrated, and profoundly sad as we realize that our efforts to control fear and guarantee fulfillment cannot work. The exigencies of life see to that.[5]

RAMIFICATIONS

Our global situation gives us a humbling perspective on the effects of our strategy for fulfillment-through-fear. We ravage the environment out of a fear of want even though we understand we are hardly leaving a legacy for our children. We go to war out of fear of losing our possessions even though so many whose possessions we are fighting for will die in the process. And on and on the list goes. Everywhere we feel this tension as humanity escalates its anxious and self-protective ways.

The rising incidence of clinical anxiety also bears witness to the havoc created by the strategy of fear. Anxiety is now the most commonly diagnosed psychiatric disorder in America, with more than 18 percent of us suffering from it. It has been aptly described as a "modern day plague" (Williamson, 2017), costing more than $300 billion in medical bills and lost productivity every year. And the statistics are mounting at an alarming rate. In 1997, we spent $900 million on anxiety medications; in seven short years that total more than doubled to $2.1 billion (Clark, 2011). Furthermore, we seem to be getting more anxious at earlier ages. According to psychologist Robert Leahy, "the average high school kid today has the same level of anxiety as the average psychiatric patient in the early 1950s" (Clark, 2011). Think of what this means: in the early 1950s, what high schoolers today have learned to tolerate as "normal" was considered a medical crisis requiring professional help.

WHAT'S MISSING?

How have things gotten so out of control? Why have we become so entrenched in fear as the way to ensure fulfillment, even when we see that it isn't working and is making us miserable? How does fear convince us to keep pace with its demands, and more importantly, what do we do about it? If we consider clinical anxiety as simply an exaggerated form of the fear we all struggle with, the problem can truly be said to be epidemic, the need universal.

Despite our most intelligent and determined efforts, we still don't have a really clear understanding of fear. Even our best psychotherapies for treating anxiety are not exactly hitting it out of the park. According to one meta-analysis from the Canadian Psychological Association, our success rate in treating various anxiety disorders averages around only 45 percent. In general, the meta-analyses show that cognitive-behavioral therapy (CBT) is the most effective technique available for anxiety. But in their study, Hofmann and Smits (2008) conclude that "while CBT is effective, there is considerable room for improvement." And one of the most noted authorities on the use of CBT has said the therapist should "fail as quickly as possible" when applying up to fifty different techniques for treating anxiety, to find one that will work (Burns, personal correspondence). While the array of techniques is impressive, we need a more targeted, efficient approach, one built on greater clarity about what is really going on with anxiety—why our treatments work sometimes and fail at other times. Again, we need to ask the vital questions: What makes anxiety so compelling? How does it co-opt the brain to become so maddeningly fixed and unyielding? What are we missing in our understanding?

The problem is that *we have not yet fully deconstructed anxiety*. We have not yet achieved a successful analysis of exactly how it works—the precise mechanisms that create it, maintain it, give it its power, and make it so intractable. Our paradigms have been incomplete. We need a comprehensive model for understanding and working with the fear at the root of our difficulties, a Rosetta Stone for cracking its code. Such a model would, according to our three postulates, not only unravel the mystery of anxiety but would illuminate its secret gift. For, as we have said, finding fear's cure reveals the path to transcending suffering in general, providing a map to deep fulfillment, healthy relationships, and a more functional world.

And why has this been so elusive? Why are we only sometimes successful in our treatments? Simply put, whenever a therapeutic intervention fails to produce the desired results, it is because it has not yet *fully* deconstructed fear in these ways. It is, in fact, rare for a therapy to find the true root of fear. Fear's trickery depends upon its ability to convince us not to look at it deeply (see chapter 2). In clinical language, we say fear is hallmarked by avoidance behaviors. We seem to be reflexively wired to respond to fear with these avoidance behaviors.[6]

THE FEAR OF LOOKING AT FEAR

Since the beginnings of psychotherapy, we have understood the importance of reversing this avoidance response, whether through insight into the unconscious, cognitive transformations, or various types of exposure therapy. Yet this wiring is powerful, our defenses are resistant, and we still have not explored the nature of fear in a complete enough way. Even if we think we are intimately familiar with it, many of the fast and fleeting thoughts behind the scenes will slip by unexamined. In truth, this is because we are subtly afraid to look at them and discover all they have to teach us (see chapter 2). We don't want to look at them because we know they will require a complete paradigmatic shift in our understanding of who we are and how we deal with life. We have become so invested in our fear-based ways of negotiating the world that we will not easily give them up. Most of us resist looking at fear as much as possible. But even those who pursue a deeper exploration of the psyche can get lost in its meandering catacombs, missing the ways in which fear is distorting their compass. The fear of looking at fear is the first obstacle to overcome in our search for freedom and fulfillment. It is the source of our human predicament and that which preserves it as well.

Our existing strategies for dealing with fear fall short of real change in direct proportion to the extent that they do not look at and deconstruct the fear fully. At the extreme, positive thinking and affirmations are rarely helpful because instead of helping us look at fear, they would have us submerge it. When they do work, it is only because the investment in fear is so minimal that it is easy to tip the scales in favor of a more optimistic view. Motivation as a strategy for moving through fear relies on a "shock and awe" campaign of overwhelming fear's influence for the moment, only to have it return in force a short while later. Prayer, too, when used improperly, can be tainted with a hidden "fear of fear," an anxious beseeching of God to keep one from having to let go of what is familiar. We must get wise to the many ways we hide from fear. We have become so accustomed to these patterns that we don't easily notice them, secretly wanting to hold on to a control that, in the end, only perpetuates our suffering.

Modern psychotherapies have made significant advances toward our goal but still have not fully addressed the root underneath all fear.[7] CBT describes only some of the thoughts underneath one's fears and not always those at the real crux of the problem, as we will see. Exposure therapy directly confronts fear to move through it and achieve habituation but only works with the presenting fear and not necessarily the fear at the root of things. As a result, the fear can come back or take another form (what Freud called "symptom substitution"). Abreactive therapies allow emotions to come forth past the inhibitions that fear tells us must be imposed but often miss a necessary insight into the fear at the source of the problem. Insight-oriented therapies can give important information into this source but still need to be combined with action so that the insights can become meaningful in one's life. Otherwise, they can unwittingly hide a fear of taking such action. We need an approach that reliably digs up the fear at the bedrock of our suffering with insight into what gives rise to the suffering in the first place.

Those who have sought out this answer, intrepid explorers of consciousness, have demonstrated enormous courage to bring back maps of the terrain they traveled. Freud at one point thought he was going crazy as he conducted his own self-analysis. Jung had to acknowledge his "shadow" in order to deal with it effectively. The Buddha determined he would sit under the Bodhi tree until he either reached enlightenment or died trying. Their courage, and that of others, has paved a way for the rest of us, showing that we must look at and examine fear, digging it up fully, if we are to become free. The hero's journey (Campbell, 1991), the dark night of the soul (St. John of the Cross, 2003), and the death-rebirth archetype (Jung, 1981; Grof, 1980) all describe the same path: we must confront and move through fear *all the way* in order to find our higher good.

Facing fear fully, in safe and manageable ways but wholly without reservation, is to be our guiding principle on this path back to fulfillment. And resolving the fear of facing fear can only come with a firm conviction that this is, indeed, a worthy path. We must be willing to follow fear to its most subterranean hideout. But when finally there, standing resolutely in the face of that from which we have been running our entire life, we may at last come to know our true "enemy," shake hands with it (M. Pressman, 2011), and even befriend it. With this, we may reveal the gift it held, discovering what it was calling for all along and satisfying its need in a new and more fulfilling way.

In traveling this path, we will come to see that the whole of humanity has been engaged in an endless cycle of fear built upon a faulty strategy for securing fulfillment. But seeing the problem clearly like this is the first step in transforming our experience. No longer are we merely a figure caught in a play. When we take hold of the fear that has been directing from behind the scenes, we can rewrite the script in more-fulfilling ways. Finding the anxiety at the root of things gives us a sort of X-ray vision where we see through our automatic assumptions about life and reveal the truth they were hiding. Like discovering the "man behind the curtain" in *The Wizard of Oz*, we lose our fear when we understand its source.

Our task, then, is to fully deconstruct anxiety, learning how to navigate through the subterfuges of fear and, ultimately, how to design a life lived from free choice. Rather than being twisted and distorted by the ways of fear, such a life reaches for a transcendent truth, one that has the potential for resolving suffering at its source and restoring us to our original fulfillment.

NOTES

1. Some may say this is an overly pessimistic view, that fear does not dominate our experience to this degree. My intention is, in fact, to create a renewed optimism, the optimism for a fulfillment far beyond what we have come to think of as possible. Certainly life can be filled with experiences of beauty and goodness. But these experiences are limited by the degree to which we have our attention on fear. We will only allow as much fulfillment to come through as we feel safe to allow. In order to find a much greater fulfillment, it is imperative that we start out with a realistic assessment of how fear obstructs it.

2. If we look at it with fresh eyes, it is remarkable that (unless there are interfering circumstances) we are born naturally happy and deeply peaceful. There are moments of distress, of course, but when needs are met, we are instantly restored to a beatific state. What if, instead of this, our natural state in childhood were emotionally neutral or morose or depressed? No, all these are learned states, the result, as we shall see, of fear. Our true nature before such learning is joyful and fulfilled.

3. This conflict between the two drives of fear and fulfillment is not dissimilar to Freud's duality of Thanatos, the death drive, and Eros, the instinct to live and satisfy desires. The new theory of terror management (Solomon and Greenberg, 2015), built on Ernest Becker's *The Denial of Death* (1976), also has parallels to this model, describing the way in which fear (or terror) is

counterbalanced by the cultural values and meanings we hold (as aspects of fulfillment). Crystal Park's (2010) "meaning making" model provides support for our model as well, stating that when trauma occurs (triggering fear), we search to make meaning out of it.

4. Csikszentmihalyi (2008) and Seligman (2012) talk about "flow" in a way that is essentially synonymous with our use of the word "fulfillment."

5. This is why the first principle in the 12-step program talks about the importance of "admitting our powerlessness" over these things, letting go of the control that has hurt us time and time again.

6. This "wiring" is being explored in neuroscience with the understanding that when confronted with a perceived threat, the amygdala, that part of the brain responsible for "fight or flight" (avoidance), overrides the cortex, the part of the brain responsible for reasoned thinking and that might provide a different assessment of the situation (Pittman & Karle, 2015).

7. Mindfulness is an important exception, as will be discussed.

2

FEAR'S SURVIVAL TACTICS
Deceptions and Manipulations

And so we realize the fantastic hypnotic power of [fear] . . . the omnipotence of the infinitesimal whisperer.

—Satprem

To begin our deconstruction: According to the second postulate, fear distorts the higher truth we seek. In order to do this successfully, it must first distort the truth about how it distorts truth—we must not know that fear is a distortion or we would no longer believe in it. So fear first draws a veil of obscurity over the way things actually are and then keeps us in darkness about what it has done. Specifically, it keeps us from realizing that it creates rather than relieves suffering, that instead of securing fulfillment, it merely fills our mind with anxiety. Of course, we think fear is a necessary tool for survival, keeping us alert to danger that we may be prepared for it. Instead, it becomes a brutal dictator, forcing us to be in constant battle-ready mode, consuming us with fantasies of threat and perils that, in the end, become our only real problem. So fear must masquerade as a "friend," seducing us into believing it is better to follow its guidance—on our toes and prepared for danger—than to let down our guard and relax. Even though fear leaves us despairing and exhausted, we choose to keep anxious vigil rather than risk some imagined catastrophe. By hiding the truth about itself, fear shrouds the real source of our troubles in mystery. We end up blaming our circumstances for our unhappiness instead of questioning our allegiance to fear.

THE FIVE DECEPTIONS OF FEAR

To find our way out of this, we must deconstruct exactly how fear hides the truth about itself, convincing us to employ its strategy for fulfillment over and over. There are five ways that fear accomplishes this goal, five "deceptions" by which it ensures its primacy:

1. Fear keeps us from seeing that it is ubiquitous, a constant way of thinking and feeling when we are not wholly fulfilled.
2. Fear keeps us from realizing it is the true source of any problem.
3. Fear keeps us from looking directly at it to see it for what it is.
4. Fear keeps us from facing and moving through it when necessary.
5. Fear keeps us from looking at or facing the correct fear.

Let's explore each of these in detail that we may become wise to the mis-directions of fear. With sufficient insight, these same misdirections can become lampposts to help us navigate our way out of fear's darkness.

Deception 1

Fear keeps us from seeing that it is ubiquitous, a constant way of thinking and feeling when we are not wholly fulfilled.

The first thing we must appreciate is that fear is ubiquitous. And we must appreciate just how thoroughly ubiquitous it is. Otherwise, we will not recognize that it is the only real problem on which to concentrate our efforts. Except at moments of true and complete fulfillment, fear has its hand, subtly or obviously, in every aspect of our life. It builds our governmental and social structures—established to protect us from dangers without and within. It fuels our economies—trade deals built on agreements for how to secure our physical needs. It directs the course of our relationships—keeping us "civil" while trying to get along. And it guides our major and minor life decisions—making certain that we anxiously try to maximize our good and minimize risk. Any field of human endeavor is driven by a quest for fulfillment, of course, but unless we have worked it through, fear becomes the strategy by which we would try to secure that fulfillment.

Karen Horney (1991) recognized the ubiquity of fear when she described a "basic anxiety" we all share, our response to living in a lonely and hostile world. She saw our neuroses as attempts to protect ourselves from this anxiety in the hope of a fulfillment (what she called "self-realization") that is invulnerable to such threat. More recently, researchers Aly and Green (2010) have shown that fear is a "key factor" in discord among individuals, groups, cultures, and religions. And according to philosopher Brian Massumi (2005), "insecurity . . . is the new normal." These statements hint at the growing awareness of anxiety's predominance in the human experience. But it is essential that we understand anxiety is not just predominant but ubiquitous in our experience, the ultimate determiner of how we relate to the world any time we are not truly at peace and fulfilled. We may try to distract ourselves, seek illusions of control, or numb our awareness in so many ways, but until we find fulfillment, we cannot escape this basic existential angst. [1]

Most of us don't recognize the ubiquity of fear or even think of ourselves as anxious because we happen to be lucky enough to be living conveniently inside our defenses. Having gained a certain measure of control over the environment, we are not seriously challenged most of the time and turn off our awareness of thoughts of danger. Eventually, however, we all meet with some experience that threatens. Having chosen "blissful" ignorance, we can be taken by surprise, our identity turned upside down, as we are forced to admit into awareness what we were so earnestly defending against. [2]

The reason fear is ubiquitous is because our search for fulfillment is ubiquitous, and as above, we use fear to try to secure that fulfillment. In other words, we become afraid of anything that can interfere with our well-being. Fear is the trigger for corrective action in the face of such interference. Think of the athletic coach who throws epithets at his players, believing that by scaring them with thoughts of failure he will motivate them to push harder. Or the person who continually searches their lover's face for signs of displeasure as a signal to make sure they are soothed. Most of our behavior, most of the time, is motivated by this kind of attempt to secure fulfillment by attending to fear's warnings. [3]

An important way to recognize the ubiquity of fear is to notice the thought continually running through our mind in the background: "How do I feel right now?" This question, no matter how imperceptibly, is literally present all the time except when we are deeply absorbed in a moment of fulfillment. It is the gauge by which we measure the meaning and value of all our circumstances. To be sure, it has many faces, such as "Do I like what's happening right now?" "Is this situation bringing me closer to (or taking me farther from) my goal?" "How do I resolve the restlessness I feel?" "How do I reach my goals so I can finally stop struggling and be happy?" and so forth. If a particular moment is not fulfilling, the thought can take the form of "How long before I can get out of this situation?" or "How do I get to where I want to be and be with whom I want or do what I wish?" All of these are variations on the search for fulfillment. But we don't simply ask these questions in a neutral, objective way; there is always at least a subtle fear behind them, an anxious readiness to spring into action should the answer not be to our liking. Even if the answer is positive, we know that our hold on it is very tenuous and it could be taken away at any time. So we continue to use fear as a whip to keep us alert to our status.

To really grasp the ubiquity of fear, we must see how thoroughly these questions inform our thoughts, feelings, and choices in every moment. *Literally every moment*, except, again, when we are truly fulfilled, we are scanning our environment for danger that could interfere with our fulfillment. We assess whether our body's needs are being met (Am I hungry? Is the temperature in the room just right?); whether a movement we catch out of the corner of our eye requires attention; whether we are progressing toward a goal, on track to meet a deadline, meeting our responsibilities to others . . . and on and on our endless list goes. We exert a constant subtle pressure in the background to make sure everything is held together, maintaining control over the natural entropy of things. Our eyes flicker with saccadic movements, darting to and fro in search of problems or fulfillments. The degree to which we assess our environment in this way, at every instant, is truly astounding.

Here's an example: Imagine there is a stimulus that enters our field of vision. The first assessment that goes through our mind may be "Is this a person or something else?" If a person, our next thoughts, taking place with lightning speed, might be "What gender, age, race, etc., are they?" We may then ask, "Do they have the characteristics I've come to identify as dangerous?" If not, our next thought is often "Are they attractive?[4] A potential mate?" followed by "Are they presenting the right gestures in their face and body to indicate that they understand the social norms—i.e., that their behavior will be predictable, sensible, and therefore safe?" If we meet the person and start a conversation, the number of cues that are assessed multiplies exponentially: "How should I interpret that inflection in their voice?" "Whom do they remind me of and how did I feel about that person?" "Are they showing signs of acceptance or even approval?" "Do I have to worry about rejection?" And so on. No wonder *A Course in Miracles* (Foundation for Inner Peace, 1975) says, "You are not really capable of being tired but you are very capable of wearying yourself. The strain of constant judgment is virtually intolerable. It is curious that an ability so debilitating would be so deeply cherished."[5]

Thoreau famously said, "The mass of men lead lives of quiet desperation. . . . A stereotyped but unconscious despair is concealed even under what are called the games and amusements of mankind" (1971). This is the ubiquity of fear. We long for Oz but are more mindful of the "lions and tigers and bears" that might come up along the way. Our solution is to engage in an insatiable search for control over that which scares us, seeking a guarantee of safety before we can relax and enjoy the fruits of our labors. Such a guarantee, of course, never comes, and we become caught in an endless maze of detours in the attempt. Think about the continual threats and challenges we encounter throughout the day—some big and obvious, most subtle and fleeting. There are the many routine demands that must be met just to maintain order and prevent chaos such as getting the laundry done, paying bills on time, meeting deadlines, etc. There are the "bigger" threats to our well-being, like problems in our relationships, health, or security. And there are also the many almost undetectable threats in the background, such as unrecognized sights or sounds, each of which must be evaluated for safety as we simply move through our day. These are the kinds of things that steal our peace in the moment and for a lifetime. We chase after money, hoping to achieve a level where we never have to worry about hunger, shelter, or security again. We work on controlling our relationships so that we never have to worry about abandonment or disapproval. The goal of the strategy of control is to guarantee a utopia of "perfection" that never ends. But knowing the goal is unattainable, we simply increase our anxiety as we fail in the attempt time and time again.

Even if we consider ourselves happy, until it is fully resolved, fear is indeed ubiquitous, always in the background, limiting our fulfillment in ways much more profound than we are usually aware of. Most of us settle for a mediocre fulfillment that is more about safety from fear, never really pursuing our ideals fully. And because of our investment in fear as a strategy for securing fulfillment, we repress our awareness of the continuous toll it takes. The path to correction is always in defining the problem. In recognizing the ubiquity of fear, we have taken a first step in that direction.

Deception 2

Fear keeps us from realizing it is the true source of any problem.

It's easy to understand that certain things can inspire fear, such as a lack of money or a medical problem. But to understand that we become afraid *any* time a situation threatens our fulfillment has the most profound implication. It means that fear is the true source of every problem. Any negative experience, regardless of the emotion it evokes, is really a fear in disguise. Anger, for example, is a forceful way of saying "Stop scaring me."[6] Greed is an anxious attempt to secure what we are afraid of not having. Sadness is a response to our fear of having to live without something that was important to us. Guilt is a way of punishing oneself as payment for wrongdoing, deflecting the fear of punishment from others. Jealousy clearly comes from the fear of losing something one deeply cares about. Loneliness is a fear of losing the opportunity for connection and the particular kind of fulfillment that comes from being with people . . . and so on, for all negative thoughts and feelings.

Once again, any response we have to a negative situation, no matter what we name it, is really a fear response. A situation distresses us because it triggers the fear of not getting what we want in life. Our distress is a way of saying "I don't like what is happening," instigating the fear that we might be powerless to do anything about it. The external situation is never the problem; we only call something a problem when we become afraid. Without the activating energy of fear, we would simply see a situation to deal with. Instead of resisting with our negative emotions, we would accept the situation for what it is and respond appropriately. For instance, boredom hides a fear of meaninglessness or purposelessness. We feel trapped in its emptiness, afraid that we will have to stay there for longer than we wish. The moment, however, we have something to look forward to, even if it has not yet arrived, our fear of being trapped is resolved and the boredom vanishes. We become peaceful in the same circumstances that caused our pain a moment before.

Once we grasp that fear is the real reason for our difficulties, we find the concept is nothing short of revolutionary. No longer can we afford to think of problems as having truly different causes. There is only one problem underneath every negative experience, and it is fear. This principle will become the cornerstone of our deconstructing-anxiety model, the sure guide we will use to find our way in any challenge or difficulty.

So fear's second deception is that it keeps us from looking at the actual source of a problem, luring us instead to focus on its many disguises. Rather than understanding our own fear when we are, say, upset with our spouse for an argument the night before, we look at the wrong problem and think it is our spouse who must change. If we are overly severe with our child for some transgression, we should first resolve our fear—for example, that they might not grow up the way we had hoped. If we wish to tackle our circumstances effectively, we must work with the fear at their origin. (In chapter 8, with an exercise called Digging for Gold, we will discover for ourselves that all problems camouflage a fear hiding underneath.)

In our effort to deconstruct anxiety and reach fulfillment, we must fully grasp this second deception of fear and realize it is absolute. It is *always* the case that fear is the real problem to address. This insight is vital. Without it, our efforts will be misdirected and the true cause of our suffering will remain untouched. We must put clothes on the invisible man; we cannot address something we cannot see or understand properly.

The very good news in all this is that we now have another step in how to resolve our difficulties. Any time we have a problem, we need only find and resolve the fear at its root. With this principle, we may cut through, like a Gordian knot,[7] all the complexities of our struggles that can leave us so overwhelmed and mystified. This principle promises a path to real freedom and fulfillment.

Deception 3

Fear keeps us from looking directly at it to see it for what it is.

The next thing we notice as we decrypt fear's deceptions is that it has us avoid looking at it directly. Even if we have gotten past the second deception and realized that fear is the true culprit behind our suffering, we still avoid examining that fear directly. By its nature, fear drives us to look away from it, to block it from our awareness. It has us do this so well that we don't usually consider there could be another way of responding to it.[8] But once again, if we fail to look at fear directly, then we are operating blindly. Still, we'd rather scramble frantically for external fixes before exploring the contents of our fear.

When we avoid looking at fear directly, we unwittingly keep it alive. We tell ourselves there must be something truly awful about it if we are avoiding it so. By refusing to look at fear directly, we never get to understand what it's really composed of. We are left to fill the void with our anxious fantasies, never finding out whether it is actually what we have been imagining. We are sure there is a boogeyman in the closet because, well, we've always been afraid to open the door! This too is fear's way of preserving itself, knowing that if we were to see it for what it is we might find something without real substance, kept alive only by our untested imaginings.

As in the second postulate, when we are anxious, we become afraid to see things as they are, insisting instead on seeing them as we wish. This is what keeps us from looking at fear directly. We prefer to keep our focus on the external situation, using our anxious interpretation of it to prepare to fight, flee, or freeze. But despite our exhaustive efforts (throughout our life and throughout the span of human history), we have never really resolved our problems or come closer to fulfillment with this approach. One problem is immediately replaced with another because the fear at their source has been left intact. This fact by itself should be enough to convince us that a different strategy is needed. The awareness of the third deception lays out this new strategy: if we want to know why we have failed to resolve our fear, we must look at fear directly, without reservation. Only then can we see what we are dealing with. And if we are to find a path to liberation, we must not be afraid to look at all of fear, fully and courageously, leaving no hidden corners unexamined.

Deception 4

Fear keeps us from facing and moving through it when necessary.

Even if we get wise to the third deception and dare to examine it, fear has another trick up its sleeve. What if, it warns us, despite having had a direct look at the fear, we have been duped? What if the only way to be sure we have assessed the fear accurately is to have a direct *experience* of it? Fear seeks a guarantee. It tells us that the only way to know with certainty what it is made of will be to face the fear, literally moving into and through it, to see what happens. But to do so, we think, could be disastrous. If our assessment turns out to be wrong, we will have exposed ourselves to all the consequences we were so afraid of. We must avoid this move at all costs.

The fear of facing and moving through fear is the natural extension of the fear of looking directly at fear. In fact, looking at it is a form of facing it. It's actually very rare that people look at *or* face fear. How often would we prefer to repress (deny, project, etc.) a problem we are confronted with, to keep things calm or pleasant or "nice" rather than dealing with the rawness of life we all struggle with? This, of course, simply relegates the problem to obscurity where we can't do anything about it. Looking at fear honestly and thoroughly accomplishes an essential step. We get to see what exactly has been chasing us, what we actually have to deal with, rather than our fearful fantasy of it. But if, after looking at fear for what it is, we are afraid to act on what we have seen, the fantasy can live on. Again, the message this conveys is there must be something about it that is too awful to face.

Deception 5

Fear keeps us from looking at or facing the correct fear.

We have said that fear is ubiquitous and that it is at the root of all problems. We have also said that it is necessary to look at and possibly face our fear. But we still have to find exactly what that fear is. The fifth deception, fear's final survival tactic and ultimate avoidance strategy, is this: we have to wend our way through the extraordinary complexities of the psyche, its many layers both conscious and unconscious, to find the correct fear that is giving rise to our struggles. True insight into the fear at the root of things—the very root—is rare. Without it, the practice of looking at and facing fear can be (and often is) greatly misguided. We can find ourselves on endless wild goose chases, feeling so very lost in the weeds of psychic debris. But with a true insight into the correct fear, one can sometimes be relieved of the problem without ever having to face it directly. If facing it is still necessary, we know just the right fear to face.

I had a client with a rather severe social anxiety. He was highly motivated to free himself of this problem and so would willingly follow through on whatever exposure task was asked of him. As an example, he would force himself to accept his coworkers' invitation to go to lunch every day. This meant sitting between two people in the back seat of the car with two others up front. Suffering through lunch, he then had to repeat the experience on the car ride back to work. No matter how many times he performed this exposure, his anxiety would not remit. It was only when we found a hidden thought he was protecting in the background—"As soon as I get out of this car I'm going back into my cubicle and I'll be safe from everyone"—that we found a way through. He was missing the correct insight into what fear needed to be faced, holding on to an escape route with his secret plan. We then designed an exposure where he had to spend an entire day with a friend (but some-one with whom he would still feel anxious), with no chance of escaping too quickly. This proved to be the key that began to relieve his anxiety in a sustained way.

Working with a fear other than that at the true source is a common occurrence, both in psychotherapy and in ordinary life. We are complex beings who have spent a lifetime avoiding fear, casting it into obscurity, leaving us bewildered as to what we are really upset about. And in any given situation we can have more than one fear, each competing with the other. We want to ask our boss for a promotion but are afraid of rejection. At the same time we fear stagnation and we long to advance in our career. In addition, we are concerned that if we get the promo-tion, our colleagues might become jealous and undermining. The multi-layered nature of fear can cause great confusion, making us afraid to move in one direction or the other. Add to this the fact that fear can take on all sorts of disguises, throwing us further off the trail of the real problem. Instead of addressing the real problem, we might, for in-stance, begin to resent our colleagues for their potential jealousy, get angry at our spouse for pushing us to ask for the promotion, or become depressed by the thought "I'll probably get turned down anyway." If we only address these surface issues, we may or may not resolve them. Either way, the root of the problem will remain intact. Like a rhizome, it will inevitably send up new shoots, different iterations of itself in various appearances. We are constantly putting out fires but missing the source that, if quenched, would finally put an end to it. Finding the right fear to work with, the one that gives rise to all the rest, cuts through enormous confusion and gives us a chance for true resolution.[9]

WHEN THERAPY WORKS AND WHEN IT FAILS

Any time a therapeutic intervention succeeds, no matter the school of thought, it is because the fear at the root of a problem has been fully revealed and worked through. And any time it fails, it is only because this root has not been reached or transformed. Even if the therapy resolves certain problems, if there is not a complete or lasting change, the correct fear at the source must remain. Let's look at several examples.[10]

Psychoanalysis and Psychodynamic Psychotherapies

Psychoanalysis, a path specifically devoted to finding this underlying root, has done us all an extraordinary service by being the first to open the doors to the unconscious. Freud's theories and practices still provide highly effective therapy when they achieve a complete insight into the correct fear at the source. However, psychoanalysis and psychodynamic therapies in general can come up short when the analyst sees many possible "conflicts" in his or her client, not appreciating the "root of the root," the one fear giving rise to all such conflicts. Furthermore, these therapies are sometimes vulnerable to the fourth deception— content to look at but not necessarily face fear. A client may achieve wonderful insight into their problem, but until they take action to move through it, they can unwittingly perpetuate a fear of such action. It's even possible that the insight can give an illusion of progress, as if something significant is happening. But if the insight doesn't actually make a change in the person's life and relieve symptoms, it is because fear is still operating anonymously behind the scenes. A complete and correct insight will fully expose this fear, enabling one to look at it objectively and act independently of it.[11] I know of many who have gone through analysis and achieved insight upon insight but only felt relief of their symptoms when they took action, determined to make some change in their life.

Cognitive-Behavioral Therapy

Cognitive-behavioral therapy (CBT) is an umbrella term that covers many approaches, including exposure therapy and thought replacement or "cognitive transformation." Traditional exposure therapy can be powerful medicine, and when performed properly, I believe it is an essential ingredient in transforming anxiety (as we will discuss). It is a direct expression of the principle of facing and moving through fear. As one does so, healing can come by discovering exactly what the fear is made of and habituating to it. But as we saw in the example above, if the client doesn't address the true source of the problem, the therapist can create exposures to the wrong fears or to fears that are too superficial to bring real healing.

The purpose of the cognitive approaches in CBT is to acknowledge (get insight into) the irrationality of one's problematic thoughts. Resolution can come by disputing such thoughts and replacing them with rational ones. Much of CBT's benefit, I believe, comes from its concreteness—clients can readily identify and concretely challenge their irrational thoughts. However, if someone is highly anxious, it's very difficult to convince them that what they are terrified of isn't "true." We all know how real and fixed our beliefs can become. This is fear's investment in seeing things the way it prefers. And even when we know our thoughts are irrational, our ability to override the fear with intellect is relatively inconsequential in most cases. It is possible to get a true insight into how a certain belief is irrational and have this insight "stick" but only after a rather extraordinary amount of repetition and persistence. Even then, the fear will only relent if one is willing to give up one's investment in it. Imagine, for example, someone who has, for their entire life, felt ashamed of their body and refused to wear a bathing suit. Telling them "Nobody really cares what you look like," no matter how fervently repeated, isn't likely to help. Each of us has our own repertoire of irrational beliefs that are powerful enough to have drastically altered the course of our life. These will not easily yield to thought replacement. We are too invested in them, too afraid to let them go. When CBT works, it is because it has created sufficient insight—for example, by labeling categories of irrational thinking such as "catastrophizing," "globalization," etc.—that we can step aside from our investment and see the faulty assumption. But it must be stressed that this will only work on fears or irrational beliefs where our investment is not overpowering.

Motivation and Positive Thinking

Motivation and its near cousin, positive thinking, of course, are not therapies per se but are often-used strategies for trying to improve one's quality of life so we will include them in our discussion here. Motivation is a way of evoking our longing for greatness, transcendence, possibility. Longing itself is the experience of remembering and being driven toward these higher truths . . . toward fulfillment. But because of the fear involved in pursuing such fulfillment, we postpone action and eventually bury our longing. Motivation is the attempt to push through this fear and reawaken our longing. When we feel a longing and use motivation to try to satisfy it, we actually set up a war inside ourselves— the same war between fear and fulfillment we discussed in the beginning. When we bought into fear, we did so for a reason, believing it was the wisest course for protecting our fulfillment. Pushing through fear means we are opposing our own decision. In this way, motivation can become a particularly painful example of what happens when we don't have insight into the correct fear, the true source of our problem. It requires drumming up enough energy and excitement that one can force one's way through the barriers set up by fear. Evoking such energy can lead to a wonderful high—that's what makes the approach so attractive—coming from a momentary feeling of having overpowered the fear. And for that moment, one can even achieve a higher perspective, seeing a greater truth, as fear gets swallowed up by this sense of power and capacity. But because the fear has been squashed rather than seen and worked through, it quickly reasserts itself when the excitement dies down. One cannot sustain that kind of physical intensity for long and inevitably becomes disillusioned when the expanded sense of potential fades.

The unfortunate consequence of all this is that in the end, it reinforces the fear. In trying to overpower it, we once again give ourselves the message that we are afraid of it and cannot tolerate looking at or facing it. I have seen many people suffer from this, continually trying to call forth more motivation in an anxious attempt to recapture the momentary truth they saw. One of my clients was involved in an ongoing seminar that took this kind of approach. She described her experience as "going through a hamburger press." In other words, she was suffering from the pressure of trying to overpower her fear and feeling "squeezed" in the effort.

Motivation, when combined with insight into the correct fear at the root of the problem, can be a wonderful thing. But this requires a deft awareness of when motivation becomes a tactic for control and manipulation—an agent of fear. Any peak experience, whether obtained through motivation or other means, can give a true insight into what is possible beyond the limits of fear. Faith is an example of this that can work beautifully for many people. But for the experience to make a real change in our life, it must be combined with the understanding that even when the "high" passes, the truth of the experience remains. In order to achieve this goal, we must look at the correct fear clearly, juxtaposing it immediately with the higher view of things, to see by comparison that the fear has no power to hold us back.

When motivation is successful, it is also because we have become willing to let go of our investment in the fear. We have achieved the insight that our fear is not important enough to sacrifice our fulfillment. But again, we cannot afford to fool ourselves about this, believing we have transcended fear when we are secretly afraid to acknowledge it.

Positive Psychology

Positive psychology, a relative newcomer to the field, has made a wonderful contribution in offering a non-pathological approach to well-being. Instead of focusing on problems, positive psychology studies our potentials so that we may reach for fulfillment directly. In *Flourish: A Visionary New Understanding of Happiness and Well-Being* (2012), Martin Seligman defines four keys to living a life of well-being: positive emotion, engagement with what one is doing, a sense of accomplishment, and good relationships. In this, he has given us a refined and elegant understanding of the components of fulfillment. But insight into the fears that can block access to these potentials is indispensable. When we pursue fulfillment, we will necessarily encounter these fears and still need a prescription for what to do about them. As we reach for the goals of positive psychology, these fears can be used for therapeutic material; once cleared out, our path is open. Otherwise, our efforts become more about cheerleading and, again, motivation. Because positive psychology is an intelligent approach, it can readily offer a kind of motivation that truly encourages one's potential. But we cannot afford to overlook the intensity of our fear if we are to adequately address the suffering it causes and find our way to a lasting fulfillment.

Gestalt Therapy and Other Body-Oriented Therapies

The abreactive (cathartic) aspect of Gestalt therapy can provide significant relief from emotional struggle with its particular method for moving through fear. This method involves discharging pent-up emotions from the body, for example, pounding out one's anger on a pillow or screaming out one's upset. The understanding in Gestalt therapy is that emotional energy gets stored in the body when we "hold it in" rather than allow its natural expression. It can be discharged by draining the physical energy of the emotions from the body in various ways, expressing what has been repressed. Such maneuvers can create a profound shift. And because the discharge is enacted with great force, it can actually create the same "high" as motivation does, with the feeling that one has gained power over the fear. Gestalt therapy doesn't help the client look for insight (believing it runs the risk of promoting intellectualization). Instead, it helps one physically face the fear that caused the emotions to be repressed in the body. Other body-oriented therapies such as bioenergetics (Lowen, 1967), Reichian therapy (Reich, 1949), the somato-emotional release technique of craniosacral therapy (Upledger, 1983), etc., can discharge the same emotional pressure from the muscles and even the fascia and tendons, creating deep catharsis and relief. Although not a stated goal, if one moves *all* the way through the physical "blockage," there will be a spontaneous insight into the fear at the root of the problem. This is because the emotions being discharged from the body are coupled with the thoughts that led to the fear (see chapter 4). One can often have flashbacks or sudden corrective realizations as they are venting on the pillow. And yet, if the release is not complete, such insight won't be realized, or if it is, it won't be integrated for lasting change. Only resolving the true root of the problem will give us the results we seek.

Existential and Transpersonal Psychotherapies

Existential therapies, we may say, work to embrace and accept the human condition (and therefore the reality of fear). Transpersonal psychotherapies focus on that which transcends fear with a higher perspective. Both can readily uproot the deep fear at the source of human suffering. Each, in its different way, helps the client feel "bigger" than their circumstances. In existential psychotherapies, one transforms a feeling of vulnerability into a sense that one is powerful enough to stand up to and accept them. In the case of transpersonal psychology, one alters their relationship with fear by identifying with a view of themselves as transcendent over it. As a result, fear "dissolves" or gets swallowed up when pitted side by side against these perspectives. But once again, without insight into the deep fear that was swallowed up, we will return to the habit of old and familiar ways of thinking. A deep transpersonal perspective or a full existential embrace of reality *can* lead to a permanent transformation out of fear. But without a conscious insight into the fear that has been usurped, they can digress into what is sometimes called a "spiritual bypass" (in the case of transpersonal psychology), or an existential despair about our human condition. Both of these responses hide and preserve the fear at the source.

Mindfulness

Finally, mindfulness, more than any other established form of therapy, I believe, can get at the root of things by addressing the fundamental nature of thought itself. Its primary method is to watch all thoughts arise and pass without "attaching" to them. By doing so, we break free of the investments that would have us identify with thoughts of fear. To become skillful in this can take a very long time. Fear's avoidance mechanisms will cause the mind to become distracted, bringing it back to familiar habits. The practice of mindfulness (in brief) is to become aware of this when it has happened and to train the attention back to our object of choice—e.g., breathing, the movements of walking—and beyond the pull of such distractions. Without doubt, practitioners can get beginning results quickly. The simple discovery that thoughts can be let go and the mind can quiet down is rewarding by itself. Most of us have so little experience stilling our mind even for a few moments. Such stillness not only brings significant relief from the pressure created by fear in the moment but shows us there is a path to freedom from fear as a whole. But it can take many years before we come to trust that all thoughts can be let go with no more fear binding us to them. While the practice of mindfulness is to let go of each thought that arises, one at a time, we can speed up the journey and more readily ensure success by targeting the root thought that gives rise to all the others. By letting *it* go, we take care of the rest.

Of course, this is only a small sampling of the wide variety of therapies "out there." Each of these and others have significantly furthered our understanding of how to work with fear. Each of them can be effective if it properly addresses the correct fear, and each of them can fall short precisely to the extent that it fails to do so. In the absence of our finding the correct fear, a problem cannot be truly resolved. It may abate for a period of time, but it will inevitably return in the same or some other form.

THE EIGHT MANIPULATIONS OF FEAR

In addition to its deceptions, fear also manipulates our perception, distorting the objective truth of things. These manipulations are the specific devices that fear would use to keep us from looking at or facing it. By manipulating our perception, it throws fantastic images before our eyes and otherwise twists our understanding. The reality we perceive when anxious can be grossly distorted and very different from ordinary perception. The manipulations of fear scare us into thinking we must give all our attention to this reality so nothing can sneak up and take us by surprise. Again, we believe this is the best strategy for securing fulfillment. But as we will see, it is all smoke and mirrors; these images are specifically designed to keep us from looking at the real fear that needs to be faced. If we deconstruct and thereby expose these manipulations, we can more readily see that they are, in fact, manipulations, or "illusions," with no objective validity. This begins our process of mistrusting fear, poking holes in its pretense, and developing the conviction that our experience of it is not absolute and fixed after all. In short, we begin to see that fear is not "real." The eight manipulations are

1. The hypnotizing effect of fear
2. The lie of fear
3. The demand of fear
4. The ruminative quality of fear
5. The impatience of fear
6. The future orientation of fear
7. The time distortion of fear
8. The self-generating quality of fear

I. The Hypnotizing Effect of Fear

Fear is a master hypnotist. It creates a sort of trance wherein we stare, truly as if mesmerized, at all the terrible things that could go wrong. This hypnotizing effect is crucial. It is as if we are put under a spell so that our rational self, that which would otherwise consider a variety of ways to respond to the situation, goes to sleep. Instead, we react automatically without considering these options at all. No matter how many times we are exposed to fear, it never occurs to us to respond in any way other than fighting, fleeing, or freezing (physically or mentally, as in a state of shock or even dissociation). The specifics of what we think will happen are so awful that we don't assess what it is we're really afraid of in the situation. Instead, we make drastic assumptions of catastrophe, ruin, and devastation. Our habitual reaction is automatic and complete, preparing us for extreme measures, assuming the worst and disregarding mitigating factors. The hypnosis of fear is such that we fixate on the threat that now looms so large in our mind it blocks out all other thoughts.

It's as if fear throws up an impenetrable wall before our eyes, or better, walls that surrounds us in every direction, a bubble we feel trapped inside. We are hypnotized by the images of future disaster that fear projects onto these walls, staring at them with a fascinated horror. Unable to take our gaze away, we remain frozen on this picture of the future as if it were the end of all things. The effect of this is that we never ask the one question that would completely undo the fear: What is on the other side of the wall, what is beyond the bubble? What actually happens when we live through fear and get past its initial moments of terror? The scenes flashing on the walls of the bubble become our only reality. We forget there is a much greater reality on the other side with a vast array of options for how to think about and respond to the situation.

Once again, we secretly want to fixate on these walls, believing that doing so will help us be prepared for the danger and not be taken by surprise. If we pay attention, we can even notice a subtle eagerness that sometimes shows up, a secret excitement to hear anxiety-producing news so that we can make good on our readiness and discharge our fight, flight, or freeze response.

2. The Lie of Fear

The hypnotizing effect of fear also creates the lie of fear. Fear makes us believe that the many possible things that could go wrong in a situation, the many scenarios we see on the bubble walls, *will all happen at once*. As we hold each of these possibilities in mind, we feel an anxious need to prepare for all of them at the same time. This is completely overwhelming and paralyzing. It causes us to scatter our thinking, fracturing it in many directions. A kaleidoscope of images fills our mind as we desperately try to keep track of all possible threats . . . and anxiously look for others we may not have accounted for. The Buddhists have an interesting phrase that describes this phenomenon: the mind is like "a drunken monkey stung by a bee." Fear does its best to convince us that these maneuvers are necessary; its lie is that we will be in great danger if we do not.

But of course, this strategy simply creates a vicious cycle. Confronted with our helplessness to master every possible scenario of danger, we become all the more anxious, frantically searching for a solution, despairing each time we find ourselves helpless once again. In truth, a threatening situation never plays out this way. If problems come to pass (and, as we shall see, most will not), they do so one at a time and are managed one at a time.

3. The Demand of Fear

Fear demands that we try to do something about it—to fix it, change it, or somehow make it "go away." It demands that we respond to it with a defense (something we will explore in great detail later). We never consider the possibility of ignoring it or engaging our attention in some other activity. Again, that would leave us too vulnerable, we believe. As above, this magnifies our anxiety. To pick up our analogy of the bubble, it's as if we see the threatening images on the walls in front of us and run in the opposite direction. As we are running, we imagine that we are being chased, heightening our fear. When we reach the back of the bubble, we press against it, trying to force our way out. But by pressing against it, we make the fear all the more real for we have to imagine something strong and solid to press against. The more we try to escape fear, and the harder we press against the walls of the bubble, the more we reinforce the idea that our fear is real and the walls are impenetrable. It refreshes our projections of danger, and we end up more afraid. The fear then increases its demand that we do something about it, and the process cycles round and round.

4. The Ruminative Quality of Fear

Next is the ruminative quality of fear. Fear makes us review, ceaselessly and tortuously, all frightening possibilities. This is connected to the hypnosis and the lie of fear. Not only do we have to stare at and be aware of all the possible threats at once, we must keep reviewing them for extra insurance that we haven't missed anything. And we do this to try to satisfy the demand of fear—by reviewing the situation over and over we hope to find a way out. Einstein's definition is apt here: "Insanity is doing the same thing over and over again, each time expecting different results." Of course, the attempt is futile because we have secretly chosen fear as our preferred strategy. We don't really want different results. We are holding out to find a way to fulfillment without having to let go of fear, still wanting to keep it close so we won't be taken by surprise. Our dearest wish, before we can pursue fulfillment, is to get control over fear with a guarantee that it will never come back. But each time we fail in this effort, we become more anxious.

5. The Impatience of Fear

Following from the demand of fear is the impatience of fear. Not only does fear demand that we find a solution to a threatening situation, we must find that solution *now* even if the situation is far off in the future. Without fear, we are naturally rather casual about a problem until it arrives. We don't think that much about it in advance, satisfied to know we will deal with it when the time comes. We realize that it is useless to dwell on it until we know whether it will actually come to pass and, if it does, what the actual experience will be like. But fear, like a child with a temper tantrum, screams at us until we find a solution. Anxiety makes us feel it is intolerable to wait. It's an extra safeguard, another of fear's survival tactics, telling us that we cannot rest until we are certain the problem has been managed. A favorite line of mine from *A Course in Miracles* speaks to this: "Only infinite patience produces immediate effects" (Foundation for Inner Peace, 1975).

6. The Future Orientation of Fear

Fear is always an anticipation of the future. It is never about what is actually happening now. But it manipulates our perception by having us imagine—and internally experience—that future as if it *were* happening to us now. Jack Kornfield (personal correspondence) tells this story that illustrates the point: A man is hiking on a trail in the woods. Looking down, he sees the paw print of a bear on the ground and starts to worry for his safety. A moment later he sees fresh bear scat nearby and his anxiety increases. In the next moment, he sees a bear down the trail and becomes even more anxious. As the bear runs toward him menacingly, the man's anxiety is at a peak. But there is nothing dangerous actually happening at each of these moments. The only problem is the man's anxious anticipation of what he believes is about to come. Even when the bear is upon him, he may of course be experiencing pain, but his *anxiety* is only about what might happen next. This is why there is never actually anything scary about the present moment. When we face the situation of the moment, without anticipating where it might lead, we are simply in action, dealing with what needs to be dealt with as best we can. The discomfort of anxiety is the effect of imagining a painful future, experiencing it as if it were happening now. The demand of fear fills us with adrenaline to try to stave off the problem, increasing the feeling that it is happening now. But with nothing real to work with, we are left frustrated, despairing, and still more anxious that we cannot get control.

It can be hard to believe that the present moment itself contains nothing to fear. Our anxiety about the future can so drastically affect our perception of the here and now. But consider this Zen teaching parable: A man is being chased by a tiger. Coming to a cliff, he has nowhere to go. He sees a branch coming out of the rock wall below and swings onto it, just out of reach of the tiger. He looks down and sees another tiger at the bottom of the cliff, pacing hungrily. Just then, two mice, one white, one black, start gnawing away at the branch he is holding. But off to the right, the man sees a beautiful red strawberry. Holding on to the branch with one hand, he reaches out to pluck the strawberry with the other and takes a bite. All he can think of is how sweet it tastes!

7. The Time Distortion of Fear

The time distortion of fear is a particularly uncomfortable aspect of it. Fear makes time seem to move very slowly, to almost a standstill. When we are highly anxious, we believe that we are facing an eternity of this agony. Time seems to stand still because we are afraid that we'll never get out of the situation—that we are trapped in a changeless hell. And without change, time loses its meaning. The hypnotizing effect of fear has us freeze time as we stare at the walls of the bubble surrounding us and fail to consider what happens after the threat has passed. We feel locked in this scene and therefore locked in time. There is no escape route, no movement out of the bubble, and no movement through time. When fear leaves, time flows fluidly again and we realize the distortion.

8. The Self-Generating Quality of Fear

Finally, fear is self-generating. It is in the nature of anxiety that we get anxious about having anxiety.[12] Because we know our strategies for dealing with anxiety can't give us the guarantee of safety we wish, we become anxious about experiencing this helplessness. This, of course, sets the whole process in motion again. It is also why (as we will see) our attempts to relieve ourselves of anxiety actually generate more of it.

Fear weaves all of these manipulations together when seducing us in its ways. We become caught in the lie of fear, for example, imagining all the terrible things that could happen as if they were happening at once. This compels us to stare fixedly at that picture, creating the hypnosis of fear. This hypnotizing effect gives rise to the ruminative aspect of fear, as we review over and over the many scenarios we are being hypnotized by, looking for a way out. And all of this generates fear's demand that we try to do something about the problem. The fear snowballs in the speed and magnitude of its effect. When we realize we cannot control it, we search even more frantically for solutions, reinforcing the entire process. Our anxiety increases as we become convinced there must be something truly awful causing us to respond this way.

As before, awareness of these manipulations—seeing them *as* manipulations—can start to loosen their hold upon us. For instance, if we challenge the time distortion of fear and remember that the problem will pass, we spontaneously wake up from the hypnosis of fear. The experiential bubble we felt trapped inside is seen to be floating in a vast universe of possible alternatives. We see this because we have imagined what is beyond the bubble walls, discovering other ways of interpreting and responding to the situation. We understand the future orientation of fear is a distortion as well; by visualizing what will happen when the fear passes, we recognize that the frightening future we have been imagining is not actually happening now. This silences the demand of fear, no longer compelling us to find an immediate fix. The ruminative and self-generating qualities of fear also give way as the illusory nature of the bubble is exposed. We want to become intimately familiar with these manipulations, catching them in the act of trying to ensnare us, finding the moment of choice before we "buy into" their illusions. With such awareness, we can stand back from and point to the process, saying, "It's only fear, doing what fear does."

When we meticulously deconstruct the five deceptions and eight manipulations, detaching from their influence by virtue of clear insight, their distortions can start to give way to truth (our third postulate). A veil is lifted from our eyes, and we may look at our situation clearly and objectively, free of the deforming effects of fear's need to see things its way. This is not meant to be a prescription by itself . . . we are, for the most part, still reading the map of the territory. But even at this early stage in the journey, we can use these principles to help relax the grip of our otherwise fixed belief in fear.

NOTES

1. Again, this is not meant to present an overly pessimistic view but rather to make us aware of the true extent of anxiety and the suffering it creates. Only by illuminating fear and bringing it into consciousness can we know what we are dealing with, find real solutions, and open up the possibility for a vastly improved experience in life. Otherwise, we simply get used to living with anxiety, relegating it for the most part to the unconscious, where it continues to do its damage in secret. This is not to say that we cannot experience fulfillment at all unless completely free of fear. Again, our fulfillment is limited in direct proportion to the amount of fear present. Until fear is fully resolved, we allow fulfillment to the degree that we have control over threats in the environment. Often what we take for fulfillment is *only* this sense of control over fear. Think, for example, of the exhilaration of finally solving a problem that has been haunting you, or winning a contentious legal battle. This is not true fulfillment but the relief that comes from feeling as though we have escaped from or established dominance over fear. Fulfillment is the realization of "good," not the escape from "bad." Think also of the thrill of a roller coaster—it gives an illusion that we are victorious over our fear. The same is true for our drive to be "great," "special," "rich," "powerful," and so forth . . . all different forms of the strategy to secure our authority over that which scares us. In the end, however, we know all control can be stripped away and we will find ourselves still longing for a more transcendent fulfillment.

2. Noted psychologist Dan Gottlieb, who suffered a severe automobile accident that left him paralyzed from the chest down, said, "All of us are skating on very thin ice all of the time; I just happen to know it better than most people" (personal correspondence).

3. This is, in large part, why children play. So much of play is designed around opportunities to practice control. Play is our primary way of learning when young, and the lesson it teaches is how to master the forces of threat by taking control. In sports, for example, one tries to get control over a ball or to achieve another physical challenge. Many sports add the element of getting more control than another team. Sometimes play is designed to scare us in controlled settings where we feel a thrill upon coming out on the other side safely, feeling a power and control over that which scared us.

4. And attractiveness is based on all sorts of things related to fear. The male ideal is often someone who looks fearless, unafraid of the challenges of life, and therefore someone who would make a good protector and provider. The female ideal is often one who is so accepting, safe, and nonjudgmental that we can let go of our fear of rejection, completely absorbed in fulfillment.

5. Contrast all this with the David Carradine character in the old TV series *Kung Fu*. His every movement was a planful, intentional meditation, a free choice based on what served his purposes best in the moment. Through his lifelong training in the monastery, he had come to master the automatic habits of fear.

6. Interestingly, the words "anger" and "anxiety" come from the same root.

7. The Gordian knot was a knot that was said to be impossible to untangle. Alexander the Great simply took his sword and cut straight through it.

8. The exception to this is when we feel cornered, confronted with something so anxiety-provoking that we cannot avoid it. The anxious client, for instance, seems to be looking at their fear very intensely, but this is different from an objective examination. As will be discussed, we can, when truly threatened, stare fixedly at fear without really looking at what it is composed of, seeing only our fearful imaginings instead.

9. We will be working with a technique later for finding the "core fear" beneath all others.

10. Of course, we can only synopsize in the briefest way this sampling of various schools of thought, and will therefore talk about those aspects relevant to our purposes here.

11. A deep insight can, in fact, be considered an action—the act of looking at fear. This is why insight can sometimes be enough for correction (with no need for overt action). But this is only if the insight is not being used to hide a resistance to action. The physical action isn't necessary per se, but the willingness to take it is. Only then can we be sure that the fear has surrendered its hold.

12. Franklin Delano Roosevelt's line is apropos: "The only thing we have to fear is fear itself."

3

THE GREAT REVELATION

My life has been filled with terrible misfortunes, most of which never happened.

—Michel de Montaigne

The five deceptions and eight manipulations are fear's way of trying to preserve itself, to keep us in its employ as we attempt to secure our fulfillment. The deceptions, taken together, could be described as fear's avoidance strategies: we avoid seeing that fear is ubiquitous, that it is at the root of all problems, and we avoid looking at or facing the correct fear—all in the attempt to *avoid the experience of* fear. The manipulations can be characterized as fear's control strategies: we stare hypnotically at fear's projections, insisting on doing something to quash them now, ruminating on this in the hope of finding a solution, etc.—all in the attempt to *get control over* fear. Of course, these strategies backfire, creating more fear and less fulfillment. So we are in search of a new approach. Instead of avoidance, we want to practice moving toward fulfillment directly, even if fear says it is risky. And instead of control, we must move toward this fulfillment with no guarantee of success. In short, we must "face our fear."

Of course, this dictum is often repeated, both in psychotherapy and in popular culture. But we are talking about something much more precise than is usually understood by the phrase. With the insights given by the five deceptions and eight manipulations, we can begin to formulate a prescription for exactly how to navigate fear's pitfalls and move most successfully toward our goals. We do not just face any fear, a simplistic formula that can easily send us down dead-end trails or even exacerbate anxiety. Instead, we use our insight into the deceptions to look at and move through the correct fear at the source. And instead of trying to gain control over this fear, we expose ourselves to it by moving in ways counter to the manipulations (i.e., we disobey fear's demand that we act on it now, we break the hypnotic fixation on fear, refuse to ruminate in advance, and so forth). This is our new path—when we use the phrase "facing fear," it is this that we mean.

THE GREAT REVELATION

When we face our fear according to the insights given by the deceptions and manipulations, a most extraordinary truth reveals itself: We discover *the fear is not real!* More precisely, we find it doesn't play out the way we thought it would, and nothing so terrible as we imagined actually happens. We see it simply cannot carry out its exaggerated and distorted threats, and so it loses its meaning as something scary.

Fear *never* plays out as we have imagined it would. When we fully expose ourselves to fear, seeing it in all its nakedness, one of two things happens: at worst, we find a problem to deal with, a problem we *can* deal with . . . and not the ruinous thing we had imagined. Most of the time, however, we discover the fear was completely made up, the result of faulty ideas learned in childhood, reinforced over and over throughout a lifetime. In one of these two ways, fear disappears or is transformed whenever we actually face it. It is seen to be an "illusion," a distorted interpretation of how things actually are.

This is the great revelation that comes from facing fear. To elaborate, whenever we face fear, we may, of course, find a problem, perhaps even the problem we were afraid of. But as we encounter fear in real time, it simply becomes a problem to handle rather than a problem to be afraid of. Understanding what is really going on (as opposed to what we anticipated), we are called simply to deal with the problem. The experience in the moment is absent of fear; our projections into the future disappear as we become focused on the present and the most effective way to handle things.[1] And we find there are always a multitude of options for handling them. Fear had us believing we would be rendered helpless to deal with it at all.

Furthermore, as we face the problem, we find it always passes—we survive it—and this by itself relieves us of the fear. The catastrophic future we had imagined was one we could not survive intact. Something essential would be lost. But when we get to the other side and discover that "life goes on," this distortion necessarily disappears.[2] In fact, all of the distortions and manipulations are spontaneously resolved when we live through what we had feared. We wake up from the hypnotic trance that had us believing all sorts of terrible things would happen; we see through the lie of fear that says these things would happen all at once; there is no more cause for fear to regenerate itself or to distort time; and so forth. The bubble of projected fears in our mind has been burst, and we wake up to the truth that was waiting behind its walls.

But it must be repeated that most of the time when we face fear, we find that there is no "there" there . . . that fear has no substance at all. It is completely without basis in reality, a fabrication built from childhood misunderstandings. For as we will later show, these ideas originate (always) in childhood when we didn't yet have enough experience with the world to build an accurate model for "danger." Nor did we have the options for responding to it that we now have as adults. When we first became afraid, we began our avoidance response and never challenged the assumption that these things were, in fact, dangerous. This unwittingly preserved and reinforced our thinking throughout our life. Psychologically, we became frozen at the level of development where these distorted ideas were born. And we remain locked into our childhood view of things by our refusal to test it out and see what actually happens. This is the basis of any neurosis . . . a failure to accept and keep pace with reality. Our childhood ideas can become so exaggerated, so discrepant with reality, as to be ludicrous. And yet many live their life terrified by these very things.

Facing fear, then, the correct fear at the root of our problems, is the great key to liberation. For a dramatic example, let's look at the Broadway version of *The Phantom of the Opera*. The heroine, Christine Daaé, has been "hypnotized" throughout the story by the Phantom, who hides his deformed face behind a mask. The Phantom is in love with Christine and uses a mixture of fear and the promise of fulfillment to win her over. At a particular moment, however, Christine lifts his mask when he is unsuspecting. At first she is horrified but then, having looked directly at what she was afraid of, the hypnotic spell is broken and she sees him for who he truly is. Her perception no longer twisted by fear, she tells him that it is not in his face but in his soul that "the true distortion lies." Without fear, her compassion is awakened, and she kisses him.[3] With this ultimate demonstration of transcendence over fear, she undoes him completely. Since he cannot scare or control her, he lets her go.

Facing fear is also the path to healing. A *Course in Miracles* agrees: "All healing is essentially the release from fear" (Foundation for Inner Peace, 1975). And this is true regardless of the school of thought. Psychoanalysts will enjoin us to "invade our anxiety." Exposure therapy is predicated on the idea of facing fear without responding in an avoid-ant way. Spiritual or transpersonal approaches pit fear's perspective against an expanded view that shows the fear to be inconsequential. Even positive thinking requires looking at the fear one wants to trans-form if one is to have a chance at success.

But once again, it is crucial that we understand exactly what is in-volved in "facing fear." First, we must be willing to look at the fear rather than avoid it. This may sound obvious but is so often the cause of misdirection, even in psychotherapy. If we do not look directly at our fear, how will we know what it is we are to face? The next step is to be willing to move into and through the fear, to discover that it has no teeth and cannot fulfill its promises. And finally, we must deconstruct our fear thoroughly (as we will do in the exercises to follow) to know that we are facing the correct fear, the fear at the root of the problem. This is essential because it is the only fear that, if faced, will truly resolve the problem. Without this, we can have at best a temporary healing of a temporary problem, while the true fear at the root will soon issue forth in a new incarnation. At worst, facing the wrong fear exposes us to anxiety with no resolution.

WHEN LOOKING AT FEAR IS ENOUGH

In fact, sometimes looking at the fear honestly is all that is required to show us that it is illusory. The action component of facing fear—moving into and through it physically—is not always necessary. If we look at the fear with no investment in seeing it other than as it is, we can achieve the same awareness of its unreality that moving through fear gives. This is the power of a deep analytic insight or a thorough deconstruction of the anxiety at the root of things. Freud (1913) was the first to demonstrate this with his "talking cure." His patient Anna O. was relieved of her "hysterical paralysis" simply by becoming aware of the investment she had in its symptoms.

In a sense, though, looking at fear *is* a form of taking action. We "move our attention" in one direction when avoiding fear and in the opposite direction when facing it. Sometimes this is all it takes to discover that fear has no power to force us to run. Still, taking physical action against the fear is sometimes necessary. Remember the fourth deception? Fear can sometimes seduce us into doubting we are safe until we have had a direct experience of living through it. Furthermore, if we only think about our fear without facing it physically, we run the risk of leaving aspects of it veiled in obscurity—it can be difficult to see the subtler levels of a fear we have become accustomed to. Taking physical action against the fear forces a confrontation with the whole of it . . . as long as it is the correct fear. Still, it's important to understand that it is really the act of looking at fear that is fear's undoing; it is a declaration that we will no longer be forced to run from it. Furthermore, if one predetermines that they don't have to take physical action for exposure to the fear, there is the high probability that they are secretly avoiding a fear of taking such action. The willingness to take corrective action is an important safeguard against this possibility.

The great revelation—that fear *never* makes good on its promises—means that we need only look at, and possibly face, the correct fear at the root of any problem and that fear will lose its power. And because fear is at the root of every problem, we have a path to the resolution of our suffering as a whole. Every time we face fear, we either find a manageable problem to deal with or we find nothing at all. And when there is a problem to deal with, eventually we discover "this too shall pass." With these principles, we no longer buy into the premise of fear, shifting out of distorted imaginings and discovering a greater truth behind them.

NOTES

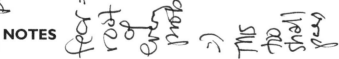

1. It is impossible to be in action handling a problem and anxious about that problem at the same time. This is why some people are surprised to find

they are "cool in a crisis." Any anxiety one experiences while handling a situation is only about future problems, never the problem they are working on at the moment.

2. Even our fear of death can give way to this truth, as we will see in our exercises. When we live through the process of dying (in our imagination), we discover that the real experience is completely different from what fear had us believe. People who are terminally ill often come to peace with death because in accepting that it is imminent, they have looked at and faced their fear in imagination. Coming out on the other side, they see death in a larger context, outside the bubble created by fear. Death is no longer the "be all and end all," their personal safety no longer the only thing worthy of attention. They have let go of their investment in fixating upon such fear and are in touch with a vaster perspective. This is true regardless of one's beliefs about the afterlife.

3. In the novel, we are told he had never been kissed, not even by his mother.

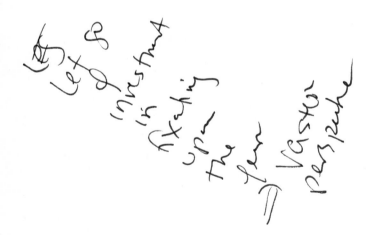

4

THREE DOORWAYS TO RESOLVING FEAR

Come to the cliff, he said. We are afraid, they said. Come to the cliff, he said. They came. He pushed them. And they flew.

—Stuart Wilde

Understanding that the great key to resolving fear is to look at and sometimes face the right fear, we will now discuss three "doorways" that can be opened with that key, the doorways of the Mind, the Body, and the Spirit.[1] Opening the Doorway of the Mind means getting a deep insight into a problem and discovering it is not "real," as we have just discussed. Again though, this means looking at it thoroughly, even imagining what it would be like to live through it, before we can truly see that it has no power to hurt us. Opening the Doorway of the Body, as we have also discussed, means taking a physical action to literally move through one's fear, giving the direct experience that the problem we were afraid of cannot carry out its threat. And opening the Doorway of the Spirit means getting so filled up with a "higher" perspective that the fear loses its power, appearing insignificant in comparison.

This is the essence of what is called holistic or transpersonal psychotherapy. The three doorways represent the whole that we are—mind, body, and spirit. It's impossible to address one part of who we are without addressing the other two. When one part is affected, the other two are as well. Therefore, if we are to *fully* resolve anxiety, if we are to achieve a true cure for a problem, we must do so in mind, body, and spirit. All three doorways are inextricably linked and must be involved in our search. We have already seen that a true *insight* into the source of fear (opening the Doorway of the Mind) will show the fear to be illusory, that it came from a childhood construct now understood to be invalid. If we have really seen this, then we will spontaneously feel "bigger" than the fear and experience an expansion of the spirit. At the same time, the physical tension in the muscles will release spontaneously as well so that we experience a deep and profound relaxation. If, on the other hand, someone starts by walking through the Doorway of the Body, using, for instance, an abreactive approach such as in Gestalt therapy (pounding, screaming, or otherwise squeezing out the physical tension on a pillow), we may know they are not finished until they have a concomitant release of fear in the mind and an expansion of the spirit at the same time. And if someone resolves their fear by getting filled with a higher (spiritual) perspective, seeing the fear as inconsequential in comparison, then it must necessarily dry up in their thoughts and "melt" out of their body as well if the cure is to be complete.[2]

ADVANTAGES OF THIS MODEL

It's not only necessary but, in the end, unavoidable that we address all three doorways if we are to heal from anxiety and discover our fulfillment. Furthermore, this holistic model provides an essential flexibility in our approach that can save enormous amounts of time. We no longer have to work out problems that arise in the mind, body, and spirit separately. Working through the problem at the root in one of the doorways spontaneously resolves it in the other two. Because of the interconnection between the three doorways, it is not necessary to spend years in meditation, work out all holding patterns in the body, or resolve all neuroses in the mind. Approaching each of these separately, and without getting at the root of the true problem, will only resolve some of our problems, while others will remain to keep us bound to anxious thoughts, physical tensions, or spiritual limitations.

In this way, our holistic model also becomes our trusted compass. It can be used to assess whether we have, in fact, faced the right fear at the root of the problem. If not, problems will persist or resurface. And it can be used to measure whether our fear is truly and fully resolved. We simply check whether the fear is released in each of the three doorways: Do we have a true insight that the fear isn't "real," a deep relaxation in the body, and a spiritual sense of new possibilities no longer hampered by fear?

It can sometimes be much easier to address our fear by opening one doorway instead of another. The flexibility of our approach lets us choose which doorway is most accessible to us in a particular situation. For example, someone who has obsessive thoughts may do well to avoid the Doorway of the Mind if it were to encourage further obsession. For another, the same doorway might be the best way to discover the fear at the root, with an insight that clarifies confusion and shows their fear to be unreal. Someone who is filled with anger may need to discharge that energy physically first by walking through the Doorway of the Body. And someone who is depressed from an existential despair or struggling with a sense of meaninglessness might well find the Doorway of the Spirit to be most effective.[3]

APPLYING THE THREE-DOORWAYS MODEL TO OTHER THERAPEUTIC APPROACHES

We can now expand upon our earlier statement: whenever a therapy fails to fully resolve anxiety, it is because it has not fully addressed the correct fear, resolving it in all three doorways. On the other hand, when anxiety is fully resolved on all three levels, there is nowhere for the fear to hide.[4] In psychodynamic therapy, for instance, a true insight can give a transformative experience that brings relief in body and spirit. This is much more than mere intellectual awareness; it is a complete cure. However, it's very possible to get an insight that only remains intellectual (the classic defense called "intellectualization"). This will never create real change though many can stay stuck at this level, the insight giving an illusion of progress. If it is to truly set us free, an intellectual insight must reach down to where we are holding tension in the body and where we are constricting our spirit as well. That is why advice-giving or motivation is rarely effective (think of the Nike slogan "Just do it"). It hasn't addressed the problem in mind, body, and spirit. Even if it helps for the moment, it cannot offer a real, complete, or lasting change because it's going to meet all of the unconscious reasons—our secret investments—for resisting such change.

If a CBT therapist offers someone the right description of their irrational belief, this too can give a true insight (Doorway of the Mind). The client can then adopt a more rational belief and experience true and lasting change. Not only are they convinced of their insight but they feel a release of tension in the body and a larger sense of self and possibility as well. On the other hand, if a correct insight into the irrational belief is not achieved, the therapist's arguments, no matter how convincing, will fall on the deaf ears of a client who has spent a lifetime believing just these things. All the hidden investments of fear will remain firmly intact. Someone, for example, who is anxious about contracting a fatal illness is not going to be moved if told the thought is irrational or the chances unlikely even when they are presented with statistics or a doctor's exam results.

Various therapies have arisen expressly for the purpose of avoiding the trap of intellectualization. Gestalt therapy, Reichian therapy, bioenergetics, and more all begin by entering the Doorway of the Body. Each of these can achieve a dramatic release of the physical tension that fear (or any of its offspring) creates. In our society especially, where so much physical expression is repressed, this can be very freeing. And if enough bodily tension is released, there will be a spontaneous shift in insight and a natural lightness of being (a spiritual shift) as well, the "weight" of the fear now released. But if one merely goes through the motions of a catharsis, they will have a hollow experience. Even if one releases significant physical energy, without the insight that the problem was unreal or the sense of spiritual elevation that can come from catharsis, the physical tension will start to build once again. I have often seen this phenomenon. The client feels the power of a physical release but has to repeat it daily to maintain a status quo, never advancing toward real freedom.

Similarly, if one begins with the Doorway of the Spirit, perhaps with a transpersonal or faith-based approach, it is possible to engage in a "spiritual bypass," as it is called, using one's ideas about a higher reality to escape from something they are afraid to address directly. This, again, can look like positive thinking, motivation, or affirmations that, unless they strike at the root of the problem, won't reach deeply enough for real change. They can actually generate more tension and suffering as one insists on their spiritual worldview, squelching the need for release in the body or refusing to acknowledge fearful cognitions.

The potential pitfall in any technique, no matter which doorway it utilizes, is that the client (or practitioner!) may have a hidden investment in the technique and unwittingly block the other two doorways. Again, it will be spontaneous and natural for the other two doorways to open up if one has a true shift in the first doorway. But one or two of the other doorways can be barred if one's model does not acknowledge—or actively resists—that these other doorways are necessary for a complete resolution. For example, if one doesn't allow for the possibility of a higher perspective, they can block their access to it. When the fear is otherwise ready to be resolved, they are left wondering why insight or physical release hasn't brought them the fulfillment they had hoped for. Instead, they feel stuck in a human experience that can't be transcended. It's also very easy to "hide" from the need for physical expression when using, say, a psychodynamic or CBT approach. There is much in our society that discourages physical expression, and people often feel it is embarrassing to do so. At the same time, our society rewards the intellectual "sophistication" or even "maturity" of someone who calmly and rationally thinks about a problem without needing to emote. And finally, those who are devoted to a body-oriented approach can sometimes squash an important intellectual insight or spiritual perspective. Because they insist that "the body has the answers," any deviation is suspect as an intellectual defense or spiritual escape.

HOW TO CHOOSE WHICH DOORWAY TO ENTER FIRST

While it is true that certain problems lend themselves more to one doorway over the others, there is a general rule of thumb for choosing which doorway to begin with. Our investment in fear makes the Doorway of the Spirit the hardest (in general) for people to walk through successfully. We are so devoted to a self-protective fear, a preoccupation with "me" and "mine," that we resist the spiritual perspective that shows there is much more going on. In the vernacular, we have a hard time "getting outside of ourselves." But for these reasons, if one *is* able to let go at this level, the Doorway of the Spirit can be the fastest approach, facilitating the release from all that investment in fear. If a spiritual experience is powerful enough (think conversion experiences), it can "blow our mind" to see how insignificant we are. No longer interpreting insignificance in a fearful way, we find it freeing to let go of constant self-absorption and anxiety. A new sense of self emerges, one that needs no protection. If we can engage the Doorway of the Spirit, the fears in the mind and body simply disperse. The perspective of the spirit washes them away like a tidal wave, their insignificance clearly apparent.

The second-fastest way to release fear is through the Doorway of the Mind. Getting a deep insight into the fact that our problems are not "real" in the way we had imagined, we can readily see them as arbitrary thoughts we have chosen. This enables us to step back from our thoughts and "choose once again" (Foundation for Inner Peace, 1975), this time without fear. And since the body holds the tension of fear, when we become skillful enough, we can interrupt our thoughts before they get locked into our physiology. It can still be difficult to achieve true insight but less so than achieving a spiritual perspective. We are more willing to examine ourselves and our neuroses than we are to let go of our self-importance. Nevertheless, a true insight will relieve the fear in mind and body, and the spirit will naturally elevate in response.

Finally, if one is too anxious to even think clearly, then the Doorway of the Body is still available to us. We can release the physical energy of the fear in any of its manifestations—e.g., pounding out anger, crying out guilt, shaking out anxiety—and then integrate a corresponding shift in insight and elevation of spirit. This is the most concrete of the door-ways and therefore easiest to access. All that is needed is to discharge the physical energy of fear. But because it is so concrete, it can more readily block the subtler shifts in thought and spirit necessary for a full cure. Still, a deep catharsis can spontaneously turn thoughts of fear into freedom and effect a powerful expansion of the spirit.[5]

Even though the Doorway of the Spirit can take care of so many problems at once, it's essential to remember that the "fastest" route is the one we are ready for. If we prematurely adopt a spiritual perspec-tive, rehearsing the idea that nothing really matters in the grand scheme of things, we may end up feeling diminished, unable to appreciate it as a key to freedom. It can even foster more fear if we interpret it as meaning we are worthless. If we implore someone to get insight into how their fear is not real while they are still invested in it, their resis-tance will increase (and the clinician can harm the therapeutic relation-ship). And if we have a particular resistance to the idea of expression through the body, we may do better to look for insight into what this resistance is about or find a spiritual perspective that frees us up for such expression. In the end, it is about knowing what we are ready for and becoming skillful in choosing which doorway is most helpful in a given situation.

SEEING THE THREE DOORWAYS AT WORK WITHIN US

Let's look at how the three doorways live inside us to appreciate the importance of their interaction in our life and therefore in healing. It's easy to see mind and body interacting whenever we have high emotions of any sort. The thoughts involved make for obvious physical changes in the body, like a racing heart, sweating palms, adrenaline surges, and so forth. At the same time, an unexpected pain in the body can certainly provide a direct trigger for plenty of unpleasant thoughts. Freud's (1913) success in curing conversion disorders demonstrates how walking through the Doorway of the Mind with a correct insight can create a change in the body. And we are all familiar with at least some of the many ways in which hormones and neurotransmitters interact with thoughts. For an obvious example, we only need to realize how powerful our physical response to sexual thoughts can be and how sexual touch can inspire thoughts just as easily.

Sex is, in fact, a helpful way to see how all three doorways interact. As sexual excitement builds, the spirit swells to fill the body and make it breathe more deeply. The chest, sex organs, and the whole body, in a sense, swell. Thoughts of problems, inhibitions, and limitations of any sort transform into thoughts of love, or some approximation of it. The swelling continues past the body to reach out to and include the other in its embrace, the two melting as one in a vastly expanded sense of the "bigness" of the spirit. Ultimately, with the physical release of orgasm, the spirit seems released from the confines of the body altogether. Afterward, the spirit "rests" in this open state, the body deeply relaxed and the mind still and at peace.

Here's an example of walking through the Doorway of the Body to open up the mind and spirit. I once had a patient who had been raised to be "proper" and "nice." This, not surprisingly, led to a highly repressed personality style. In the context of other things, I inquired about his sex life and particularly if he felt free in sex—free to express himself the way he wanted, free to ask for what he wanted from his partner, and so forth. After discovering that, in fact, he was embarrassed to make noise during sex, we worked through the fear behind this inhibition. At the end of the session, he announced he was going home to make love to his wife and "open up." The next time we met, he was quite transformed. His entire demeanor had changed. Where before there had been great tension and self-doubt, he now carried a powerful sense of confidence and a new kind of relaxation. I asked him what happened to cause such change. He said that he did indeed go home that night to make love with his wife. As he approached orgasm he resolved to open up his voice and let himself make all the sound he wanted. He found himself roaring with a sense of power, wild with the excitement of letting loose so thoroughly, surrendering his inhibitions and getting fully taken over by the moment. With extreme satisfaction on his face, he said, "It changed me." And indeed, from that moment on, he was different, maintaining the same level of confidence and power—a sort of spiritual magnanimity—that he came in with that day.

For an important example of someone who resolved their fear by walking first through the Doorway of the Spirit, we have this story. Martin Luther King Jr., shortly before his assassination, had been receiving anonymous phone calls from people threatening to bomb his house. One anxious night, he could not sleep and began pacing up and down in the kitchen, worrying for his and his family's safety. His fear was at a peak and he longed for a way out. But with everyone counting on him to continue to lead the movement, there really was no escape. At that moment, he felt he had a spiritual "visitation"; he described an intuitive certainty that he was doing what he was supposed to be doing. With this, a calm came over his mind and body and he no longer doubted himself. He knew what he had to do and was ready to do it. A few days later, he gave his magnificent "I have a dream" speech on the mall in Washington. All three doorways had been fully integrated, his fear clearly vanquished.

THE NEXUS POINT: SEAT OF EMOTIONS, SEAT OF THE SELF

To really understand the interaction of the three doorways, we want to look at the "mechanism" that ties them together. Starting with the Doorway of the Body we may ask, "How exactly does fear manifest in the body?" and "How does its release in the body lead to a shift in intellectual insight and an expansion of the spirit?" Notice that there is a "place" in the body where we feel our emotions most intensely—a ganglion, if you will—where all the relevant "information" gathers to create an emotion. It is a sort of central processing station, the primary area where our emotions are experienced. We will call it the Nexus point. This Nexus point is situated just behind the sternum, pretty much positioned in the center of the upper body (perhaps a little closer to the back). As more than just a physical experience, its location can be hard to pinpoint precisely. It may be more helpful to look for it on top of the middle of the diaphragm, just below the level of the heart. In fact, it must certainly be what we mean when we say we feel something (emotionally) "in our heart." You may never have thought of it before as having a physical location, but it is easily recognized as simply the place where, again, you feel emotions the most intensely. Tension, fear, stress, and other negative emotions are primarily felt here, as are love, excitement, fulfillment, and other positive emotions. You can also recognize it as the place from which arises the deep sigh of relief when fear is released. When we are anxious, the Nexus point causes us to tighten our diaphragm, and we feel the "angst" or "squeezing" sensation at this spot.[6] In fact, all of our emotions affect and are affected by the contraction or relaxation of the Nexus point. It may be understood as "the seat of emotions."

One may ask about the sensations we feel with emotions that are located in other parts of the body. There are, of course, many such sensations (e.g., tense trapezii, sweaty palms), but these are physical-only sensations that do not, by themselves, stimulate emotions.[7] If relevant to us (those that are irrelevant go unnoticed, like the feel of your clothes against your skin, for example), the information from these physical sensations is sent to the Nexus point where they get interpreted by our thoughts and spiritual perspective. This is how meaning gets assigned to the sensations. Until then, we don't have an emotional response to them . . . we don't "feel" them (emotionally) in the Nexus point. For instance, someone who, under hypnosis, has been given the suggestion that contact with an ice cube will be experienced as burning heat can actually develop a blister. The thoughts and spiritual context assigned to the physical sensation are what create the meaning of it. Therefore, physical sensations not registered in the Nexus point are emotionally neutral. They are sensations without meaning; the meaning is given by the composite of physical sensations, thoughts, and spiritual "movements" (contractions and expansions).[8]

So the Nexus point is the primary seat of emotions. But what do we even mean by "emotions"? We say we "feel" an emotion, but the word "feeling" can refer to an emotional experience, a cognitive opinion, a physical sensation, or a spiritual impression. In our model, emotions are the amalgam of thoughts, physical sensations, and spiritual movements that occur in response to a situation, real or imagined. Here's how it works: we encounter a situation and have our emotional response to it. This means (to start somewhere) we have thoughts about it. These thoughts create automatic and corresponding physical sensations at the Nexus point (notice that there is always a physical sensation associated with any emotion). We feel these sensations as tension or release of tension in the Nexus point. There is also a corresponding expansion or contraction of the spirit; expansion with release from fear and contraction when we are engaged with fear. All three of these responses interact, shaping and informing each other in a way that combines to create our total emotional experience. For example, when the emotion is anxiety, we have thoughts about how a particular situation is dangerous. This stimulates physical tension, felt in the Nexus point. The spirit contracts, becoming focused and engaged with the threat. All this gives our thoughts further material to interpret, the interpretation creating more physical and spiritual responses, and so on. In another situation we might feel an emotion of excitement. Our thoughts might be about a goal we hope to achieve; the physical response may be described as a fluttering sensation; and our spirit expands, giving us a sense of power and capacity to rise to the challenge. Again, all this is felt most poignantly at the Nexus point.

Because thoughts and spiritual experiences are non-physical, we must understand that the Nexus point is not just a place in the body.[9] The Nexus point is the vehicle by which non-physical thoughts and the non-physical spirit are focalized, made manifest, into physicality. This is how they become something that we can "feel" in the body. The physical sensation attached to an emotion is the manifest expression, we may say, of thought and spirit. To experience the non-physical in a way we may "know" with the senses requires contracting it from an unmanifest state into something condensed and tangible. The natural state of the spirit, for instance, is infinite expansion; we experience this as a sense of "bigness" or "magnanimity." When the Nexus point contracts, it is not just our body that contracts but our spirit as well. We have the sense of feeling "squeezed" into too tight a container.[10] Our mind also can "tense up" or relax, focusing narrowly on the problem when tense, lying still and quiet when relaxed.[11]

If we examine it further, we notice that the Nexus point employs the diaphragm and the breath to help actualize its contractions.[12] Physical tension, by definition, is a holding pattern in the muscles, and emotional tension includes most of all a holding pattern in the very large muscle that is the diaphragm. With tension, we hold or restrict our breath, causing a pressure upon and contraction of the diaphragm. When the tension is released, the diaphragm is released as well; we can breathe freely again, often heaving a deep sigh of relief. And with this release, we feel a shift in our thinking and an expansion of the spirit (literally, more room to breathe).

For example, when stressed, we spontaneously take deep breaths (this is different than when we sigh with relief) as if we're struggling to get more air. On the inhalation of such breaths, the ribcage expands, giving the diaphragm more room so it is not so "cramped." The exhalation presses down on the diaphragm to squeeze out some of its excess tension. The combination of movement in the diaphragm and breathing is involved in the expression of so many emotions: exasperation—a quick burst of exhalation; surprise—a sharp inhalation; being stunned— inhaling and holding the breath; feeling let down—deflating the lungs.[13] Similarly, crying, laughing, screaming, roaring, etc., all affect, are affected by, and also are effected by contractions of the diaphragm and breathing patterns. Even hiccups (repeated contractions of the diaphragm) can be caused by too much excitement or, so it is rumored, dispelled by being scared. All this is registered primarily in the Nexus point.

Think also of the expressions "uh-huh" and "uh-uh," casual versions of "yes" and "no." "Uh-uh" uses a harder glottal stop, with greater force in the contraction, than "uh-huh" does. In this way, it releases more of the tension associated with "no" than does "uh-huh." At the same time, the extra *h* in "uh-huh" releases more breath or spirit, as one would expect with the meaning of "yes." This is why the words "spirit" and "breath" or "wind" are so linked, as for example with the word "inspiration" in English, *ruach* in Hebrew, and *pneuma* in Greek.

Stress, we might say, is the accumulated tension of the many subtle fears we carry throughout the day and throughout our life. The diaphragm contracts, usually on a microscopic level, each time we react to a problem with stress. This contraction helps us bear down on the problem as we try to contain and get control over it. Contracting the diaphragm limits the capacity of the lungs to breathe freely and causes us to "strain." We may hold our breath to contract the diaphragm even more. By straining in this way, we concentrate our energy to use against the problem; as we press down upon the diaphragm, we press down upon or push against the problem. Ultimately, we hope to push the problem away from us, "pushing out" the accumulated tension as we do so. The grunting, groaning, or roaring sounds that can happen when straining against problems results from the combination of holding our breath and pushing on the diaphragm at the same time.

When stress is relieved, such as when we go on vacation, come home after a hard day at work, or simply go to bed for the night, the relaxation in the Nexus point causes the diaphragm to relax and our breathing patterns to become more regular. Our anxious thoughts calm down, and we let go of the spiritual "armor" we use to fight our way in the world. When this happens, we often heave deep spontaneous sighs, further relieving tension in the Nexus point. These may involve sound as well, created as the diaphragm discharges its tension by pressing against the lungs, expelling the necessary air to make the sound. Yawning sometimes happens too, the result of the diaphragm relaxing and allowing the body, mind, and spirit to "breathe" more freely.

A MODEL FOR THE SELF

While we started with the Doorway of the Body, this model describes not only how the mental and spiritual realms get translated into the physical but also how our physical experience and mental life have their "reverberations" in the spirit and how our spiritual and physical experiences shape our thoughts as well. How can we say which came first? Do we first have a thought of fear, for example, that warns of a specific threat? Or is it a spiritual contraction that comes from a sense of being small and vulnerable? Or is our initial experience a physical sensation of fear with an undefined dread or even a biochemical imbalance? The three doorways are so connected as to be indistinguishable . . . in fact, they are inseparable. When we have a physical release of tension in the Nexus point, we experience a release of fear in the mind and spirit as well. When the spirit swells and soars, the body is flooded with "streaming" sensations[14] and the mind dwells on nobler things. And with the recognition that our anxious thoughts are fabrications born of mistaken ideas, the body relaxes and the spirit softens once again.

If we fail to appreciate the full interaction of all three aspects of the self—mind, body, and spirit—we will not only lose an essential understanding of how emotions work but we will lose the chance to deal with them effectively. If, for instance, someone is focused only on the physical sensations of anxiety, they can misinterpret a panic attack as a heart attack.[15] Emotions are more than a set of physical sensations. Again, in the case of anxiety, we know it can be an extremely uncomfortable physical experience, causing a powerful constriction in the area of the Nexus point. But the physical experience is always accompanied by an intense focus on anxious thoughts and a sense of spiritual binding. An emotion is a living, dynamic thing. It is the functional interaction of mind, body, and spirit.

The event called an emotion, therefore, is an integration of all three, the total experience we have of a thought, which triggers or is triggered by a physical sensation, which triggers or is triggered by contractions and expansions of the spirit. It's impossible to have one of these without the other two occurring simultaneously. The combination is felt in and as the Nexus point. And while this describes the origin of emotions, it also describes the origin of the "self." All emotions taken together, the countless thoughts, physical sensations, and spiritual impulses that comprise each moment's experience, create the infinite facets of who we are, the extraordinary complexity of human experience.[16] The Nexus point may be called the seat of the self just as much as the seat of emotions. It enables us to peer into the inner sanctum, the secret throne room at the center of all our experience. When we look there, we find the creator of our private world, transforming the non-physical into the physical and manifest reality into an ethereal mental or spiritual experience. But we must remember, this is our doing . . . it is ourselves that we "feel" at the Nexus point. This is where "we" live. If we can get behind the controls of what occurs in the Nexus point, we may take our seat in this throne room and transform our experience. And since all such experience boils down to fear or fulfillment, we may become the master of our life by learning to shift the thoughts, physical sensations, and spiritual movements in the Nexus point from those of anxiety to those of our higher self.[17]

TECHNIQUES FOR WORKING WITH THE NEXUS POINT

There are many techniques for healing that work with or try to manipulate the Nexus point (even if not consciously intended). In meditation, for example, one is often instructed to train the attention on the breath and sometimes specifically on the "stillpoint" at which the breath flips from breathing in to breathing out. As we develop our concentrative ability, we discover this stillpoint is the same as our Nexus point. Ram Dass, a spiritual teacher, once described it as "a little muscle" that moves up and down in correspondence with our breathing. Rocking is another example: it is not only a way children self-soothe but is used in many spiritual traditions (Jewish davening, for example) to balance and soften tension in the Nexus point. It creates focus and stillness by finding the center of the rocking motion. This center is the physical aspect of the center of the Nexus point. Chanting causes a resonance that vibrates and breaks up tensions in the Nexus point as well. As mentioned earlier, sound requires constricting or closing the throat and then pressing down on the diaphragm to create a release of pressure. This release is felt as a lightening in the Nexus point. In Gestalt therapy and other abreactive techniques, one is sometimes encouraged to discharge the tension of their fear by screaming, roaring, or yelling. This creates a powerful contraction of the diaphragm, draining the physical energy of whatever the negative emotion happens to be. The result can be a profound relief felt in the Nexus point. And when one undergoes a relaxation exercise, for example a guided visualization, one experiences a melting away of the stress stored in the Nexus point. By focusing on soothing images and sensations, our attention is stolen away from the fears that were energizing contractions in the Nexus point.

There are several types of "breathwork" techniques used for healing purposes, most notably Stanislav Grof's holotropic breathwork (1988). Each employs some form of altered breathing—in Grof's case, breathing quickly and deeply for a prolonged period. There is much to say about these techniques, but for our purposes here it is important to note that they mimic what the body does naturally when emotionally stimulated. Babies preparing to scream and mothers giving birth—any of us when in a heightened emotional state—will spontaneously begin the same rapid, deep breathing. This often leads to a powerful expression of sound, as the breathing stimulates repeated convulsions of the diaphragm. Often there is a buildup, concluding in one long, loud sound that forces a great contraction of the diaphragm, spilling out the emotional contents it was holding and releasing the Nexus point. Because these techniques usually employ all three doorways, accompanying such a release is often a deep shift in thought and expansion of the spirit to a higher perspective. If you take a few fast, deep breaths right now, you will feel the Nexus point become highly energized, your rapid breathing "charging up" the emotions stored there.

CONCLUDING THOUGHTS ON THE THREE DOORWAYS

Hopefully by now we have a deep feel for each of the three doorways and their interaction. It bears repeating: We need this holistic orientation for a successful resolution of anxiety. Our approach must reach down to the source of a problem—the fear at the root rather than the symptoms at the surface—and it must do so in all three doorways. Without this, we have, at worst, psychopharmacology at the expense of psychotherapy.[18] At best, we will treat only one aspect of the constellation of factors that make up anxiety.

We need this holistic view as a society as well. We are (still) reluctant to talk about mental health and psychotherapy, averse to exploring our own internal state. We fixate instead, almost exclusively so, on what we can control outside of us. And the resistance to including a spiritual perspective as a real and valid part of the cure can be stronger still. As in our second postulate, if we are not willing to consider the possibility, there must be a fear insisting on a particular point of view that prevents us from investigating things in an unbiased way. What is it that accounts for our society's preoccupation with the external, material, corporeal, sensorial, and empirical focus? Why is exploring and giving voice to the interior world so often derided, even considered anathema? The answer must be that we are *afraid* to look within. Our society as a whole is obsessed with this external focus. All the while, the extraordinary degree of emotional suffering goes largely unaddressed. Mother Teresa, when she came to America, said that she had never seen such suffering before. In our country of relative material wealth, security, and comfort, she was overwhelmed by the degree of loneliness and isolation she encountered—"spiritual deprivation," she called it. It is crucial that we train our attention on the mind and spirit as well as the body and material surround. To help in the effort, we will now explore how we arrived at this state—the origins of our experience of separation, of manifest form, and the worldview that arose from it.

NOTES

1. The word "spirituality" can evoke much resistance in our society and it doesn't need to. Here is my workable definition: Spirituality is that which transcends the limits of our usual, empirically based understanding of who we are and what reality is in a way that coheres (i.e., is not psychotic or psychologically disorganized) and is fully integrated (i.e., all parts of the understanding relate to each other in a logically consistent way), giving a sense of purpose and meaning to existence. Because of its interaction with mind and body, a spiritual experience is actualized when it effects insight and action. As an alternative, Elkins, Hedstrom, Hughes, Leaf, and Saunders (1988) define spirituality as "a way of being and experiencing that comes about through awareness of a transcendent dimension and that is characterized by certain identifiable values in regard to self, others, nature, life, and whatever one considers to be the Ultimate." Because spirituality is not a physical or mental phenomenon, we

don't have much in the way of language for it, having taken only the physical and mental as "real." And yet we do know the experience of something "other" than just physical and mental phenomena. We say that we have a "sense" of the spiritual or an "impression" of it. Both of these words are based on physical descriptions. It is not a sense like the other five senses. It does not make an impression as in impressing upon something physical. It's easier to describe mental phenomena than spiritual ones because thoughts, while also non-physical, have more of a discrete, separate, nature . . . one thought is clearly seen as distinguished from another. But thoughts are no more physical than the spirit, and yet we know the experience well. Similarly, we know we exist even though we cannot describe how we know it. Before the time of Newton and Descartes (Laszlo, 2016; Grof, 1980), people accepted the existence of a spiritual domain more readily than many do today. Descartes and Newton began the trend toward empiricism; they wanted to grab hold of experience in a concrete way and measure it. Descartes said, "I think therefore I am," getting as close as he could to acknowledging the existence of spirit—the "am" part of "I am"—but still making it dependent on thoughts. With their attempt to measure our experience empirically, they built a consensual reality where only what we could know with the senses would be taken as real; we would deny the existence of anything we could not get our hands around in this way. Neuroscience today tries to explain thoughts by reducing them to biochemical and neurological processes. Consciousness is supposed to be an epiphenomenon of the brain. But it is impossible to create a non-physical experience from a physical one. There is no way for physical processes to capture or explain the *experience* of consciousness. Neuroscience has only explained physical processes that correlate with consciousness. And yet we know consciousness is "real." Without the cultural bias against the possibility of a spiritual reality, we would simply know of it as we know that we are alive and aware . . . that we have consciousness.

2. For additional discussion as well as exercises for walking through each of the three doorways, see *Radical Joy* (T. Pressman, 1999).

3. I once had a twenty-three-year-old young man come to me for depression. He had just graduated from college and was feeling the pressure to "get a job" rather than a true vocation, despairing at the prospect of an unfulfilling future. In one session his depression lifted completely as we discussed his need for meaning and purpose. He spontaneously realized that he had been trying too hard to satisfy others' expectations. This gave him the intellectual insight into what was wrong, released the physical energy that had been "depressed," and filled him with a powerful, spiritual sense of purpose as he left the office ready to pursue his own direction.

4. Freud had a marvelous analogy that speaks to this: "If the right of asylum existed at any one point in town . . . how long will it be before all the riffraff of the town collected there?" (1913, 135).

5. I remember my first experience with Gestalt therapy at the Esalen Institute when I was twenty-three years old. After pouring out a heavy store of pent-up emotions for the first time in my life, I sat there quietly. My thoughts were completely still while I had a sort of spiritual "vision." In my mind's eye, I saw white sparkling light filling the empty space inside that had just been cleaned out with the catharsis. It was accompanied by an extraordinary buoyancy, deep peace, and abundant gratitude for the facilitator's help and caring.

6. The German word *angst* means "a narrow passage," and this is most apt—when anxious, we feel that our energy is squeezed in a narrow passage at the Nexus point, causing the uncomfortable pressure and tightness we associate with fear.

7. If, by way of analogy, you lean over a pot of simmering soup and inhale through your nose, the molecules in the steam register as wonderful smells. If, however, you close your nose and inhale through your mouth, you can tell there are molecules registering on your tongue but they produce no "meaningful" sensation of flavor.

8. To illustrate this further: if we have a neutral sensation that we then learn signals a medical problem, we may become worried or anxious (even if not physically uncomfortable). We have assigned meaning to the sensation, developed thoughts and spiritual contractions in response to it, and so it has become an emotional experience. Think of the child who scrapes his or her knee but doesn't start crying until they see the blood. Or the anxiety client who is sure they feel a lump until the MRI shows nothing there. And of course, there is plenty of work being done on the relationship between biochemistry and emotions (cf. Pert, 1999). We all know, for instance, how sexual hormones are released in response to sexual thoughts and how a "spiritual" experience can fill the body with endorphins. Then too, the same sexual touch can be interpreted in one situation as "safe" and in another as "unsafe," causing entirely different chemical responses. Hormones, neurotransmitters, etc., must be considered physical-only phenomena that don't actually create emotions until they are allied with thoughts and spiritual responses as well.

9. The Greeks thought the mind was in the heart—we may presume, where our Nexus point is. Of course, thoughts are not located in any physical headquarters, but they are so closely associated with the physical aspect of emotions that the confusion is understandable!

10. When the spirit expands, we feel the physical sensations of our emotions in a much larger area of the body. Think of how sexual feelings flood the entire

body (and even seem to expand beyond the body), while sadness, felt as a more localized sensation, almost literally contracts the body to become smaller.

11. Interestingly, the body mirrors these movements of spirit and mind. Notice, for example, that when tense, we contract our muscles as we contract our spirit, our eyes narrow and focus as do our thoughts, etc.

12. You can readily feel this by taking in a somewhat deep breath and holding it. The pressure is experienced in the diaphragm, the back of the throat (where you have blocked the flow of air), but even more so in the Nexus point which seems to connect the two. If still unclear about this, try holding your breath until you can't hold it any longer; the "aching" sensation that compels us to breathe brings the Nexus point out in bold relief. Or you can expel all of your breath and hold it while pulling the diaphragm up. As you do so, you can clearly feel the diaphragm pulling up against the Nexus point.

13. Notice again the mirroring movements of facial muscles with each of these.

14. Alexander Lowen's (1994) concept of "streaming" sensations in the body fits well with our tripartite model.

15. The Schachter-Singer two-factor theory of emotion (1962), which suggested that physiological cues can create emotional experience without the input of "accurate" cognitions, leaves us with a rather robotic view of the human experience.

16. This accounts for the fact that when in fear, we experience ourselves as an endlessly shifting state of relative experiences, as in our postulates. When fulfilled, we integrate all our separate parts into a unified whole, resolving these many states into a singular, constant self that transcends the limits of relative experience.

17. In certain of our exercises, we will become acutely aware of the Nexus point and "penetrate" the tension in its centermost point to dissolve and release the fear that generated it.

18. While psychopharmacology has its place and can be life-saving at times (as well as a potential adjunct to therapy), I am complaining about when it is used as a substitute for psychotherapy.

5

COSMOGONY AND PSYCHOLOGY

Separation as the Source of Fear

The knowledge of the ancients was perfect. How perfect? At first, they did not know that there were things. This is the most perfect knowledge; nothing can be added. Next, they knew there were things but did not yet make distinctions between them. Next, they made distinctions between them, but they did not yet pass judgments upon them. When judgments were passed, the Way was destroyed.

—Chuang-tzu

How did fear come to be so ubiquitous, the overarching experience of the human condition? How did we come to believe that being afraid was the most effective way to ensure we would protect ourselves and find fulfillment? It may seem there is no alternative, but that is only because we are so used to living this way. Why, for instance, do we instinctively avoid looking at or facing fear? Why are we not "wired" instead to be curious about it, to investigate it, especially given how much trouble it causes us? To understand this as we continue deconstructing anxiety, we will now look at the origins of fear, both in the evolution of humanity and in the psychology of the individual. We start with a re-visioning of the creation story, placing our focus on the birth of fear. [1]

THE STATE OF ONENESS

"In the beginning," there was an original state of Oneness, an all-encompassing "field" where everything was unified in a single whole. Because it was all-encompassing, it was a field of infinite potential . . . any limit on its potential would render it less than "all-encompassing." Sometimes called the "Plenum" or the "Void," it was the "Ground of Being" from which manifest reality would spring forth. If everything were part of Oneness, then "we" were part of it, too, our mind joined in a "Universal Mind." This mind co-arose with Oneness, giving it its existence. Our awareness of it calls it into being just as much as it gives rise to the Universal Mind. [2]

The state of Oneness is characterized by perfect peace, stillness, eternal changelessness, "bliss." There can, by definition, be no problems or suffering of any sort because of its all-encompassing nature. For if everything is contained in Oneness, nothing can be missing; there can be no lack or unfulfilled need. The solution to any problem is ever- and immediately present. And so everything functions harmoniously, is perfectly coherent and integrated. [3] We do not long for anything, we do not want for anything because we are infinitely joined with whatever we need. We are "complete."

Mystics, peak experiencers, and advanced meditators all talk about this state of Oneness in some way or another. Meditators keep all their attention on one point; thoughts disappear, and there is a spontaneous opening to the unitive experience. They jettison their sense of separateness and feel joined with the object of meditation, and eventually with all things. Peak experiencers who enter "the zone" and mystics both describe the experience of boundaries and limitations dissolving into the same state of wholeness. All of us can relate to this, perhaps in an attenuated version, when we feel "joined with" a person or a group of people that we love. Even the identification with one's culture, country, or all of humanity derives its fulfillment from this experience of Oneness as we lose our attention for the small "self" and invest it in the larger whole. This identification with the whole can be so strong that one experiences their boundaries dissolving, as in lovemaking, or surrenders their individual identity to adopt the identity of the group, as when they become willing to die for their country.

Starting our creation story with this idea of Oneness is inevitable. Intuitively we understand that there must be a single, ultimate state from which the universe was born. It is also inevitable logically; we have to assume an original and absolute source as a baseline, a measuring point for comparison, to give meaning and value to the many things that arise from it.[4] Finally, we can observe the echoes of Oneness all around:

> Everywhere we look in nature, said the philosopher Jan Smuts, we see nothing but *wholes*. And not just simple wholes, but hierarchical ones: each whole is part of a larger whole which is itself a part of a larger whole. Fields within fields, stretching through the cosmos, interlacing each and every thing with each and every other.
>
> Further, said Smuts, the universe is not a thoughtlessly static and inert whole—the cosmos is not lazy, but energetically dynamic and even creative. It tends . . . to produce higher- and higher-level wholes, ever-more inclusive and organized. (Wilber, 1980)

THE SEPARATION

In the eternal, unchanging state of original Oneness, something then began to stir. Suddenly, there was a breach and a rent, from which issued forth . . . manifestation, the first "thing."[5] This gave rise to a separate world, an experience or "place" other than Oneness. By definition, such a place cannot exist since Oneness is all-encompassing and all-inclusive. There cannot be something "other" than "everything." Eternal changelessness cannot truly change. In order for this new world to seem real, we (Universal Mind) would have to "dream" that it was so.[6] In this way, the universe of phenomena began with a thought.

This is the origin of the world and our human experience of living in it. In every way, life as we live it is an experience of separation from Oneness, our original state and a state we still intuitively "remember." We remember it as a longing, the longing for fulfillment that drives us throughout our life. Where else would this longing come from if not an experience we somehow know already? It is the impulse to reclaim our wholeness, filling in the missing pieces of our life, putting an end to the emptiness and loneliness that comes from being separated from our good.

This separation story is the template for so many religious cosmogonies. In the Old Testament, light is separated from darkness, water from sky, earth from water, and so forth. The ancient Egyptians conceived of the "benben mound," often portrayed in the shape of a pyramid, appearing out of *Nu* (translated as "inactivity"), the deity of the primordial waters. In "Chuhwuht," the "Song of the World" in Pima Indian legend, darkness "congeals" in certain places to begin the creation. In Taoism, all things are said to spring forth from the Way, a state of fundamental unity. In Zoroastrianism, Angramanyu is created as a distinct entity (representing evil) from Ahurumazda, the overarching god of goodness. And in the *Chandogya Upanishad*, one of the "Grand Pronouncements" is *Tat Tvam Asi* ("Thou art that"), revealing that our identity comes from the unchanging source of all that exists. Either bit by bit or in a big bang, these cosmogonies describe a primordial state of Oneness out of which the world of multiplicity arises.[7]

Because it cuts us off from what we need, the separation creates suffering—we become separated from the experience of being whole, complete, and fulfilled. Our good has been lost and we must begin a search for it "out there." The perfect unity has been fractured into many pieces, each piece containing part of the original harmony but, in itself, incomplete and inharmonious. We begin a search to reclaim and reunify our missing parts, to find our fulfillment once again. But it is this *search* for wholeness, reifying the idea that we are no longer whole, which signals the arrival of fear. We become afraid that we will fail in our quest. We then use this fear to alert us to danger and maximize our chance for success. The moment we set out on our expedition, we take fear's hand, using it as a technique to ensure our fulfillment, becoming afraid of anything that could interfere with the goal.

Let's look at the Garden of Eden story as a metaphor for this. The garden itself is a place and experience of perfect unity. In eating from the tree, Adam and Eve learn for the first time of the difference between "good" and "evil." Before this, they were blissfully unaware of such a distinction. All was still "good," as God proclaimed in the beginning. When they do eat the apple, they become afraid—the first fear. They hide from God, feeling that they have done something "wrong"— the first guilt. They cover their nakedness (the first shame) with an awareness of what it is to be vulnerable and exposed (the first sense of "self"). Finalizing this plunge into separation, they are cast out of the garden to begin a life of labor and toil.[8]

This can be translated into the human condition as we live it. Again, in the beginning there was only one Universal Mind in which, we may say, all of us were joined. Being one mind, we had no need to discern or judge differences. But with the separation, we saw ourselves as distinct individuals, each containing our own "piece" of the Universal Mind, capable of having our own thoughts. We consolidated this experience by housing these separate minds in bodies, physically walling off our thoughts from others. Now the separate self had become fully autonomous, moving in its own body without depending on anything else for its existence. It is specifically this idea of the separate self that is described as the source of suffering in so many traditions. If we are separated from the whole, then we are cut off from our source like a drop of water pulled out of the ocean and left to evaporate in the sun. With the separate self comes a feeling of being on one's own, having to fend for oneself, no longer supported by the whole. In this is born the struggle for survival and fulfillment, the incredible power of the "self-preservation" instinct that occupies us every moment.

At the same time, we secretly enjoy, even lust after, this sense of separation . . . we want to eat the apple.[9] We want to be our own gods, the creator of our own experience. We are determined to make our own decisions, passing judgment on all that we see. Think, for example, how this plays out in human relationships. If we have our own mind, hidden from others by the separating walls of the body, then we may harbor secret judgments of them, making ourselves feel "special" by comparison. This establishes our autonomy even more securely. But at the same time, these judgments alienate us from the whole, emphasizing our separateness from that which we are judging. And of course, as we judge others, we become afraid of their judgment upon us. In the end, the separate mind is vulnerable to the many miseries of fear: we feel guilty that our thoughts are "impure," anxious that we will be found out, shameful that we are masquerading as someone we are not. In trying to gain power over others with our judgments, we end up feeding our fear. Knowing they are judging us as well, we are afraid we will lose the power struggle. All the complexities and challenges of human relationships, in fact, arise from the idea that we are separate and must remain so, while at the same time longing to rejoin as one. In this we can already see the beginnings of the great conflict between fear and fulfillment and how fear came to be ubiquitous in the world.

To continue our creation story, once the world was established as a place of separation from Oneness, time and space were born. Together these created the matrix in which we could move and breathe and live out our autonomous experience. In Oneness, there would have been no change and therefore no need for time and space.[10] There would be no possibility of "here" as a separate point in space from "there," or "now" as a separate point in time from "then." Instead, it may be said we were "everywhere always." But with the separation, we experienced ourselves in a place other than where our needs would be fulfilled and at a time other than when they would be fulfilled. If time and space are marked, as Einstein said, by separate events, then we learn how to experience them (it is not innately given)[11] according to our thoughts of how close or far from a goal we are. Our experience of time is the span between when we are and when our fulfillment is, and our experience of space is the span between where we are and where our fulfillment is. For this reason, we may say time is fear laid out sequentially and space is fear laid out in three dimensions. In other words, we know time and space by our assessment of how long and far we must travel to reach our goals. When we are fulfilled, when we have reached a goal, we are in the moment—time disappears and our sense of a separate, vulnerable self in space disappears as well. When we are far from a goal, fear increases and the time and distance to get to fulfillment seem long. On the other hand, as the goal gets closer, we become more confident—time speeds up while the space seems to shrink. We all know the experience of trying to find a new place we have never been. The trip to get there can seem much longer than the return when we know where we're going and how to get there. The fear that we might not reach our goal, that obstacles to our fulfillment may intervene, determines our perception of space and time.

Once time and space are established, we need to orient ourselves accordingly. Our bodies, designed to carry out the will of the mind they are housing, need an up, a down, a front, and a back in order to move effectively through space and time toward fulfillment.[12] This further reifies the experience of space and time as we move toward or away from our goal, some things behind us and some ahead, etc. Evolution is a matter of physical adaptations to accomplish this goal more and more effectively. We build a sensory apparatus (primarily in a face oriented "forward") that reads the environment; learn to walk upright, freeing our hands that have developed opposable thumbs; grow a neocortex that can plan through time; and so forth. All this in the effort to manipulate our experience successfully. All this in the attempt to reclaim our missing parts and find our fulfillment once again.

Gravity too becomes a necessary ingredient in building a matrix of space and time. It pulls discrete "things" toward a central focal point in space and determines the rate (time) at which they arrive there. Without gravity, everything would float randomly without relationship to each other—there would be nothing to create a *relative* frame of reference, no way to assign meaning and value to things. Assigning value to things makes it possible to establish relationships among them, recognizing the relative value of one thing compared to another. Otherwise, all is randomness and chaos. But once it is so ordered, our mind can interpret the universe, assigning ideas of good and bad, pleasant and unpleasant, fulfilling or fearful.

All of this reflects the choice for separation, believing that it gives us an autonomy and control that is preferable to Oneness. This is the choice to use fear as a strategy for the fulfillment of the separate self. But this is also the source of our struggles. We have cast ourselves out from Oneness and are trying to reclaim it without surrendering our separation. Human suffering, the whole Pandora's box of our problems, comes from the separation. It is the great labor against gravity and the forces that press against us, the effort of moving through time and space to reach our goals. It is the longing for what we don't have and the anxiety that we might not get it, or the anxious hoarding of what we have for fear of losing it. It is the feeling of being cut off and trapped inside our body, yearning to connect with others but having to navigate the complexity of relationships to do so. It is the lust to aggressively pursue what we long for. It is the grief over the loss of what we had and are now separate from. It is the source of competition and war, separate people or groups vying for the same prize. And it is the ultimate separation from life called death. In sum, suffering is the result when we attempt to recapture our missing parts, to become whole again and become afraid of what might keep us from our goal. [13]

Just as the separation shatters the Universal Mind into many minds, it shatters the wholeness of each separate mind into a kaleidoscope of anxious thoughts. Our mind races here and there, checking out possible threats and seeking opportunities for fulfillment. The saccadic movement of the eyes reflects this. If a person comes into our sphere, we instantly look to see if they might be our "savior," someone who can give us the love we need, or if they pose a potential threat to our well-being. We continuously scan the surroundings in search of opportunities to "get ahead," gaining control over fear with more money, safety, love, prestige, and so forth. Notice the power of the compulsion, for example, to look at the driver in the car that pulls up next to you, as if to check out whether they hold some key to our happiness (or whether they offer perhaps some opportunity for judgment). Try resisting looking at your cell phone the next time you get a text—every "ping" generates a compulsive urge to check it, with a subtle anticipation that perhaps it holds some prize or answer to your longing. These are some of the living effects of believing we are separate from our good, using a strategy of fear to reclaim our wholeness.

THE SEPARATION IN THE BIRTH PROCESS AND BEYOND—ONTOGENESIS (THE GENESIS OF BEING)

The story of the creation of the universe is the story of the individual as well: ontogeny (the genesis of being) recapitulates phylogeny. The birth process represents a similar journey from Oneness to separation—from the womb into the world. Let's take a closer look to see how each of us buys into fear.

Otto Rank, in *The Trauma of Birth* (1952), wrote that while in utero, we experience a state of what may be called oceanic bliss, just as in the Oneness before separation began. After birth, he said, we spend our life trying to recapture that state, fantasizing about a return to the womb. As a trauma, birth is our first and most important experience of fear. This parallels the creation story perfectly . . . before labor, as before the separation, every need is met and there is no distinction between self and other. We feel joined with the whole in perfect peace. Then, as the birth process begins, we experience a disruption in this blissful state. Moving through the birth canal, the walls of the uterus press against our skin. This creates our initial "contact" with separation, letting us know where we stop and the rest of the world starts. Finally, we are expelled from the womb and our separation is complete.

Stanislav Grof introduced his powerful model of the four stages of birth in his book *Realms of the Human Unconscious* (1996). He agrees with Rank's idea that the pre-labor experience is a blissful one and that the birth process as a whole has profound psychological impact. Grof then elaborates specific ways in which the experience of birth creates a template for how we meet later life challenges. He grounds his work in the reports of those who have had experiences, through various means, in which they seem to relive their birth, gaining insight into the way it shaped and informed their life. Not only are their reports remarkably consistent with Grof's model, regardless of culture and time period, but many contain facts about the circumstances of their birth that have been verified and could not have been known by alternate means.

In his model, Grof delineates four "basic perinatal matrices" (BPMs).[14] These correlate the stages of the birth process with the psychological experiences we can have in those stages. In BPM 1, the stage before labor begins, we are, as per Rank, in a unitive state inside the womb. Assuming no medical complications, all our needs are instantly met through the umbilical cord and we float freely in a perfect, warm environment, nothing interfering with our satisfaction. There is no awareness of the possibility of fear or struggle for nothing has come along to challenge us.

However, in BPM 2, the first stage of labor, we feel an extraordinary break (separation) from the beatific state we have known up to that point. We encounter, Grof says, a hellish experience of "no exit" as the uterine walls contract and bear down upon us, causing great pain. A feeling of being trapped and utterly helpless accompanies this pain. This becomes the template for later life experiences where we might feel similarly trapped and helpless. It is also a potential precursor to the helplessness of depression. This stage not only is characterized by profound pain and fear but also gives us our first awareness that something can threaten our well-being.

In the next stage, BPM 3, we begin moving through the birth canal. We become engaged in a life-and-death struggle to get to the "light at the end of the tunnel." This acts as a sort of initiation, we may say, into the experience of separation. The edges of "who we are" become well-defined as we pass along the uterine walls. This establishes our sense of being an individual in a body, separate from "mother," separate from our previous state. How we progress through this stage informs how we will meet later life struggles that similarly involve moving toward a goal and fighting oppressive forces. It is our first taste of personal will (as opposed to the helplessness of the prior stage) as we exert our own efforts to get out of the womb.

Finally, in BPM 4, we arrive outside the womb with a sense of having conquered these challenges. We have emerged victorious over the forces of life and death and discovered our ability to exercise control. This stage is characterized by a return to the homeostasis and (relative) bliss of BPM 1, but this time with a difference: we are aware of the potential for danger and the need to be prepared for it. [15]

Let's examine these ideas in light of the separation from Oneness and the development of fear. In BPM 1, it may be said we are truly in a state of Oneness before there is a world of separation (or an awareness of that world). The experiences described by those who purport to have relived this stage of the birth process (or analogous experiences in later life) are the same as those suggested by the creation mythologies—a Oneness with all things, the absence of separating limits, and a profound and complete fulfillment. Then in BPM 2, as the uterine walls close in, we have our first encounter with fear. Our sense of perfect wholeness is now under siege. What was our home, where we floated freely in an infinite "cosmos," is now a prison cell that would trap us, causing great pain and threatening to squeeze us out of existence. In the next stage, we become engaged in a life-and-death struggle to escape this scene. Thus arises our first opportunity to use our will and exercise control over fear. And finally, in BPM 4, we come out the other side. While in one sense, we have a return to homeostasis and the restoration of peace, there is at the same time a new sense of separation. We are outside the Garden of Eden once again, separated from our "creator" and left alone to fend for ourselves in a world we now know as dangerous. As the umbilical cord is cut, our separation is completed. We have been "born" into an individual, discrete, and separate body. [16]

As we progress beyond the birth process and consider the rest of childhood (and even lifelong) development, we see a continual deepening of the experience of separation. Before the umbilical cord is cut, our mother essentially eats and breathes for us, delivering nutrition, oxygen, and other gases directly into our bloodstream. There's no need to do anything or "think about" even that. But after a titanic struggle to get out of the womb, we enter a cold world with blaring light and we fight to take in great gulps of air in lungs that have never been used as the tether to our former world of perfect peace is severed. The umbilical cord is cut, and we must begin to survive on our own. If we are placed on our mother's breast and given milk, warmth, and love, we feel an approximate return to the safety we knew before. Still, we have been through a trauma and that cannot help but register. And we must take in nourishment at our mother's breast by our own efforts. This is a return to safety but with a world-changing difference. From that moment forward, we know of the possibility of fear and we know also that at some level we are fundamentally alone in life . . . that it is up to us to get our needs met. Others may help, but we must be vigilant about making sure they do. This directive continues throughout life.

Still, if all goes well, our infancy can be a time of relative peace and satisfaction, with loving parents providing for our needs. But bit by bit we must individuate from them, learning to take care of ourselves, consolidating the experience of separation and autonomy. What is called "healthy" development is really a matter of empowering this autonomy and developing a solid sense of self. Of course, this is necessary for survival and for the realization of our potential, but our success depends on how well we understand and negotiate the ways of fear, learning about the many dangers our environment poses and becoming skillful in managing them. Over time we develop extraordinarily sophisticated models for judging situations and people. We use these to navigate an all-too-often-hostile world, assessing whether something poses a threat or signifies support. As individuation progresses, we identify more and more with our autonomous bodies and our private thoughts, compelled to protect our separate identity.[17]

It's fascinating to watch a newborn, still very much "in" the Oneness, with their undifferentiated, non-separated consciousness. Without much going on in the way of thoughts or self-awareness, they have not yet formed a unique "identity." You can see this identity trying to form: they open their eyes for a bit and attempt to focus on this world. They seem to stare in wonder at it all, not yet able to make sense out of things but trying to collate impressions of the world. It is as if they are exercising the "muscle" of consciousness, contracting it from its previously undifferentiated state, to focus on the external world. You can almost feel them attempting to process the information coming in through the senses, watering the first seeds of "personality." Then their eyes glaze over and they drift into the uncontracted state once again, melting, we may imagine, back into Oneness.

If not mirrored properly, if this emerging sense of self isn't nurtured, encouraged, and reinforced, problems can arise. The child needs this mirroring to ground their fragile identity, making it more "solid" and developing confidence in it. Without it, they won't learn to individuate in a way that is necessary before it is possible to return to Oneness. If all proceeds as it should, the child is naturally drawn to becoming more and more autonomous. Adults delight in watching this autonomy unfold as the child finds its way through the world, trying things out and venturing forth in increasingly more independent fashion. The child builds a distinct identity, developing their unique ways of understanding and responding to circumstances, while becoming part of the social norms we have all agreed to. Our delight is in seeing them "become one of us," joining in our common culture. We welcome them to the tribe and feel the joy of initiating them into the experience of being human.

While there is fulfillment in the emergence of this autonomy, we can't afford to forget that it promotes self-protection and therefore fear as well. We anxiously tense when our individuality is threatened, physically or emotionally. This tension, over time, rigidifies us; it concretizes the sense of being a separate self in need of protection. We can become evermore devoted to making sure our circumstances turn out the way "we" want. This is fear's strategy for fulfillment, protecting the autonomous self by maintaining a constant readiness to do battle. It saps us of our life energy and, in the end, diminishes our joy as we sacrifice our well-being in the moment for an idea of fulfillment in the future. We end up spending too much of our life protecting this idea of a separate self, forgetting to get on with the business of really living.

Whether talking about the birth of creation, the story of our individual birth, or the archetypal birth of the self, we see the same process: we emerge from a state of Oneness into a separated experience of existence, buying into fear as we do so. In our search for fulfillment, we seek release from this fear, joining once again with the whole and finding completion. But to realize this goal, we must understand and reverse the process by which we bought into the separation, that which created our fear in the first place. This process, as it turns out, has everything to do with the mechanics of perception, which is where we will turn our attention now.

NOTES

1. This version of the creation story is heavily influenced by *A Course in Miracles* (Foundation for Inner Peace, 1975).

2. It is meaningless (at least for us) to say a thing or state has an existence if there is no awareness of it.

3. This is our first postulate.

4. To further explain, if we assume two or more sources, we have to then imagine a preexisting source from which they arose. The existence of two or more sources already presupposes that there are differences between them, and these differences can only be measured by comparison to a prior, single state . . . it is only by this comparison that we can notice the differences between them. To say it another way, there has to be an original, uniform experience from which we can create a boundary or dividing line that would separate two or more forms. Einstein said this when developing relativity: there must be an ultimate frame of reference to measure all relative frames of reference. This is why, in our first postulate, we talk about an ultimate or absolute truth rather than the experience we have of relative, shifting "truths." The question is sticky only because our thinking takes place "outside" Oneness. Our time- and space-bound mind, our duality-based thinking, can't truly conceive of the origin of all things outside these parameters. As soon as we say "this" was the beginning of time or "there" is the end of space, we automatically ask, "Well what was before that time?" or "What is beyond that place?" Our questioning will never come to a final, ultimate point. This is the problem with thinking about Oneness with a mind that sees itself in the world of plurality. But logically, we realize there had to be a single original source, and one that is beyond this realm of space and time, meaning it was always existent everywhere. If we do not assume this single source, then we are already playing in a world of duality, assuming the existence of two or more things that have differences. The idea of an original Oneness (i.e., monotheism) was an important development in the evolution of religious thinking. But there are plenty of religions still that postulate the existence of two or more creative sources ("gods"), and the debate about the "myth of monotheism" is alive and well (see for example Eck, 1998). Nevertheless, it is inevitable that we end up with the idea of Oneness. Those postulating a pantheon of gods, for example, still must answer the question "Who or what gave birth to them all?" Many pluralistic

religions, in fact, answer with a kind of composite; they imply a singularity, a type of unity "behind" the plurality (as in Zoroastrianism or the Brahman-Atman behind the many faces of the Hindu deities).

5. Or more likely, as Lemaitre proposed with his Cosmic Egg theory (later called the Big Bang), all the "things" of creation emerged at once.

6. Many wisdom traditions talk about this dream. Buddhism's goal is to "wake up" from it, while *A Course in Miracles* (Foundation for Inner Peace, 1975) would have us put an end to the "tiny mad belief" that such a dream is possible.

7. For a fascinating discussion of these principles played out through a physicist's understanding, see *A Universe from Nothing* (Krause, 2013), in which the author describes universe upon universe issuing forth from a background field of potential, like bubbles erupting in a pot of boiling oatmeal!

8. We also see in the Garden of Eden story, as well as in many other creation myths, the theme that male and female, two of the major "parts" divided by the separation, must rejoin in order to achieve wholeness. Adam is lonely and so God creates Eve. Therein is born the eternal search for the "soulmate" who is supposed to complete us.

9. We can understand this as the urge to be an autonomous individual. In adolescence, especially, we experience the pull to establish our own identity, separate from that of our parents. We have great resistance to giving up our autonomy. Doing so would require giving up our preoccupation with who we are and what we want. We are driven to preserve our separate selves and avoid returning to Oneness. This is why we believe fear is the best way to protect ourselves and try to secure fulfillment.

10. People often imagine that a state of eternal changelessness would be "boring," but boredom is a temporary, changing state, a relative identity ("I am bored") that will give way to other states and identities. It cannot be the state of Oneness. If there were problems or challenges in eternity (something to work on to avoid boredom), they would necessarily imply a threat to our well-being, a potential end to our experience (as in death). But in eternity there is no end so there can be no threat. The experience of eternity, then, is an experience of a fulfillment that never abates.

11. The classic "visual cliff" experiments in perception psychology attest to the fact that spatial perception is learned.

12. As above, a spherical body would not be well suited to a world of differentiation.

13. Once again, if you think this sounds too pessimistic, remember that the same bodies that make us feel separate and cut off can be a source of great fulfillment once fear is out of the way. The excitement of being in a body that is healthy, virile, and energetic is certainly fulfilling. It is the excitement of "feel-

ing alive," that we can "conquer the world." The question is whether we are being driven by fear or fulfillment. If we are trying to conquer something, the thrill can be the result of a fear-based excitement about obtaining control and avoiding failure. If, on the other hand, the experience is free of fear, then it can be about the expansion of the spirit to embrace a larger sense of self and participate in a greater reality.

14. The word "perinatal" means "around birth" or that which has to do with the birth process.

15. Of course, all of this assumes a normal birth process, and Grof discusses the impact of various alternative scenarios such as Cesarean birth, medical complications, and so forth. He also gives examples of how specific birth stories came to be reflected in a person's later life work, including the work of H. R. Geiger, the plays of Sartre (e.g., *No Exit*), and even the speeches of Hitler.

16. It is interesting to consider the origins of the thinking process in utero. A fertilized egg certainly wouldn't have the ability to think. When then does this ability first arise (as pre-verbal experiences that register in consciousness)? We can imagine that before labor there would be no trigger to stimulate the thinking process, no contrasting experience to have a thought about. Thinking must start with the first significant change in the fetus'sl experience. So it would be our first exposure to contrast, something "different from" (separate from) the state of Oneness, that launches the thought process. We need thoughts to discern and interpret difference. It makes sense to assume that the beginning of labor, as our first significant experience of fear, would be something we'd need to think about, to register and try to make sense of. Like any trauma, it would force us to "wake up" and pay attention, searching for ways to protect ourselves and resolve the situation. Perhaps there were glimpses of thinking before labor, trial runs, so to speak, such as when the baby kicks, sucks its thumb, or seems to play in the womb. But it seems likely that the first real experience of thinking, the first call to focus consciousness and attention, would be at the beginning of labor. As "we" are born into the world of separation, so are our thoughts.

17. Joan Kellogg, the brilliant art therapist, developed a model that parallels what we are saying beautifully (Kellogg, Mac Rae, Bonny, & DiLeo, 1977). This model, which she called the Great Round of Mandala, is built upon Jung's ideas on individuation. It describes twelve stages of development through life. In the first stage, we start out in the "void," a state of "bliss" that is likened to being in our mother's womb. Later we move into "a trusting state where we are in the mother's world" then into "separation from paradise, an awareness of self as separate" and so on. This characterizes the first half of development, leading to a fully individuated self, or "ego." The second half requires that we "reverse" this process, little by little dissolving the ego and ultimately arriving

at a state of "transcendental ecstasy," wherein we have "returned home" to the original void.

6

PERCEPTION

Architect of the Separated World

A human being is part of a whole, called by us universe, a part limited in time and space. He experiences himself, his thoughts and feelings as something separated from the rest . . . a kind of optical delusion of his consciousness. This delusion is a kind of prison for us, restricting us to our personal desires and to affection for a few persons nearest to us. Our task must be to free ourselves from this prison by widening our circle of compassion to embrace all living creatures and the whole of nature in its beauty.

—Albert Einstein

In the creation story, we saw how a thought of separation gave rise to the world of multiplicity as well as the fear of not being able to get what we need in that world. Since we know the world through our senses, our experience of fear must be the result of how we perceive things. We therefore want to make a thorough deconstruction of just how the senses perceive separation and cause this suffering.

Perception is the apparatus through which the thought of separation puts on clothes or becomes "flesh" . . . manifest reality. As we will demonstrate, we use the senses to pull out separate and discrete "things" from a background of Oneness. We then make interpretations of what the senses show us by assigning meaning to these separate things. This meaning makes them appear objectively "real." In fact, they are artifacts of perception. When it seems our senses are passively receiving information about an independently existing reality, perception is actually overlaying its interpretation on top of the original nature of Oneness.

Remember too that there is a logical inconsistency in our creation story: if Oneness is everything then there can be nothing other than everything—no place other than everywhere, no time other than "everywhen." So the separation can't be real in the ultimate sense; as we have said, it is often referred to as a dream. Still, of course, we do experience it . . . we certainly seem to be in separate bodies moving in a world of manifold things. To resolve this paradox, we are forced to arrive at the same conclusion—that there is a perceptual distortion going on, an "illusion" of separateness, superimposed upon an original Oneness. Because we want to believe in separation, we fool ourselves into forgetting that we generated the whole thing in the first place.[1]

We can understand this in everyday terms as well. To experience the world, we *project* our ideas onto it through the mechanism of perception.[2] Here's how it breaks down: We first decide (unconsciously, of course) what ideas we want to perceive in manifest form. We make an internal representation of what we want to see and the experience we would have of it. When data comes in through the senses, it is at first neutral and raw, without meaning. We apply meaning to it (interpretations, judgments, etc.) according to how well it corresponds to the internal picture we have constructed, the picture of how we *wish* things to be. We then selectively perceive—allow, deny, transform, or distort—the sense data so that it will conform to our predetermined wishes. And it is this that we project and take as objectively "real."[3]

In this way, our senses only show us the world of separation we have chosen to see. Perception is the out-picturing of a mental image we have already formed, lifting out separate parts from the background of Oneness that will confirm our ideas.[4] Like a cookie-cutter stamping shapes out of a uniform sheet of dough, we break up Oneness and perceive a world of multiplicity. As we will show with forthcoming examples, we literally can't perceive something until this happens. We may now understand our postulates more thoroughly: it is the act of perception that obscures the truth by having us see what we are invested in seeing instead.

It's perfectly understandable that we would have huge resistance to this idea. Not only have we been practicing faith in our perception of separation for a lifetime, but this perception is consensually agreed upon by everyone else. They too are assuring us that what our senses show us is real.[5] But let us not mistake resistance for objective truth. Our second postulate still is unavoidable: fear, by creating an investment in seeing what we want to see, obscures objective truth. We are afraid to see it as it is. If we are to find freedom from the suffering created by separation, we must be willing to cast doubt on our assumptions and consider an alternative view.

DRAWING THE BLUEPRINTS OF REALITY AND PROJECTING THE HOLOGRAM

How exactly does perception accomplish this extraordinary illusion, generating the appearance of solid things and discrete phenomena like a prism transforming white light into many colors? Going back again to our creation story, we remember that with the idea of separation, we conceived of the Universal Mind as many separate minds, each housed in a body. These bodies would interact with the field of potential that is Oneness through a sensory apparatus that could "define" separate parts in the Oneness. Our eyes perceive (interact with) the Oneness by defining edges, limits, separating boundaries around what then become discrete "things." And so we say our eyes "see" these things. Similarly, our ears "hear" discrete sounds that begin and end in time, each distinct from the other. Our fingers "touch" solid objects, letting us know where they start and stop, and so forth. As *A Course in Miracles* says, "You use [the body's] eyes to see, its ears to hear, and let it tell you what it is it feels. It does not know. It tells you but the names you gave to it to use, when you call forth the witnesses to its reality" (Foundation for Inner Peace, 1975). This is how we overlay perception on top of the original nature of things.[6]

We simply cannot "see" (perceive) objective sense information. We first project the separating boundaries that circumscribe a "thing," pulling it out from an undifferentiated background, and then assign value to it. This gives it its meaning and identity—its existence (to us). Without this, we wouldn't be able to make sense out of it or relate to it; we can only do so by comparing its value to the rest. This is how we organize our experience of reality, a vast network of relative values, comparing the meaning of one thing to another. And the ultimate measuring point, the ultimate frame of reference for assigning value, is whether and how a thing promotes our fear or fulfillment.

If we could see objective, raw sense information, it would necessarily appear as neutral "energy" or "isness," sometimes called "suchness" or "thusness." William James in *The Principles of Psychology* (1890) imagined the infant's world, before he or she could organize experience into something meaningful, as "a blooming, buzzing confusion." He described a similar process to ours by which we distinguish one thing from another through "associations," relative meanings. Helen Keller, before she developed language, had the same confusion. She had no fixed ideas about things to bring forth a coherent experience of reality. But when Anne Sullivan placed her hand under the pump and wrote the word "water" on her palm, the whole "world" suddenly came together and made sense.

Once we build a frame of reference, a measuring stick for assigning value to things, we can create mental constructs of our experience. And it is these constructs that get projected as what we perceive. The perception is like a stamped-out form from an internal template, creating a projection that we can see, hear, taste, touch, and smell. The world we perceive is literally a three-dimensional, multisensory hologram that we believe we are living in, projected from our mind and appearing to surround us in every direction.[7]

Everything about this hologram gives testimony to the reality of fear or fulfillment. When we are in fear, we project a very distinctive experience. The perceived world contracts, shrinks, "darkens." The separating walls of fear shoot up to block out the "light" of wholeness and fulfillment.[8] This darkness is accompanied by a sort of heaviness, like a weight bearing down upon us, robbing us of the freedom and expansion we feel when fulfilled.[9] It creates an entire atmosphere, with a specific palette of colors, in which the lines of perception are drawn: we see the world in a darker way; we hear sounds in a less harmonious, more shrill and jarring way; we feel things in a more prickly way; and things taste and smell less sweet. What we need appears distant and inaccessible. The safety and relaxation that comes when we can trust in a constant state gives way to the anxious uncertainty of relative realities. We are left feeling as though there is no solid place to stand, no steady truth to depend upon, and no way to know who we really are or how to relate to the world.

Each time we react to the idea of a threatening world, we reinforce its apparent reality, forgetting it is a projection of our own making. It's a self-referential loop. We come to a situation ready to be anxious, heart racing and thoughts scrambling. We see the situation according to our expectations. Having confirmed what we expected to see, we feel our heart and thoughts race all the more, and the process repeats. The more we do this, the more fixed our perception becomes. The same is true when we practice a perception of fulfillment. Whichever our choice, we "vivify reality with our attention" (M. Pressman, 1999; 2011).[10]

It is imperative to understand that our experience of reality is *only* the result of projected perceptions. Projection is responsible for everything we perceive. There is a helpful Hindu metaphor in which we are asked to imagine scooping a cupful of water from the ocean. The separating boundaries of the cup make it possible to label what is inside as a distinct and real entity—a cupful of water—but the distinction is artificially made. It is we who decided to put a cup around that bit of the ocean. Chief Seattle said it poignantly in his letter to the "great chief" in Washington, DC. When asked to sell the land of his people, he wondered at the way Americans created imaginary borders to claim a piece of the land as their own: "How can you buy or sell the sky, the warmth of the land? The idea is strange to us. If we do not own the freshness of the air and the sparkle of the water, how can you buy them?"[11]

And it is imperative to understand as well that fear projects a perception that obscures truth. It overlays its distortions on the background field of Oneness. Fulfillment projects a perception that more closely matches Oneness, with greater wholeness and fewer lines of separation. Fulfillment is the natural result of withdrawing the projections of fear. Therefore, if we can get our hands on the controls of projection, we can choose which projections we prefer, the interpretations of reality that work best. We will now approach this goal with many examples that show what we perceive is not fixed but the result of what we choose to think. We will spend a good deal of time on this effort to loosen the grip of our belief in the separation and the world of suffering that arises from it. Look for and encourage this effect, like the advanced meditator who sees the universe of phenomena as a masquerade covering Oneness, the forms of perception becoming transparent, unable to hide the ultimate truth behind them.

EXAMPLES FROM EVERYDAY LIFE

We can actually see the process of perception forming along the lines of the thoughts we are holding. We can witness our thoughts drawing the blueprints of what we will see before we see it. And we can watch as our projections then flesh out this blueprint with three-dimensional shape, color, texture, and mood. Here are some examples: I remember taking a tour through a cave. The cave was filled with gorgeous geologic formations that had taken millions of years to build. But our tour guide was busy pointing out the "ice cream cone" and the "carrot" that we were supposed to see in the formations. Everyone searched along the lines of her description, looking for the point here and the edge there, when suddenly the shape jumped out at us and came to life (though I preferred the more natural perception). Similarly, when hunting for a new house, we set our expectations for the kind of house, neighborhood, etc., we are interested in. Somehow, For Sale signs that we have never noticed before seem to pop up out of nowhere. When we see one such sign, we immediately scan the house to see if it will match our expectations and hopes. The house becomes either a source of excitement or disappointment, very different from how we might look at it under other circumstances.

For an obvious example, if we look outside in the morning and see the sun shining, our thoughts go to ways we might enjoy the weather. Even before we step outside, our spirit expands and our body feels energized. If, on the other hand, we see that it is cloudy and gray, we make up a different scenario in our head and can feel heavy with a sense of being cut off from life.

Next, imagine you hear that a friend said something hurtful behind your back. The next time you see this friend, they literally look different as you project a darker image upon them. But if you then learn they didn't actually say what you thought, your perception changes accordingly—they are your friend again. This has important implications for our relationships. If we can appreciate that any time someone upsets us they are actually fending off fear in some form, then we have a ready path to forgiveness. And since this alters *our* perception, resolving *our* fear, we end up doing ourselves a favor.

Our self-perception—how we think others perceive us—is usually grossly distorted. We focus only on what we believe is wrong and how to fix it, or perhaps we affirm what's right, taking reassurance in it. Here's a surprisingly powerful little exercise you can try: Look at yourself in the mirror with another person or people standing behind you. Make sure you can see them in the mirror as well. Study yourself in the context of these other people. Compare what you actually see in the mirror to the image of how you thought you would appear. The distortion of your self-image will become immediately apparent as you observe yourself in "real" time and space, measured against the fantasies in your mind. This can be very healing since the distortions are usually, again, about what is wrong that needs to be fixed. Seeing yourself as a real person interacting with other real people, rather than as the fantasy in your mind, shows how "normal" and fine everything really is, a demonstration that what we fear never comes to pass as we imagined it would.

In fact, any time we are afraid of something that then passes, we have an opportunity to see our perception responding to our thoughts. You think your boss is calling you into the office for a reprimand but instead you get a promotion. Someone is driving more slowly than you'd like and you later learn they were in a terrible car accident. Or you feel guilty because of something you did and your therapist shows you it wasn't your fault given the fears you learned in childhood. In each case, the contrast between the before and after experience is clear. We get a glimpse into how we were projecting our ideas onto reality before we looked to see what the reality actually was.[12] As the fear passes, we discover the perception was "made up." And we can see the truth that was waiting behind the perception. With practice, and we will do this in our exercises, you can even step back into the "place" from which the perceptions were projected, resting in the Oneness from which they all arise, free to create the perceptual reality you choose.

The contrast between perceptual realities is especially easy to see upon first waking up in the morning.[13] In the sleep state, the world has "disappeared." Upon waking, we can watch our thoughts about the world come back into focus. We can further watch, as if in slow motion, these thoughts projecting out as our perception of the day. If you are looking forward to it, your perception will be vastly different than if you have only drudgery and problems to handle. For example, upon waking our first thought might be "What day is this?" We then review the schedule for the day, asking ourselves with each line item whether there is anything we have to be prepared for, whether our plans for the day will make us happy or unhappy, whether we will be pressured or busy, lonely or bored, etc. But with awareness, we can hold the state before these thoughts take over and then carefully practice the perception we wish to project.

Coming out of a meditation or relaxation exercise also gives this opportunity. Having released, to whatever degree, our contracted focus on the external world, we can then observe how our mind wants to latch onto that world once again. Because our thoughts are usually about fear and protection, they are accompanied by a physical tension that prepares us to respond accordingly. With careful discernment, we can play with the very moment when our mind tries to "stick" to those thoughts—the very moment when tension arises—and relax back into peace. This cultivates our ability to choose how we think about the world without tension, projecting a perception that doesn't require the same degree of fear.

For advanced practice, we can play with the thought that it is time to finish our meditation and get back to dealing with things in our usual way. What if we let that thought go? Our fear says we could lose all we have invested in if we're not anxiously attending to the world we have built. But we can, in fact, take care of things while in the meditative state and function very well. Imagine what it would be like to rest in the Oneness instead of re-energizing the perception of fearful imperatives. In the end, we give the perception all of its power. We bring it to life by thoughts of its reality and can let it go by choosing different thoughts. [14]

EXAMPLES FROM CINEMA

In the remarkable film *Brainstorm*, we have a visual depiction of all this. The main character undergoes a near-death experience. Sense data from this world explodes in a kaleidoscope of sound and color as it loses the meaning he would normally have projected onto it. His attention is invested in a different reality. The same sensory material comes into his awareness but is interpreted in a spectacular new way as he leaves "the world" behind.

For another example from the movies, we have the equally extraordinary film *Life Is Beautiful*. Having been sent to a concentration camp during World War II, a father is determined to protect his young son from the horrors all around. With extreme courage and creativity, he builds a different perception for the boy by pretending the entire experience is a game. To ensure his son's compliance with the protocols of camp life, the father tells him he must follow the rules of the game in order to "win." In this way, he protects his son not only physically but emotionally as well. The father continually helps him re-interpret what would otherwise be perceived as extreme deprivations as worthy sacrifices for a higher goal.

Perception can be used as a tool for fear or fulfillment. We choose what we perceive according to the thoughts with which we interpret a situation. One person described a "mystical" experience of this phenomenon: Every time he took a step forward, a new layer of the visual horizon would form where none existed the moment before. He realized it was forming in response to his expectation that there would be a new layer to see and that the details of what he saw matched the details of his expectation.

RESEARCH IN PERCEPTION PSYCHOLOGY

As an undergraduate student, I had a wonderful class in the psychology of perception. We learned about a litter of kittens raised since birth in a room that had no horizontal lines. They were then placed in a different room where they encountered chairs, with horizontal bars connecting the legs, for the first time. The kittens behaved as if they didn't see the bars at all; they simply bumped into them. The explanation given was that they had not learned to see the horizontal bars and so the bars literally didn't show up in their world. In the same class, we learned of the inverting goggles experiment. These goggles have prisms for lenses that make the world appear upside down. After wearing the goggles for three weeks, one's perception of the visual world rights itself! What's more, upon taking the goggles off, your see everything upside down for a while until, once again, things shift back to "normal."

But the process by which perception creates reality is more than simply a matter of learning. If we see a row of two or more blinking dots lighting up in rapid succession, our eyes naturally fill in the blanks and perceive a single, moving dot.[15] You can try something similar right now. Look at the series of dots in figure 6.1. These are random dots on a page with no inherent meaning. But if you look for the "plus" sign (where the middle two columns and the middle two rows cross), your eyes lift this now-named "thing" out from the page. Or you can see four squares of four dots each, four overlapping squares of nine dots each, or any of a number of other combinations. This is the experience of projecting meaning, making reality, in action.[16]

Not only do we project our reality as individuals, but groups of people project their common experience as well. In a testament to the Universal Mind, the meanings we agree upon together inform the perception we all share. Jung's theory of the collective unconscious (1981) and Plato's concept of Ideas or Forms (1997) speak to this notion of a consensually built perception. Both suggest that as individuals, we derive our experiences from a field of potential contributed to by us all.

perception creates reality

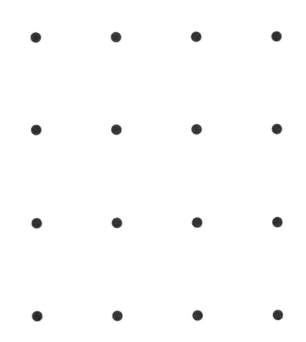

Figure 6.1.

For Jung, this field is a composite of our individual thoughts and experiences organized into certain archetypal themes we tap into. For Plato, our perception of particular "things" is based on an ultimate, ideal version of those things, an unmanifest potential we draw from when giving particular forms their meaning.

The "hundredth monkey phenomenon" (Keyes, 1984) makes the point more specifically. In the 1950s, research was being conducted on several islands in Japan. Each day a ration of sweet potatoes was dumped on the sand to feed the macaque monkeys that were being observed. Eventually, one of the monkeys on one of the islands discovered that washing the sand off the sweet potatoes in the ocean made them taste better, and it taught the other monkeys on the island to do the same. At a certain point, monkeys on the other islands then started washing their sweet potatoes in the ocean as well at a rate much greater than chance would suggest. The hundredth monkey theory states that when a critical mass was reached (the proverbial "hundredth monkey"), the idea of washing the sweet potatoes was somehow transferred to the monkeys on the other islands.

Although challenged on its details, the idea is compelling. It coordinates with the fact that shamanic rituals among disparate groups in time and place have, for many thousands of years, practiced remarkably similar traditions. New breakthroughs in science have sometimes occurred simultaneously at different points on the globe, one scientist having had no contact with the other. There is also research attesting to the validity of this phenomenon. Rupert Sheldrake (2009) developed his theory of "morphic resonance," proposing that our joint experiences create a "morphogenetic field." This field, like Jung's collective unconscious, gathers strength as more people experience the same perception. Eventually, when the field becomes potent enough, it influences the perception of others so that they too start experiencing reality in the same way. I participated in an experiment Sheldrake conducted to test the theory. Approximately five hundred of us at a conference in Switzerland were shown an image of black-and-white blotches on a screen. These blotches camouflaged an image of a horse. We were told there was an image in the blotches but were not told what it was. The blotches were arranged so that the image was not obvious and only a certain percentage of people would naturally see it. At the same time, approximately five hundred people at a conference in Japan were being shown the same set of blotches, but they were taught how to see the image. The study was designed to discover whether we in Switzerland would see the horse more often than a control group as a result of a possible morphogenetic field created by our counterparts in Japan. The results proved statistically significant.

All of this becomes relevant when we translate it as instruction on how to shift our perception from fear to fulfillment. When we recognize that, indeed, our perception is the result of the thoughts we choose, we may "choose once again" (Foundation for Inner Peace, 1975). This is not simply a matter of positive thinking—not at all! We must become aware of the hidden investments of fear, creating thoughts that shape our perception just as much as any conscious thoughts we may choose. Otherwise, our positive thoughts will compete with our fearful thoughts, creating conflict, tension, and contraction. Furthermore, we have to be aware of the "pressure" to perceive things as the consensus would have us perceive them. This too creates a fear: the fear of defying the norm. Still it is always a matter of choice, and once we become aware of our fears we can begin to step back from them, creating a new perception. A friend of mine put it nicely, saying, "It takes great courage and generosity to cut the net of agreement [when everyone around us is choosing thoughts of fear]" (Almayrac, personal correspondence). But this is our task. And because of our interconnection, doing so for ourselves helps others to do it as well.

EVIDENCE FROM QUANTUM PHYSICS

There is an experiment in quantum physics that, to my mind, should be proof enough that perception literally shapes reality. If a beam of light hits a screen with a slit in it, we would expect to see the light that passes through the slit register on a screen in the back in the same shape as that slit. And we do . . . sometimes. If the experimenter is observing the event, we will, in fact, see such a slit. But if the experimenter is not observing the event, the beam shot through the slit registers as a wave form.[17] This famous experiment suggests what has come to be known as the "observer effect": Our observation affects what we observe.[18] In our model, we would say our observation shapes what we perceive according to our expectations. If we expect to see the same shape as the slit the light passed through on the back wall, that's what we see. When no one is around to perceive it as such, what registers is a wave form, or what is called a "probability field." When we impose our expectations, assigning meanings and values, the wave form "collapses" into what we expect to see, literally taking shape according to our expectations. This is the Copenhagen Interpretation of quantum physics, that light (for example) is in potential both a particle (a discrete thing) and a wave (a field of possibilities). What we expect to see pulls out one of the possibilities and collapses the field into a separate, distinct "particle." Before that, the light remains as undifferentiated potential, registering on the screen as a visual approximation of Oneness.

Schroedinger's Cat is a thought experiment built from these same ideas. Schroedinger imagined a box with a Geiger counter in it. A Geiger counter has radioactive particles that have an equal chance of decaying or not decaying. Schroedinger set his thought experiment up so that if any particles decayed, a lethal substance would be released inside the box. He then imagined a cat inside the box along with the Geiger counter. The experiment states that if no one can observe what is happening inside the box, not knowing whether particles have decayed or not, the cat is in a state of "superposition," both alive and dead at the same time. It is only when an observer opens the box that the wave form collapses into a specific reality. [19]

Werner Heisenberg discovered the same thing when, as in his uncertainty principle, he found that if one observes an electron at a particular place, it is impossible to say precisely what its momentum is at that place. Or if one specifies the electron's momentum, it is impossible to say precisely where it is. Rather, it exists as a probability field, like a wave form. As per our creation story, it exists in a state "before" space and time (velocity being a function of time) are projected into manifest reality. And yet we depend on knowing its speed and location in order to make things happen. It is the act of observation (projecting perception) that allows it to function as a discrete object.

I remember seeing a video of a karate master chopping through a very large stack of bricks. The video was taken with high-speed photography and as a magnified, extreme close-up. Watching the hand come down upon the bricks in super slow motion, the camera zooming in on what would become the exact point of contact between the bricks and the hand, I saw the moment when the hand should have struck the bricks. But as was unambiguously clear, there was no physical contact. Instead, the edge of the hand splayed out as if being buffeted by high winds, and the bricks simply started to crack. The explanation given, of course, was that it was the karate master's *ki*, or energy, that cracked the bricks. We know, at the microscopic level, that when we touch something, our perception of solidity is actually the result of electrons repelling each other with no direct contact between our "hand" and the thing touched. Was this a visual demonstration of electron fields repelling each other, creating the appearance of a "physical" hand breaking through "physical" bricks?

Einstein would concur. He said, "Concerning matter, we have been all wrong. What we have called matter is energy whose vibration has been so lowered as to be perceptible to the senses. There is no matter." Twice nominated for a Nobel prize, Ervin Laszlo (2016) writes, "We do not need matter to explain what we find in the world—'matter' is not needed in medicine and in healing, nor in the economy and in communication. It is a superfluous concept that only complicates our understanding of the world. The time has come to say good-by to matter as an element in the real world." And Fritjof Capra (1983) demonstrates that we only know of certain subatomic particles by virtue of their effects on other subatomic particles. We cannot see them, but once they are hypothesized to exist, all sorts of phenomena occur to verify that, indeed, they must account for the effects we are seeing.

EXAMPLES FROM ANTHROPOLOGY

There is interesting work being done comparing the perceptual abilities of different cultures. The "carpentered world" theory (Segall, Campbell, & Herskovits, 1963) proposes that people in non-industrial societies have little experience with right angles since these are primarily found in modern buildings and rarely in nature. We would therefore expect them to respond differently to optical illusions (perceptual tricks), such as the Mueller-Lyer illusion, than do people in industrial societies. The Mueller-Lyer illusion consists of two lines of equal length side by side. Each has arrows at its ends but pointing in opposite directions: one line has arrows pointing out and the other has arrows pointing in (see figure 6.2).

People from industrial societies tend to see one of the lines as longer than the other, while people from non-industrial societies do not. Here again we are given the same hypothesis: people from non-industrial societies have not "learned" to perceive the illusion the way we have due to their lack of familiarity with the angles of the arrows.

Legend says the Aztecs were so vulnerable to the Spanish conquistadors because, when their ships appeared on the horizon, the Aztecs did not see them. Never having had any experience with anything appearing on the horizon, they were unprepared when the Spaniards came on shore. In the same way, aborigines in Australia, upon looking at a photograph for the first time, are unable to make out the contents of the photograph. Apparently, we must learn to interpret the patches of color and light in a meaningful way.

EXAMPLES FROM NEUROSCIENCE AND BIOFEEDBACK

Rick Hanson (2009) uses the language of neuroscience to talk about the ability of thought to affect physiology. He states that when we repeat a thought over and over, we actually build neural structure in the part of the brain that corresponds to that thought. Imagine the implications for shaping our response to stress, disease, and other assaults on the body (Pert, 1999; Chopra, 2015; Barasch & Hirshberg, 1995). In fact, biofeedback has been developed precisely from this idea. In the 1960s,

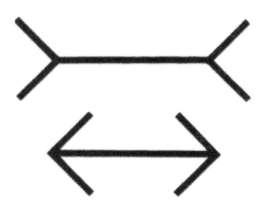

Figure 6.2.

Elmer and Alyce Green were conducting research with a man named Swami Rama at the Menninger Foundation. Swami Rama was an Indian adept who had the ability to alter certain aspects of his physiology at will. As they placed the electrodes that would measure his body's response to various intentions, it occurred to them that they might hook up ordinary people to the same instruments, employing relaxation techniques and visualization to induce a similar response in the body. With this, the science and practice of biofeedback was born. The Greens' daughter, Patricia Norris, published one of many accounts about the success of this strategy. In the book *Why Me?* (1985), she describes her work with coauthor Garrett Porter, a young boy who was suffering from brain cancer. In a deeply relaxed state, he would visualize Pac-Men eating up his cancer cells. Garrett became skilled enough with the visualization that he could intuit just how much the tumor had shrunk before getting an MRI that confirmed his prediction. Eventually, the tumor disappeared altogether. The Greens believed so thoroughly in the power of biofeedback that Elmer once said, "If you can place an electrode on it, you can heal it" (personal correspondence).

A final example from neuroscience also demonstrates the power of our thoughts (and spirit?) to affect the body. In an experiment, sixteen married women were exposed to the threat of an electric shock. Each experienced a significantly diminished level of neural distress when holding her husband's hand compared to her level when not holding hands. The level of diminishment also corresponded to the reported quality of the marital relationship. When they were holding a stranger's hand, the level of distress was also diminished but not as much as when holding their husband's hand (Coan, Schaefer, & Davidson, 2006).

HOW TO HEAL OUR WORLD(VIEW)

There is a story about a samurai and a monk. This samurai was feared throughout the land. One day, he approached the monk, sitting peacefully in his monastery. The samurai commanded in his most imperious voice, "Monk, teach me about heaven and hell." The monk looked up from his meditation seat and after a while responded, "Teach *you* about heaven and hell? I couldn't teach you anything. You're filthy, you smell, your sword is rusty . . . you are a disgrace to the samurai!" On this, the warrior drew his sword, readying to strike the monk down dead, when quietly the monk said, "That's hell." Stopping in his tracks, the samurai was taken aback, realizing that this monk was willing to even sacrifice his life to teach him the meaning of hell. He slowly began lowering his sword and was filled with a strange and overwhelming peace, where-upon the monk said softly, "That's heaven."

If the perception we project is determined by the thoughts we choose, and if this perception creates the world we know, then the thoughts we choose moment by moment have the power to change that world. Again, this is not simply a matter of thinking the "right" thoughts. We must resolve the thoughts of fear that would block our way. As we have seen, these thoughts of fear project a world where we are separate from our good, cut off from wholeness. Release from fear shows a world that reflects more nearly the unitive state. Our objective then is to withdraw the projection of our fearful thoughts, recognizing that it is not only arbitrary but unnecessarily painful. As we learn to master per-ception in this way, we have our hands on the controls of our entire experience of reality and can reshape it according to our wishes, bring-ing a natural and spontaneous fulfillment.

We *can* alter our experience of life. We are not the hapless victims of a predetermined set of affairs but have free choice and the real possibil-ity of a way out. Viktor Frankl demonstrated this powerfully in *Man's Search for Meaning* (2006). Reflecting on his experiences in a Nazi concentration camp, he concludes that nothing can take away

> the last of the human freedoms—to choose one's attitude in any given set of circumstances, to choose one's own way. . . . [In] the final analysis it becomes clear that the sort of person the prisoner became was the result of an inner decision, and not the result of camp influ-ences alone. Fundamentally, therefore, any man can, even under such circumstances, decide what shall become of him—mentally and spiritually. He may retain his human dignity even in a concentration camp.

Healing—in mind, body, and spirit—is the result when we withdraw our projections, creating "a shift in perception" (Foundation for Inner Peace, 1975) from fear to fulfillment. In our exercises, we will learn exactly how to effect this shift. But first we must let go of our belief in fear as the best strategy for securing our good, and that has been the purpose of our work so far. We have spent a lifetime with this belief in fear, convinced that letting it go would invite tragedy and loss. But as *A Course in Miracles* states, "Where [we] anticipated grief, [we] find a happy lightheartedness instead" (Foundation for Inner Peace, 1975). The symbols of fear that populated our world are then seen to be empty projections, meaningless without our investment of belief. We are given a clean slate, an open and infinite field of possibilities with which to create our world anew.

NOTES

1. Since the brain is the instrument through which thoughts create perception, it's interesting to notice the correlation between different stages in brain evolution and different stages in the experience of separation. Ants or bees, we can imagine, don't know much about separation—they function as a group with very small brains. Dogs, as pack animals, still function as part of a larger whole but at the same time have plenty of "personality" . . . we may say each is an "individual." Human beings, with their prefrontal cortex and the ability to make their own decisions, judgments, and so forth (tools of the trade for separating perception) are still social animals but highly skilled at functioning as separate individuals. It's also interesting to consider that by means of the same prefrontal cortex, we may come to the realization that separation causes suffering and choose to transcend our individuality, becoming part of the larger whole once again. Many have called this the next stage of our evolution.

2. Projection is a helpful description since, like a movie projector, we throw images "out" from Oneness into the world of separation. Again, projecting "out there" reifies the separation. Otherwise, everything would be here and now.

3. We will be working with plenty of examples shortly to see this process in action.

4. For example, the three-dimensional world we see is really a two-dimensional image on the screen of our retinae, transduced by rods and cones into electrical signals in the back of the brain. Projection uses the trick of depth perception to give it the appearance of three dimensions.

5. Before Descartes and Newton brought their influence to bear, the universe was interpreted in a much more "fluid" way. Cause and effect were attributed to forces beyond mechanical "laws." We had epistemologies beyond empiricism (Laszlo, 2016; Grof, 1980). The insistence that only what we can perceive with the senses is real comes from a fear, I would propose, of living in

this more fluid reality. It gives a sense of security to be able to explain things so concretely even if, as quantum physics shows, the explanations fall apart in a wide variety of circumstances. Still we cling to this view, devoted to believing only what we can "prove" with the senses. In the same way, people in Western society are often loathe to "look within" at their feelings and intuitions, choosing to stay "grounded" in what is concretely knowable.

6. Have you ever noticed how we seem to live behind our faces? Why do we experience ourselves primarily in that part of our body? The answer is likely because the face contains most of our sensory apparatus. But it's not to be assumed that we should take up residence in the face, locating ourselves "in" the senses. In tai chi, for instance, we train our attention to reside in the *tian tien* and to "move" (physically and in our awareness) from this point three finger-widths below the navel. Various forms of meditation focus on the same spot. In the Hindu tradition, there are seven primary centers of attention, or *chakras*, each expressing a different quality, a different aspect of human experience. And some psychotherapies cultivate awareness of the "wisdom of the body" or "the body's knowing." If we loosen our identification with what the senses alone show us, withdrawing from a contracted focus on the face, we can expand our awareness to inhabit the whole body and then beyond, incorporating larger and larger aspects of the whole.

7. There is an episode in the original *Star Trek* series when mysterious synchronicities keep occurring on a new planet. It is Dr. McCoy ("Bones") who finally realizes that whatever one thinks on this planet will occur in "reality" the next moment. He tests out his theory by thinking of a medieval maiden. Suddenly, from behind a rock, the very maiden appears. In the next moment, however, a knight in full armor starts charging toward McCoy on his horse, lance in position to strike the good doctor down. As the knight approaches, McCoy keeps repeating, "It's only a thought, it's only a thought . . . it can't really harm me"—a powerful metaphor for what we are working on here!

8. This sounds, not coincidentally, like a description of the second stage of birth, when the uterine walls close in upon the fetus.

9. I find it fascinating that virtually every time I'm with a client who resolves a fear, their description of what has happened includes an experience of darkness in some form transformed into light.

10. In the *Harry Potter* books, wizarding students are taught to transform their fearful projections, given form by a creature called a Boggart, by imagining them in a silly way and commanding the spell "Riddikulus!" The creature takes whatever shape the student is holding in their mind.

11. And yet today, one can even purchase "air rights" to the empty space that exists above a building!

12. See www.youtube.com/watch?v=PnDgZuGIhHs for a really beautiful demonstration of not only how our projections are arbitrary—assumptions that distort the truth—but also how we can transform them, for a perception that comes closer to a universal Oneness.

13. In Zen, the hours of first waking are called the "magic hours" because of the potential for this awareness.

14. In the Carlos Castaneda books (e.g., 1985; 1991), Carlos's teacher, Don Juan, tells him he must "stop the world." His meaning is precisely the same as what we are talking about here. Similarly, in Zazen the student is commanded to "die" on their meditation cushion, to put an end to the world of perceived phenomena by letting go of the thoughts that create them.

15. See www.youtube.com/watch?v=foWq1L05TtU for an interesting example.

16. If I point to an object at a distance with my finger, my dog looks at my fingertip wondering why I'm holding it in midair. Humans project an invisible line from the fingertip to the object, but my dog just sees me placing my finger in a random ("meaningless") position, sniffs it to try to make sense of it, and seems to shrug her shoulders as if to say, "No clue."

17. For simplicity's sake, I have taken liberties with this explanation. The actual experiment relies on two slits. If light were a wave passing through the two slits, we would expect to see a pattern on the back screen showing the interference of the two waves after passing through the slits. If light were particulate, we would expect to see it register in the discrete shape of the two slits on the back screen. Again, what we see is determined by what we expect to see—a wave pattern when no instruments are observing or two slit-shaped patterns when measuring the results.

18. Alternative explanations have been offered but none that account for the phenomenon as well as this one. See https://www.youtube.com/watch?v=G7n5V9nlloY/.

19. Blake Crouch's disturbing but thrilling novel *Dark Matter* (2018), based on this thought experiment, shows one version of what it could be like if we were to master our ability to re-create perceptual reality. The realities created are largely fear-based until the protagonist becomes more skillful at choosing his reality.

7

THE CORE FEAR AND CHIEF DEFENSE

A New Model of the Psyche

Just as the twig is bent, so is the tree inclined.

—Alexander Pope

So far we have seen how the original decision to separate from One-ness manifested as distinct bodies that would house distinct minds, each of which would experience separation through the development of a sensory apparatus. This sensory apparatus would give perceptual form to our thoughts of separation. We have also said that these thoughts of separation are sourced by fear, for fear reifies the separation. All of this gives rise to the individual "I," separated from the whole and therefore vulnerable to further fear and suffering. To fully understand how this sense of an I, this separated self, emerges from the thoughts we choose, we must deconstruct its elements. In so doing, we will propose a new model of the psyche, one with the power (as we shall see in our exercises) to liberate us from the perceptual distortions of fear.

THE CORE FEAR

Assuming all goes well during pregnancy and delivery, each of us is born into a state of relative peace and well-being. The trauma of birth has left its mark, but with the nurturing of our caregivers, we are able to return to a fair semblance of wholeness and fulfillment. This is wonderfully obvious whenever we see a healthy baby. Their pleasure in the simple experience of being alive is infectious. It is a time of innocence and purity when, still mostly fused with the mother as in the womb, we feel a nearly undifferentiated state of harmony. All our needs are for the most part met, and our balance, if momentarily disturbed, is quickly restored.

But then life happens and things begin to get messy. Our mother leaves the room and we think it is forever. Our father is distant and cold and seems to withdraw when we need him most. A sibling is born and we imagine we are no longer valued as before. Love is sometimes withheld, our needs sometimes left unmet. Perhaps we are exposed to actual harm by accident, illness, or malicious intent. Whether it is a specific danger or an undefined atmosphere of threat, we learn that the world is not always safe. We have our first encounter with fear.

Because we are so young, the magnitude of this encounter shakes us to our very vulnerable core. With no prior experience to mitigate the impact, we find our world has gone full tilt, our distress extreme and intolerable. The deep peace we have known is suddenly ripped away from us, and we feel as though our well-being—even our identity—is in jeopardy. Having nothing to compare it to, we take this threat to identity as a threat to survival.

The first exposure to fear is felt so powerfully in our psyche that our entire being organizes itself around the event. We lock our attention onto it and stare at it fixedly.[1] We begin a reflexive, frantic search to regain our footing, to make sense (even if pre-verbally) of what's happening. All the while, we maintain our gaze, never letting the threat out of our sight. Because of this fixation, because of the import of this moment, we develop a new understanding of how the world works, one that incorporates the possibility of this kind of threat. This understanding becomes what we shall call the "core fear."

The core fear is our most basic interpretation of danger—how the world can hurt us, deprive us of our needs, or somehow threaten the integrity of who we are. In other words, it is our primary understanding of how life can interfere with our fulfillment. As such, it becomes the foundation of our entire fear-based worldview. From the moment we land on this idea of danger, we begin looking for the signs of it everywhere. And this becomes fear's strategy for survival. Only by this hypervigilance, we think, will we be ready for the danger when it comes again.

The formation of one's core fear can happen in a single, "traumatic" moment (e.g., the loss of someone significant, a serious medical problem) or over time if the child is exposed to a general atmosphere of threat (e.g., a bully at school, an alcoholic parent whose behavior is unpredictable). But once it forms, we begin projecting perception accordingly. Because we are now vigilantly on the lookout for signs of this new danger, we pick out those features in the environment that match our expectations. We organize perception around these thoughts and begin to live in a world that is inhabited with their reflection. Of course, we are doing this in the attempt to stave off threats, believing it to be the best way to ensure our return to wholeness. But as we embark on this mission, determined to root out all potential dangers, our orientation to life begins to shift from fulfillment to fear.[2]

THE FIVE CORE FEARS

There are five basic core fears. These five describe in broad strokes the fundamental interpretations of threat that people hold. Any essential fear that drives a person's life will be found in one of these categories. The five core fears can also be understood as universal themes of loss since the separation cuts us off from an experience of completion we once knew. In this sense, a core fear is that which threatens some basic aspect of wholeness and fulfillment.

The five core fears are

1. Abandonment (loss of love)
2. Loss of identity
3. Loss of meaning
4. Loss of purpose (the chance to express oneself fully)
5. Death (including the fear of pain and sickness that might lead to death)[3] (security)

It's appropriate that we start with the fear of abandonment for we all know the importance of giving and receiving love. But when fear comes along, we engage in faulty strategies for protecting our experience of love. Betrayal, rejection, loneliness, disinterest, caretaking, shame, and neediness are some of the disguises for this core fear. It describes the universe of relationship struggles most of us are very familiar with.

Identity is here defined as who we truly are beyond the relative, shifting roles we play and masks we wear. Authenticity is a rare thing. Most of us hide our true selves to some degree in the interest of protecting our integrity and avoiding other losses. The fear of losing our identity, nevertheless, remains, and we long for the freedom to simply "be" as we actually are, without judgment, without pretense.

Fear of the loss of meaning is fairly self-evident. Meaning is simply that which gives value and worth to our experience—the experience of ourselves and the world around us. Without such meaning, we are exposed to an inherent sense of emptiness, along with a feeling of being cut off from where (meaningful) life is happening. This is the essence of depression and existential isolation. It too is one of the basic categories of human suffering and fear. This is why we continually project meaning onto our circumstances, trying to make sense out of things in a way that promotes fulfillment but all too often finding the opposite when fear dictates our projections.

Purpose is closely associated with meaning. It can be defined as the action component of meaning, the movement to actualize meaning in our world. This is the *drive* for fulfillment, that which impels us to create (i.e., to create what is meaningful). Our purpose is that which will make positive change, bringing us closer to fulfillment. It is the urge to realize our potential and reach our goals. Where meaning is an assessment of the value of things as they currently exist, purpose is the drive toward improving that value in the future. To lose our purpose stimulates a fear of having nothing to look forward to—no hope. This can readily evoke a fear of losing meaning as well.

And of course, the fear of death is fundamental as well. It is a constant pressure in the background for most of us, most of the time. As the ultimate form of loss, death takes away all chance to reach fulfillment in this lifetime. While many come up with different belief systems to soften its impact, bargaining with our experience to find some comfort until we have fully resolved the projections we have attached to it, the fear of death remains a powerful influence in our life.[4]

It's important to remember these are only labels for experiences we all share.[5] But when we deconstruct anxiety to its root, these are the five kinds of experiences people report, the interpretations of fear we all make. They are the universal themes of loss that each of us buys into, archetypes of the fearful aspect of existence. Of course, many subdivisions are possible because there are many different ways these fears manifest in the great variety of human circumstances. But we will soon be performing an exercise that reliably demonstrates there is always one core fear at the root for each of us. It is the most fundamental layer of our psyche, the underpinning of how we interpret everything that is not "safe."

As you have no doubt detected, each of the five core fears is intimately related. Purpose, as we have said, is tied to meaning. If we lose our sense of purpose, life feels empty of meaning. And usually this meaning will have something to do with our connection to other people—love. If we are abandoned by a loved one, life can easily seem meaningless and also without purpose (as opposed to the "high" of being in love when everything is imbued with meaning and purpose). So too with identity: we can't really find or be our true selves in a vacuum (i.e., if abandoned)—who we are is built in large part on our relationships with others, the impact we make on them and they on us, the mirroring we give and receive. So much of the meaning as well as the purpose of life comes from our identity as a member of a tribe, family, community, etc., where we love and are loved. If cut off from this membership, we can suffer from any of the other core fears as we lose a significant source of love, meaning, and purpose. We can also fear exposure to death, a "genetic memory" of the importance of the group for survival. This fear of death, however, can arise even when connected to others since it promises to take away our chance for fulfillment in the other core fears as well. Coming to terms with death, on the other hand, gives us an extraordinary freedom to live life fully as our true self, giving and receiving love without fear of abandonment, finding a renewed meaning in being alive, with the purpose of soaking up all that life has to offer and sharing it with others.

Because of their interconnection, we each carry some of all five core fears. Being universal in nature, describing the most important aspects of fulfillment and the biggest threats to it, they are inescapable as we go through life. Still there is going to be one of the five that is at the "core" for each of us, one that explains our essential fear more fundamentally than the others. So in the end, even though the lines between these five overlap significantly, it will be important to discover our unique core fear, the primary interpretation beneath all others of how life can be unsafe.

THE CHIEF DEFENSE

Our first encounter with the core fear is so distressing that we naturally begin looking for ways to protect ourselves from it. If very young, for example, we may scream reflexively when our mother leaves the room. As she comes running back with care and concern on her face, we make the connection that our screaming is responsible for this wonderful result and get the first inklings that we just might have some agency in the situation. We try the same response again and again. Each time it works, it becomes mightily reinforced and the behavior gets locked in. If confronted with a fear that is significant enough, it can get locked in in an instant, interpreted as a life-saving measure.

When we are a bit older, we explore more sophisticated variations on the theme. If, for example, our father is distant and cold, we may become extra solicitous in the hope of engaging his attention and winning his love. If we are one of several siblings, we may become highly competitive to get our needs met. If someone has abandoned us, we may become compulsively "good" or "pleasing" to ensure they will stick around the next time. Some of us choose a style of being overly responsible, others, of being a peacemaker. Still others may learn to act out for negative attention or may become a narcissist, inflating their own importance. There are, of course, myriad ways in which, through trial and error informed by circumstance, we choose our responses.

The response we ultimately commit to becomes what we will call the "chief defense." *The chief defense is our primary strategy for protecting ourselves from the core fear.* It is the strategy we believe will best manage the threat. With the arrival of the chief defense, we have discovered our ability to make ourselves safe, returning to our previous state of well-being by exercising a control to meet our needs. The relief we feel when we first land on the chief defense is extraordinary. Because exposure to the core fear is so overwhelming, the restorative impact of the chief defense is equally profound, making an indelible imprint upon the psyche.[6]

With the arrival of the chief defense, we have taken the next step in becoming an autonomous being. Each time we use it successfully, we build a little more of our individuated identity, one that can regulate and have some command over its environment. The discovery of the chief defense gives us our first experience of "I can take care of myself." This is an experience of power and control that, because it relieves so much fear, becomes addictive. It waters the seeds of the separated sense of self with an intoxicating feeling of authority. But with it, our focus becomes more about increasing our command over the environment and less about fulfillment.

Even though the chief defense is a response to the core fear, we cannot say there are five chief defenses. The complexity of our circumstances creates an equally complex set of possible ways we can respond to them. For example, if exposed to the threat of losing love, one person may build a chief defense of clinging (e.g., dependent personality disorder). Another may become depressed, defending against the pain of disappointment by giving up the hope of ever getting love. A third person may become very demanding or presumptuous (e.g., narcissistic personality disorder), while someone else may test the limits of others' love to ensure it is secure (e.g., borderline personality disorder). In short, there are too many options for how human beings respond to the core fears to group them neatly in a set number of categories.

MAKING THE VOW

Upon first discovering our chief defense, we feel safe once again and return to balance and peace. All is well, it would seem, in our personal little universe. We had quite a scare but have found a way to make things right again. Suddenly, a new thought occurs to us: *What if the threat comes back?* This is the thought that will change the course of our life. We now realize that we no longer live in a world where we can fully rest as before, oblivious to the potential for danger. Instead, we must stand guard, ready to use our defense should the threat arise again. We make a solemn vow—often literally[7]—to be vigilant, prepared at a moment's notice, never to be taken by surprise as we were before.

This course of events is unavoidable; we really don't have any option when we are young. Because of the relief our chief defense provides, because the feeling of power it gives is so addictive, we see it as our new path to fulfillment, our assurance of safety and the guarantee of happiness we seek. We will perfect our ability to use the defense so that we never have to feel threatened again. We have found the key not only to survival but, we believe, to salvation . . . not just relief from the core fear but the promise of a return to wholeness. We will make sure we always have this key at the ready, having made a vow never to let it go.

As we mature, we fine-tune and perfect our proficiency in using the chief defense. This is why it becomes such an automatic and fast response. With each repetition we reinforce the habit, becoming highly skilled in manipulating our environment and negotiating life. Each time we successfully stave off fear, we reinforce the message "This is what I am good at, what I know how to do well" and also "This is who I am." As a result, the core fear and chief defense become all-consuming in our life, ultimately leading to the ubiquity of fear and our attempt to find fulfillment through fear's strategy.

SECONDARY DEFENSES

Of course, just as with the core fear, our response to a problem is not always going to look like the chief defense. In fact, we have developed a huge array of intricate, subtle, and highly sophisticated "secondary defenses." These are the many faces of the chief defense, adaptations to the particular requirements of the moment. The variety of secondary defenses we can develop accounts for the complexity of what it is to be human, the multifaceted ways we interpret and respond to life.

Secondary defenses provide the flexibility we need to enact our chief defense in a way that is appropriate to the situation. It would not, for instance, be appropriate to yell at our boss even though it can be an effective defense with our spouse. With our boss, our repertoire of responses is restricted. So instead of yelling, we might manipulate, cajole, become passive-aggressive, and so forth. Think of the many instant choices we make when having a conversation. At the speed of thought we decide whether, in response to an insult, we should reply sarcastically, attack, act hurt, apologize, become charming, act haughty, etc. These and many more are the secondary defenses we use to express our chief defense most effectively, according to the circumstances of the moment.

We could actually create a hierarchy of defenses. The first level, of course, would be the chief defense. The next level—secondary defenses—would be those adaptations of the chief defense developed when very young. Arriving early on the scene, they have more impact on our thinking and behavior than those discovered later in life. They are more fundamental and broad, less specific and focused on details (corresponding with the abilities of our developing neurology). If someone, for example, has a chief defense of "being the best," a secondary defense might be to become very knowledgeable, always ready with the best answer. Later in life, they may develop what we could call a tertiary defense, becoming very knowledgeable in a specific domain, such as an occupation, trying to be the best in their job. This tertiary defense would not have as much influence on the person's overall behavior and strategy for living as would the secondary defense, which wouldn't have as much influence as the chief defense. And so on. We make new defenses all the time, always variations on the chief defense. Those made more recently are ways of fine-tuning our strategy for living, details on how to live life a little more successfully, get a little more control, make things slightly easier, work out a bit better, etc. For simplicity's sake, we will stick to the label "secondary defense" for any behavior that is spun off from the chief defense.

In looking for our secondary defenses, we must not assume that a particular behavior equates with a particular defense. The same behavior can be used as a secondary defense in the service of more than one chief defense. Someone who pursues money, for instance, may be seeking security from starvation or homelessness, with a core fear of death. Another person may acquire money in order to feel important, trying to procure a sense of identity. Someone else might focus on money as a defense against meaninglessness, donating financially to worthy causes that make them feel fulfilled. Yet another person might try to buy someone's love with their money, and so on. For a different example, consider the secondary defenses used in a conversation. Most of us are socialized to keep the exchange "pleasant"—to be polite, maintain eye contact, smile, look interested, and so forth. But one person can use these behaviors as a narcissistic defense, adding a twist of charm and charisma. Someone else can use them to ensure they are thought of as caring, emphasizing eye contact, and a look of concern. And a third person may purposely avoid following these social norms to look "cool," dispassionate, and independent.

I remember one summer when, in my twenties, I interned at a psychiatric hospital. There was a particular patient in the locked unit who displayed psychotic symptoms. These symptoms, we discovered, were a defense whose purpose was to get others to "leave him alone." The prospect of being around too many people was overwhelming for him, and isolating himself had become his chief defense. Each day, the staff of the hospital would encourage him to come out of his room and participate in group therapy, for example. He wanted none of it and was clearly bothered every time they would interrupt his isolation. One day I watched with some amazement as he interviewed to be released from the hospital, presenting as completely normal, well-adjusted, and so forth. His request was denied as the interviewing psychiatrist understood his reasons . . . he wanted to leave the hospital so that he could maintain his isolation without the interference of the hospital staff. Both the psychotic features and his presentation at the interview were secondary defenses against the fear of being overwhelmed by people.

All our efforts to get life to be the way we wish, from grand schemes to momentary impulses, employ our chief and secondary defenses. For example, dreams of being famous, finding a soul mate, or acquiring power are all attempts to conquer fear and restore our original state of wholeness. If we are famous, we think, we'll never feel worthless again. If we find our soul mate, we will finally feel loved. If we have power, we can dictate our own terms, no longer at the mercy of fear. Every moment that we are not deeply fulfilled, feeling complete and at peace, we are holding some fear of loss and therefore defending against it.

WHY ALL DEFENSES BACKFIRE

Our defenses do work to alleviate the fear of the moment—that is why they are so compelling. But they come at too great a cost. In fact, they create further fear. Because their strategy requires that we are always prepared for problems, we have to be on the lookout for situations to defend against. We scan the environment for signs of threat, projecting

① Chief defense → Isolation

Examples { ② fame → not worthless

a perception of imminent danger to overlay on top of things. Again, this fills our mind with anxiety as we become more and more preoccupied with danger. But our defenses go further than this . . . they can actually create fear out of nothing! Not only do we look for signs of danger in the environment, we anticipate problems that aren't actually there. Living in the distorted perception of our mind, we experience this as if the problems were real here and now, becoming just as anxious as when defending against something concrete.

In short, all defenses backfire. They cause the problem they were designed to fix. We may say our core fear creates the potential for suffering but our defenses actualize it. Without defenses, our core fear would have nothing to attach to. We would experience our circumstances as neutral, perceiving no threat to defend against. Nothing would require our anxious response and we would simply move to meet our situations effectively.

So it is our defenses that project the perception of threat. They take the blueprints drawn by the core fear and project them as something real that we must defend against. We focus our attention on danger so we can be prepared for it at a moment's notice, ready to parry its blow or strategize a solution. This constant readiness to do battle, this vigilant attention to threat, is what creates the "clutch" of anxiety. It also accounts for the hypnotizing effect of fear, keeping us entranced by what could go wrong as a preparation for dealing with it. And because we experience our projections as if they were actually happening, we feel these imagined threats as real. Unless checked against reality or otherwise worked through, this is how fear's dimensions grow out of proportion.

There are two ways in which our defenses backfire. First, they increase fear by making the problem real, as we have been describing. The act of defending gives us the message there must be something real to defend against or we wouldn't be responding as we are. Second, we have the unsettling realization that our defenses may not be up to their task, that they may not fully ensure our safety in every situation. This creates the anxiety that we are helpless against a fear. So we ramp up our efforts, becoming even more vigilant, even more determined to win the fight. But each time we do, we discover that, still, it is not enough— we don't have a guarantee of safety. No matter how determined we are, no matter how prepared, we cannot be sure our defenses have taken care of all possible opportunities for danger, now and in the future.

Here's another way to explain the backfiring phenomenon. Exercising a defense requires pushing against something solid. Our fear is a projection—nothing solid. But by pushing against it, we reify it, giving ourselves the impression that it is "really there," pushing back. Again, we tell ourselves there must be something to be afraid of or we wouldn't be reacting so. But the reaction makes the fear. We then realize that we haven't defended against it sufficiently and become scared all over again. This impels us to push harder with our defense, which in turn makes the fear seem even "bigger"—more solid and more powerful—and we have our vicious cycle. When this process spins out of control, we call it an anxiety disorder.

THE CORE FEAR–CHIEF DEFENSE DYNAMIC CREATES OUR REALITY

To review, our core fear is the template for all our perceived problems. And our chief defense is the template for all our responses (secondary defenses) to these problems. The core fear–chief defense dynamic is what ultimately traps us in an anxious stance toward life. We saw in chapter 6 that whenever we meet a new situation, we project meaning onto it. We can now understand that this meaning is derived from our core fear and chief defense. Our perception is an overlay of the core fear and chief defense on top of the situation. Like placing a colored transparency over the scene, it blocks out certain features and highlights others. It gives the situation its meaning as we judge it to be either safe or threatening. If threatening, we next judge how best to engage our chief defense, projecting the various scenarios that will result from this form of the defense or that. Once we make a choice and our defense is deployed, we then project fantasies of what will happen next: will our efforts succeed or will they be met with a new attack and if so, of what sort? We ready ourselves to parry with a range of alternative defenses, each of which leads to further fantasies. And around and around we go.

To break the process down in slow motion, the core fear has us anticipate problems in the future. We look at these anticipated problems and become anxious, preparing to defend ourselves against them. We use the instruction of the chief defense to determine the best response. This has us tense up in such a way that we can carry out that response, ready to fight, flee, or freeze in the prescribed manner. Fully engaged, we then look outside for the enemy we have conjured. Of course, we find it, since that was our mission. But in the end it is a perceptual distortion, an overlay of our expectations on top of reality-as-it-is.

Again, all of this becomes our automatic way of responding to life. In every situation, from the first moment a new stimulus meets our senses, we rise to the occasion to see if our core fear is returning and prepare to use our chief defense in protection. *Literally every experience gets processed through the understanding of the core fear–chief defense dynamic.* It becomes the lens through which we filter all information. Our experience gets fashioned accordingly. Unless we have assessed that a situation is safe and promotes fulfillment, we overlay the perception given by our core fear and seal that perception with our chief defense. As such, it may be said that our core fear and chief defense are responsible for our entire experience of reality whenever fulfillment is not predominant. The perception they create is the only reality we know.

THE SECOND DECEPTION OF FEAR REVISITED

Now we may understand the second deception of fear in a more thorough way. Not only does every problem have fear at its root, but every problem has specifically the core fear at its root and a chief defense that locks the fear in. Because we make a vow to perceive reality through their lens, the core fear and chief defense become the source of *every* upset, difficulty, challenge, or threat we experience. In other words, every time we have a problem, we are experiencing it as a problem because of the core fear interpretation. It is always the same core fear that projects our various perceptions of the world. We are upset by a situation *only* because our core fear has been triggered and we have responded to that fear with our chief defense.

This principle, when we see it in action, is truly life-changing. It will become the foundation through which we can know with certainty that our problems are only ever an "illusion," a projection of the core fear

given reality by the chief defense. We never have to be mystified or
confused again about why we are suffering. In our exercises to come,
we will trace the true source of any problem down to the same core fear
and chief defense—every time.

TWO EXAMPLES AND A CASE STUDY

Let's illustrate with examples to bring some Technicolor to the picture.
Think of a young girl who has been ridiculed for having a birth defect.
She might develop a core fear of abandonment and be ready to assume
that people will judge her every flaw. In response, she adopts a chief
defense of "going into hiding." She refines this defense through the
years into a reclusive lifestyle. One day she learns of a social engagement she cannot avoid. She spends weeks filled with anxiety, running
through all the possible scenarios she can imagine, trying to polish her
defenses accordingly. Because she realizes she can never prepare adequately to feel comfortable, her anxiety builds, stimulating further projections about what might go wrong in an attempt to defend more
successfully. Finally, the event arrives. She has worn drab clothing and
covered her face with her hair so as not to be noticed. As she steps into
the room filled with people, she is sure everyone is staring at her. She
fabricates (and projects) all sorts of ideas about what they are thinking,
imagining their secret critiques. She quickly moves to the table of food
where at least she can look occupied. Whenever someone tries to start a
conversation with her, she makes an excuse to go to the restroom. After
a while, she runs out of defensive options and finds a reason to leave
early.

Or imagine someone who is beaten up by the school bully. More
than the physical pain, he suffers from the humiliation of "losing face"
in front of the other kids. If he internalizes this, it can create a core fear
around identity—feeling inadequate and worthless. This might lead to a
chief defense of victimizing others. Later in life, he becomes a business-
man and plans the hostile takeover of a competitor. Projecting what the
future might bring, he begins an anxious cycle of plotting and scheming
on how to ensure the outcome he wants. He rehearses over and over
any scenario that could threaten his goal (stimulating his core fear) and
prepares his defenses to deal with it. The timing has to be just right, he

GOAL 1 => ① see how core
fear / defenses are
running life amok

must check and countercheck that his associates are trustworthy, he must make sure everyone knows the plan inside and out, and he must come up with backup plans for this eventuality and that. Finally, he is relatively secure that his plan is sound. But even then he is on high alert, ready to discover something he hasn't accounted for, ready to engage his defensive strategies even more rigorously.

We spend most of our time being run by these kinds of fantasies, rarely in the present moment of what is actually happening. The projections we make from the core fear and chief defense are the great shaping forces of our life. Any time we are not experiencing a deep fulfillment, the core fear and chief defense are making decisions for us, choosing our thoughts, feelings, and behaviors. We fill our days obsessively taking care of responsibilities, securing money and other protections, fending off attacks and keeping up with obligations . . . all dictated by our core fear and chief defense. This is fear's strategy for securing fulfillment, the attempt to achieve control over that which threatens it. We are exhausted from the endless fight against reality, knowing that our efforts will never be enough. This Sisyphus-like task creates enormous frustration, leading to depression, suffering, and, as we have said, further anxiety. Our first goal must be to clearly see how the core fear–chief defense strategy has run amok in our life so that we may seek an alternative solution.

I once worked with a client who was a very capable woman in her fifties. I'll call her Sylvia. She essentially ran her household, having chosen a husband who was rather passive. This worked out well as it gave her the control she wanted to do things her way. But after a lifetime of taking care of everything and everyone, always having to be so capable, she was severely burned out. This was her reason for seeking treatment. One day, Sylvia came into my office looking especially forlorn. Her doctor had just diagnosed her with a serious illness that came from working with the exotic animals that were her business. The doctor told her she had to quit the business or she would die. As we explored her response, she finally admitted to me, "It doesn't seem like life would be worth living if I have to give up the business." As I inquired further, we realized it wasn't so much that she needed the pet shop. She simply couldn't tolerate a disease that would take away her control in life.

from core fear

core fear → defense running amok

fulfilled → core fear → defense running amok

Digging for the origins of this powerful projection—that life just wasn't worth living if she couldn't be in control—she revealed that she had grown up with an aunt who was very cruel. Her mother felt she couldn't take care of her and had sent her to live with this aunt. When Sylvia was only eight years old, she took her dog and walked three miles to her mother's house in the dead of winter. She was determined to live at home instead of at her aunt's house. But when she arrived, her aunt was waiting for her, ready to take her back. Sylvia grabbed her mother's dress and held on so tightly that no one could pull her away. Finally, her mother relented and she was allowed to stay.

In recounting this story, Sylvia had a sudden illumination . . . this was the source of her tremendous drive. At the moment when her mother relented, she learned that if she took control over her circumstances, if she was extremely competent (even to the point of walking three miles on her own to her mother's house), if she was thoroughly determined to make something happen, she could succeed. Her core fear was a loss of security (fear of death) born of the abuse at her aunt's house. And her chief defense was to take matters into her own hands and turn things around. Now, as a grown woman who had lived by this strategy her entire life, she had become highly skilled at "making things work." But with the diagnosis of an illness she could not control, she felt utterly helpless to find a reason for living that made sense to her.

This insight, however, gave her some distance from the projection. Motivated by her burnout, she understood that taking control was not the only strategy for living. With my encouragement, she began looking for other sources of fulfillment that didn't require such control. She started spending more time with her grandchildren and began painting as an expression of her creative side. Eventually we found a way for her husband to take over the pet shop while she supervised from a distance, giving her just enough control to make the transition to a new way of living.

HOW TO CREATE REALITY

The idea that we "create our reality" often gets bandied about casually, but the clarity of our model makes it possible to understand the concept in a more sophisticated way. The reality we know is indeed the result of our perception, and our perception is indeed the result of the thoughts we choose (see for example Chopra, 2005). But as we have discussed, this involves much more than consciously choosing certain thoughts and expecting reality to comply with our wishes. Rather, we must clear out all opposing thoughts, born of fear and for the most part unconscious. Popular teachings such as the law of attraction—attracting that which we consciously choose to think—are appealing to positive thinking enthusiasts. But this is only a partial truth. We do create our reality by the thoughts we choose, but our unresolved fears are usually the greater part of that creation.

Furthermore, the law of attraction falls apart when we consider what happens when two or more people try to create conflicting realities. One person wants the new guy in town to ask her out on a date while another is vying for the same reality. The new guy in town also has his own ideas. Who wins? The answer given by our model is whoever's intention is clearer, i.e., whoever has fewer opposing thoughts blocking the way. Usually it is a combination of everyone's intentions that makes up the final mix. This is not metaphysical but easily understood. One of the competing girls has a core fear of rejection and defends against it with shyness. The other has a defense of exhibitionism. She perhaps has more of a chance of getting noticed by the boy, but his defenses may make shyness more attractive to him than exhibitionism. As in our discussion of the hundredth monkey phenomenon, our collective perceptions build a consensual reality—the person whose perception is reinforced by the greater number of people wins the day.

So in order to truly create our reality, we must clear out all obstacles (unconscious opposing thoughts) to that which we wish to perceive.[8] Even psychodynamic therapy, which directly seeks these unconscious thoughts, can come up short unless it finds the source of them, the core fear at the root. Without this, our ability to heal from suffering and create a different reality will be compromised. Unless we cut through to the core, we encounter too many layers of fear, new ones being created all the time, to ever make our way through. But with the understanding that our negative thoughts come from a core fear that generates them all, we simply need to resolve that core fear. This is the key to taking control over the projection process and creating the reality we wish to perceive.[9]

PERSONALITY DEVELOPMENT: THREE PHASES

Our core fear–chief defense model of the psyche provides a new definition of personality. Personality is the combination of how we interpret the environment (the thoughts and feelings we have about it) and how we respond to that interpretation (our behavior). In our model, except when inspired by fulfillment, all of these interpretations come from the core fear and all of our behaviors come from the chief defense. So the core fear and chief defense, plus the drive for fulfillment, literally combine to create our personality. They determine the unique way we interact with the world, the particular style with which we understand and respond to it, the colors and qualities that make us who we are. We may also say that personality is our way of perceiving the world. This too, we have seen, is built upon the core fear and chief defense and any impulse for fulfillment we allow to come through.[10]

There are three distinct phases in the emergence of a personality, three periods of development in the evolution of the core fear and chief defense.

Phase 1: The Birth Experience

Personality formation actually begins in the womb. Earlier we discussed how fear and separation are first experienced in the birth process and that these experiences become imprints, patterns, and templates for later life experiences. Let's review this through the lens of personality development.

Grof's four-stage model of the birth process (1980) sheds important light on the establishment of the core fear and chief defense. The first stage of birth is the state before labor begins. Again, all needs are met in an experience of undifferentiated Oneness and fulfillment. Barring health complications, the possibility of struggle doesn't exist for the fetus.[11] In the second stage, this utopia is interrupted as the vaginal walls clamp down upon the baby, causing great pain and the experience of being trapped. This, in our model, represents the first moment of fear, the moment when the infant makes their first projection about what is happening and the fact that they are unsafe. Grof describes this as a hellish experience of "no exit" . . . the fetus is totally helpless. In other words, he or she has no defenses to come to their aid. The third stage shows the infant now moving toward the "light at the end of the tunnel," struggling to get out of the womb. This is the stage where one starts using one's will, trying to get free. It is the first defense, the first attempt at self-preservation. Finally the baby is out of the womb. He or she has a sense of victory over danger. This seals the idea that their defensive efforts were effective. They are free of the threat, back to their previous state of comfort and safety. Only now they know of the possibility of future dangers that must be defended against. Their personality begins to bend around these awarenesses.[12]

We mentioned earlier Grof's holotropic breathwork technique for accessing expanded "states of consciousness" (1988). In it, people often have direct experiences of these stages of birth, sometimes getting information about specific details of their birth they previously did not know about (and can corroborate). Such an encounter may give tremendous insight into the fears and defenses behind one's present life difficulties. I regularly see this with my clients in an adaptation of the technique I call "transpersonal breathwork." The freedom that comes when one re-experiences these first moments of the core fear and chief defense is often life-changing by itself.

Phase Two: Early Childhood

As we said previously, if all goes well, after the birth experience we do come back to relative homeostasis. But inevitably we have our next encounter with fear in early childhood. Whether a specific event or a general atmosphere of instability, something happens to disturb the peace and fulfillment of our protected state. Because our brains are more developed than in utero, more capable of making meaning out of things, we begin to interact with the world around us. This is where the core fear and chief defense really start to take shape. We can see the infant practice approach-avoidance behaviors, venturing out further and further away from the parent, always turning around to check for safety. In this way, they gradually develop their understanding of what is risky or dangerous (the core fear) and build a strategy to find their way back to safety (the chief defense). With each experience of success or failure in the world, their personality congeals a bit more and a bit more. If something significantly threatening occurs, the impact upon the psyche can be enough to set the core fear and chief defense in a moment, effecting a more sudden evolution of personality.

Phase Three: Adolescence—A New Birth into the World of Adulthood

But then in adolescence there is a shattering of innocence once again. Like a second birth, this time into adulthood, we have an identity crisis, as our former world undergoes a radical transformation. We realize we are not the center of the universe, not all-important, challenging the defense of childhood narcissism. We begin a deep individuation from our parents, understanding that they are not the "gods" we had taken them for. We meet the big existential questions for the first time: "Who am I?" "What is the meaning of life?" "Why are we here?" etc. And we comprehend the reality of death, feeling our fundamental aloneness in this world of separation. Whatever level of security we felt from living in a protected bubble gives way to an appreciation of the limitlessness of the universe and our smallness in the face of it. The meanings we projected onto the world, the tidy frame of reference that gave our world its order, is lost. We have our first encounter with the "Void."[13]

This is the separation experience, now lived in its most raw pure form. It is often described as "existential angst" because we experience the full impact of what it is to be cut off from wholeness. The fear this can incite is extreme and accounts for why adolescence can be such a time of turmoil. We feel the force of all this powerfully molding our personality, shaping our core fear and chief defense, like the pressures upon coal that form a diamond. Many will use some form of avoidance in their defense, shutting down to the experience because it is too painful.[14] Many also build into their defense a powerful external focus away from their inner experience. They become preoccupied with what they can control in the environment, distracting from the emptiness they have seen underneath it all. Seeking stimulation and satisfaction of the senses, seeking money, power, fame, etc., are all different forms of this kind of defense. There are many other possible responses, of course, some people getting anxious in the face of these existential truths, others getting depressed. There is a wide variety of personality styles we can choose from. All of them are built upon a core fear–chief defense strategy for how best to return to the fulfillment we knew before. Unfortunately, because of this strategy, they backfire, leading us to less, not more, fulfillment.

But we must understand that our way of interacting with the adolescent experience is shaped by our previous learning—i.e., by the core fear and chief defense that have been forming through birth and early childhood. One doesn't suddenly come up with a new interpretation of life in adolescence. We don't develop a brand-new behavioral repertoire out of the blue. Instead, we draw from lessons already learned about how to make sense of and respond to life. We are, after all, talking about personality, and while we may explore different variations on the theme when young, our basic personalities start to emerge very early. There is already a fairly fixed structure in place by the time we reach adolescence.

Our encounter with the existential void seals the deal. This is where the "vow" we spoke of earlier, the promise to be ever-vigilant, takes full hold. It is a vow to look at every situation, *literally* every situation (except when deeply fulfilled) through the lens of the core fear, ready to respond with our chief defense at a moment's notice. From adolescence on, this is "who we are." As you think about your own experience, see if you can identify a particular moment when this kind of decision was made, a moment that set the course of your life in a certain direction. Many of us know the moment well since it is such a pivotal event. Others may not have noticed it as it was occurring but can look back and see how their personality changed through adolescence. This is the moment when who we are becomes fixed for a lifetime. [15]

CASE STUDIES

Peter was a forty-eight-year-old man who suffered from generalized anxiety disorder. He was born by C-section without labor. According to Grof (personal correspondence) and English (1985), those born Caesarean without labor "skip" the second and third stages of birth where much of the struggle and fear of birth is experienced. As such, says Grof, babies born by C-section without labor can have greater access to transpersonal realms but can also suffer from lack of grounding in the "real" world. Peter exemplified this perfectly. He was especially devoted to finding transcendence in life, and he struggled with the limitations of being human. If we grant that this may have begun at birth, then we can understand how his childhood furthered the experience; he had an overprotective mother who shielded him too well from the exigencies of life. At nine months old, however, he became very sick and was hospitalized. He must have been in significant physical pain. More importantly, he must have been terrified at being separated from his mother, in a strange, cold environment, with strange people poking and prodding him. When he returned to the security of his home, he regressed, clinging tightly to his mother and showing behaviors he had already grown out of. He stayed young and dependent (especially on his mother) throughout his childhood. Then when he was fourteen years old, he began a tumultuous adolescence, feeling the hormonal changes as an overwhelming challenge to his identity. His first response was to try to "cling" to his parents for comfort, but for the first time since the hospital experience, they were not able to calm him. This increased his anxiety all the more. His response at that point was to embark upon an intense philosophical and, later, spiritual quest in an attempt to reclaim the happiness he knew in childhood. This time, the source of comfort would be God, as he chose a chief defense of "clinging" just as tightly to a spiritual ideal as he ever did to his mother.

Helena was a fifty-nine-year-old woman. She didn't know the details of her birth but described a highly anxious childhood, eating little, throwing up often, and afraid to speak much, sensing extreme tension in the house. Her general strategy for safety was to hold in her feelings and "stay away." In later years, her mother would say, "I never knew what you needed because you never cried." Her father was a narcissist, by her report. Her mother became progressively more depressed as a response to his self-absorption. When she learned he was cheating on her, they separated. Helena was ten years old. She remembered the moment when her parents told her and her sister that they were going to live in separate places. Helena thought, "My life will never be the same again." Still, her chief defense had not fully set. She tried to be close with her father but he would not reciprocate. As her mother's depression worsened, Helena became highly independent, taking care of herself by getting up and out for school, making meals, etc., while her mother stayed in bed. Her defense of holding in her feelings deepened because she understood that it was pointless to express her needs or expect a nurturing response. Then in later adolescence, when Helena was visiting her father and trying desperately to connect with him, a decisive moment occurred: after she had asked her father to be sensitive when talking about her mother (daring, against much fear, to express her needs), he soon started blaming her mother and speaking badly about her. At that moment, Helena told herself, "That's it; I'm never going to trust anyone again." The defense of holding in her feelings, taking care of herself without depending on anyone, became powerfully locked in. She would spend the next several decades following this strategy. Romantic partners could get only so close, and many would complain that she "wouldn't talk" about her feelings or needs. She also used anger as a secondary defense, as if to show the world (and specifically her parents) how hurt she was, how in need of nurturing. But like any defense, this plan backfired . . . if someone did try to offer support and nurturing, she could not accept it. Doing so, she said, would mean "letting her parents off the hook." She was caught in a perpetual loop, using anger as the only safe way to show how hurt she was and at the same time unable to receive the nurturing she needed. Still, she would never let her anger at her parents come out *fully* for that might mean losing them altogether. This further reinforced the whole dynamic as she tried earnestly to ask for help but only felt safe doing so with anger, never expressing herself directly. And yet she held on for dear life to this defensive style, too afraid of the alternatives. It was, she believed, her only protection from the pain of opening up to the love she longed and being disappointed when it was not given.

Gerry, a forty-two-year-old client of mine, was the oldest of five siblings. She had always been proud of the fact that her brothers and sisters looked up to her. As a child, this gave her a sense of identity that she used to compensate for a significant degree of neglect by her parents. When Gerry was twelve years old, her mother had a psychotic break. Her father, never one to express his feelings, became very busy taking care of the household while Gerry's mother stayed in the hospital. Gerry saw her opportunity to win favor with her father and so took over her mother's role. She made meals for the family, cleaned the house, and provided emotional support. Her father's approval was powerfully reinforcing, and her chief defense was set. This was the point at which she made her "solemn vow"—that she would take charge of things from that moment forward. By the time she had come to see me, she was exhausted from a lifetime of too many responsibilities and too much hard work, with no opportunity for rest or nurturing.

Stephen came to see me for social anxiety when he was thirty-three. He was the youngest of three siblings and had been overly praised for being "adorable" as a child, especially by his mother and grandmother. When he became an adolescent, he struggled with the fact that others did not treat him the same way his family did. As he explored different ways of handling this including isolating socially, staying close to his family, and so forth, he ultimately landed on a chief defense of being "nice," a people-pleaser. He became highly attuned to others' facial expressions, gestures, and inflections. If they showed signs of approval, he would "put on" the charm and become "adorable" again, trying to ensure their goodwill. If they were disapproving, he would "go invisible." Each was a secondary defense driven by a chief defense of preserving his childhood identity. Like all defenses, this had a silver lining—he was a highly aware and sensitive person—but being fueled by fear and tension, it came at too great a cost. Then, in tenth grade, he had a philosophy class at school where they were discussing the possibility of perfection. This idea lit him on fire and became the moment at which his chief defense took on its final form: he would try to become "perfect"—perfectly good, kind, and loving—ensuring that no one could ever find fault with him again.

A NEW UNDERSTANDING OF SUFFERING

The core fear–chief defense model lends new understanding to our suffering. To explain, we must introduce the word "resistance" into our discussion. Resistance, the act of resisting, is the action component of a defense. The defense is the wall we put up when we resist. Resistance is the action of using that wall to press against things, push them away, or at least actively keep them out. Of course, we resist that which we don't like (and in some form are afraid of) and use the defense to avoid or try to change it. [16]

Suffering is the result of resistance; the act of resisting is the source of suffering. When we push against things as they are, attempting to get control over that which we fear, we create the tension of our distress. [17] We experience resistance in the body as the act of tensing up physically, resistance in the mind as the act of thinking about our objections, and resistance in the spirit as a contracted sense of self whose energies are gathered to focus on the problem.

But not only is resistance the source of suffering, resistance *is* suffering. In other words, the act of contracting physically, mentally, and spiritually is what hurts. Until we contract in mind, body, and spirit, we may have a physical sensation, but we don't suffer until we think of it as "pain." We may have a sense of being limited spiritually, but if this is not experienced as a confinement, we won't feel squeezed by it. And we may have an upsetting thought, but if we're feeling well physically and spiritually, the thought just doesn't seem to trouble us.

It's important to emphasize that *only* resistance is suffering. There is no other source or experience of suffering to consider. We never suffer because of the "thing" we are upset about. It is only our reaction to that thing—our resistance, born of our defenses—that needs to be addressed. This is very good news, in fact, because it puts the power of healing squarely back into our hands. If the source of suffering were outside us, we would have no opportunity to truly escape it. Remember, defenses create anxiety by reifying it, projecting it as something real we must defend against. If we put our attention on our internal response, the external situation disappears as the cause of suffering. It is seen as a wholly neutral phenomenon, waiting for our projections to be laid on top of it.

For this reason, all healing comes from letting go of resistance (and the defenses that source the resistance). But as in our deceptions, fear persuades us to look away from the true reason for our suffering. Instead, we continually place our attention on the external world, trying to resist and change its circumstances. The exercises to come will teach us how to let go of this resistance, transforming our defenses as we do so, facing the actual source of suffering hidden under the defense. And because it is the actual source, each time we do so, our suffering resolves. With this, we discover the need for resistance and defense disappears, for the fear we imagined turns out not to be "real."

ASSESSING OUR JOURNEY TO THIS POINT

Whether beginning in utero, early childhood, or adolescence, we make decisions about how to interpret and respond to life at an early age. We build a core fear and chief defense from these decisions and assign all situations their meaning accordingly. We assume that our thoughts about life are fixed and true, inherent in the nature of things, and that our automatic way of responding is our only viable option. But these decisions were made when we were very young. We didn't know back then about choosing different strategies. And so we now live in a world of projection, our three-dimensional hologram, patterned upon these decisions. As children, this was the best we could do. In fact, it was necessary for survival. Making sure our mother was always within sight, for instance, could have meant the difference between life and death. Obviously this is not so when we are adults. But we have never challenged these projections and they have become stubbornly fixed from a lifetime of practice. So our suffering comes from looking at the world with the mind of a child, assuming it is ready to threaten us at any moment and we must always be on guard.

Projections take place with lightning speed. They seem to be nearly automatic and instinctive, which is why it can be so hard to change our behavior. But the first step is always insight, and we must fully "catch" these projections at work inside of us. We can do so by noticing where we resist, tensing and bracing against a reality we want to control. We can actually feel the separation occurring each time we apply resistance. We push away that which we don't like so we can stay separate from it. But we never reach the goal, we are never secure enough. Instead of freeing ourselves from fear so we may pursue fulfillment, we end up spending our life defending against perceived problems.

The core fear and chief defense must no longer be our tools for navigating the world. They do not make us safe or foster wholeness. With them, we have been living a life that is more about staying away from danger than it is about pursuing fulfillment. Still, we long to express what is highest and finest in us. When we become tired of suffering, when we have become exhausted from the endless effort of defending against fear, we will start to question our assumptions. And this is the beginning of wisdom. We challenge the belief in fear with the understanding that it distorts truth. Realizing we have been following the wrong guide, we withdraw our investment in it, no longer needing to defend against fear. With this we reveal the natural path to fulfillment that has been waiting all along. This is how we heal and this is how we resolve suffering. It is time to rework our projections, letting go of resistance, usurping the core fear and chief defense as our strategy for fulfillment. And that is exactly what we will do in part 2.

NOTES

1. This is our first experience with the hypnotizing effect of fear.

2. William Blake's *Songs of Innocence and Experience* (1977) speaks exquisitely to this transition.

3. The fear of death can be thought of as the fear of losing our chance to fulfill the other four domains.

4. The fear of sickness and the fear of pain are also important in most people's thinking, but they are not quite at the core, as we shall see. They lead to the deeper fear of death. There's no question that our relationships with others are fundamental in our experience of fulfillment and therefore play a key role in our core fears. Each of the five core fears can be said to involve our interpretation of threat or fulfillment in the face of other people. With abandonment, it is obvious. Identity is built largely from the mirroring and feedback we receive from others. Meaning has much to do with the fulfillment (or lack of it) that comes from our connection with others. Purpose is the expression of that meaning and almost always has to do with making a difference with other people. And our fear of death includes, of course, the fear of being cut off from life and especially other people. There is much to say about how relationships play into our model, but that is beyond the scope of what we can cover here.

5. And it is important to be flexible in our labels, choosing words that bring the experience to life most effectively.

6. For a wonderful example of a child who is just finding her chief defense, see www.youtube.com/watch?v=MLErNXIYjMg.

7. Many clients in psychotherapy will identify a pivotal moment in their development when they made such a vow. Finding this moment can be very helpful in the course of treatment.

8. And again, because of our interconnection, we must also clear out any fear of breaking from the perception of the consensus, i.e., our social conditioning. After all, we want to be able to choose our own way regardless of what other people think.

9. When the core fear is fully resolved, however, we do not need to impose our individual wishes upon reality. Rather, we calmly accept things as they are, with no fear or need to defend a certain reality, and act on what serves the greater good (see chapter 15).

10. With practice, we come to see that all of human behavior—our individual and collective ways of being—is built on these principles. Of course, our parents have a powerful influence on shaping our personalities. We model our core fear and chief defense in large part upon what we learn from them. We pick and choose aspects of each parent's personality, observing how they interpret and respond to life. As we grow older, we have more of our own experiences, and our personality can diverge from theirs. Other significant people in our sphere, siblings, friends, and teachers, lend their influence as well. Culture, in fact, can be said to be the "personality" of a society or another group, with its own core fear and chief defense that set the social norms.

11. For a remarkable example of what this "feels" like, see the first 45 seconds of www.youtube.com/watch?v=RVlVcsp-ed4. (I recommend turning the autio off to get t he full experience.)

12. There is a common observation among nurses who work with neonates. In the case of twins, the smaller of the two babies often develops a feistier personality. The hypothesis is that because the smaller baby is under greater strain in the womb, receiving a reduced share of nutrients from the placenta and getting bumped around by their larger twin, they learn to fight harder and assert their needs more firmly. This is interesting evidence of personality forming in the womb.

13. In fact, this moment can be nicely described as an exposure to the five core fears: seeing our parents as ordinary human beings with flaws and limitations, we lose the idea of perfect love we knew before. We realize they cannot protect us from the Void, and we feel fundamentally alone (abandoned). In undergoing the radical shift in our bodies, hormones jumbling up our thoughts, etc., most of us ask the question "Who am I?" feeling lost to our previous identity. Similarly, with exposure to the infinity of the universe, we lose our frame of reference and all can seem meaningless. Without a sense of meaning, we can lose our purpose. And as we have seen, there is an awareness for the first time of our mortality, a confrontation with the core fear of death.

14. Existentialism as a philosophy grew as a reaction to this very defense. The existentialists declared they would not turn their backs on this experience. Acceptance of it makes it possible, they believed, to create one's own meaning in the face of what otherwise presents as empty and meaningless (see for example Camus, 1993).

15. We might also include a fourth stage in personality development when one reaches old age. At this time we are confronted with the reality of death in

a more imminent way. As we examine our life retrospectively, questions of meaning, purpose, identity, and love come to the fore once again. Of course, some people become rigid, bitter, or depressed in old age, using the same defenses to struggle against these new fears. But others let go of their defenses to varying degrees, recognizing their ineffectiveness. Still others become worn down, too tired to keep fighting against reality, and they undergo a "mellowing." Defensiveness is replaced, to whatever extent, by acceptance, and they become softer, less controlling, and more loving. It can sometimes seem as though we adopt a personality style in adolescence very different from who we were prior to it. A client of mine once said, "I'm clear that my chief defense in childhood was to be very obedient but then I rebelled in adolescence, becoming angry and defiant." Someone else said, "I was a happy child, became withdrawn in adolescence, feeling lost and confused, but now I am very involved in life again." These examples actually confirm our model nicely. We do try different defenses—all of which are generally informed by our first exposure to the core fear—until the point in adolescence when something "clicks" and we make a final decision about which defense or which combination of defenses will be most successful in meeting our goals. This becomes our chief defense, the overall response style that we settle on, built from previous trial and error. It's also true that personality shifts, changes, and grows after adolescence but only within the parameters of the core fear and chief defense. Someone who develops an anxiety disorder, for instance, experiences the same core fear in a more exaggerated way. Even traumas are interpreted and responded to through the filter of the core fear and chief defense. Similarly, many of us "settle in to ourselves," feeling more confident as we mature than we did in adolescence, but only when our core fear and chief defense are not ignited by circumstance.

16. We could use the word "defensiveness" instead of "resistance," but since it is more abstract, it doesn't convey the action component as well for what we are about to describe.

17. It is important to distinguish between the words "pain" and "suffering." Pain, we may say, is a physical-only experience of sensation. As discussed previously, it does not have the meaning of "suffering" (an emotion) until we add the mental and spiritual elements to it. Only then does pain acquire the definition of something "bad," registering in the Nexus point as suffering.

Part 2

The Exercises—Bringing the Principles to Life

8

DIGGING FOR GOLD

Finding the Core Fear

The cave you fear to enter holds the treasure you seek.

—Joseph Campbell

It is time now to bring these principles to life, freeing ourselves from anxiety and opening up to the fulfillment we seek. We will start with exercises for finding the core fear, the source of all our difficulties, and the chief defense, that which preserves and agitates the core fear. Next we will discover how to dismantle the chief defense so that we may face the core fear (the correct fear underneath our struggles) and find it has no power over us. As we do so, we will become highly skilled in withdrawing the projections that create our picture of reality, the manifest forms of the core fear and chief defense. This naturally results in a transformation of personality as well. We stand as the creator of our experience rather than a creature bound to it, free to choose a path that serves our higher purposes. The distortions of fear have dissolved and we have an unobstructed view of the truth they were hiding.

So we begin with finding the right fear to face, now understood as the core fear. Digging through the layers of defense that have concealed it, the deceptions and manipulations that have distorted it, we will find the "gold" waiting at the bottom. Our technique for doing so represents a major breakthrough in finding the true cause of suffering in our life. It is a powerful, remarkably fast, and effective way of getting to the root of things in the unconscious. It is the cornerstone of our model, the foundation for freedom and fulfillment, and the gateway to everything else we will be doing.

The process for finding your core fear, Digging for Gold, is vital. Like an archaeologist, we will literally be excavating the layers of our unconscious, looking for the buried treasure at the bottom. It's impossible to overstate the importance of seeing the core fear at work inside us. Doing so is what enables us to withdraw our ill-fated projections and choose a different approach. This is an essential tool for transforming our life at the source. [1]

The exercise for finding your core fear is about deconstructing, step-by-step, the surface presentation of a problem to find the original fear hiding at its foundation. Performing this exercise, you will see that underneath any problem you have—any suffering you experience, any obstacle to fulfillment—is one core fear. Every time. [2] To discover this for yourself can be truly eye-opening, even life-changing. It reveals the secret culprit behind whatever disturbs your peace, the anonymous core fear that pulls the levers and turns the dials of your perception. Performing the exercise, we will witness the power of the core fear to drive our beliefs, our decisions, and our very personality. The entire structure of our worldview springs from the dictates of this single interpretation about how life works, made early on in childhood and accumulating associations, memories, and further interpretations throughout our life.

We will further see that our core fear takes many faces, explaining why we suffer from constantly shifting identities and endlessly variable moods. If our core fear is of losing love, for instance, it might masquerade as a fear of dying. But with this exercise we will find that underneath the fear of dying—the real reason we are afraid of it—is the fear of being cut off from those we love. Without this core fear, our interpretation of death would be very different. Of course, we have a fear of death, but it's not always primarily about the fear of losing loved ones. If the loss of love is one's core fear, it consumes them, showing up in myriad different circumstances. It is what generates their fear and suffering—not fundamentally a concern about dying. Everyone is born with a profound fear of death, but it comes to mean different things for each of us. The same is true, of course, for the other four core fears; our interpretation of them depends on our original contact with fear and the lessons we learned from our exposure to it.

Remember too that when we experience our core fear, we may experience some of each of the other core fears as well, which is why it can sometimes be confusing to pick one. One is still predominant, however, and it is important to get a very clear picture of your unique core fear. Ultimately, it's not the labels of the five core fears but this picture—the living experience of it—that matters. You are not trying to force your experience to fit the label but merely using the label as a guide to give parameters for insight.

The exercises for finding your core fear and chief defense, taken together, are a remarkably fast and powerful way to uncover the deep structure of your personality, revealing exactly who you are, how you perceive life, and why you make the decisions you do. Of course the insight you can get from doing these exercises once will not be as complete as when you do them repeatedly. To glean their full benefit, you'll want to apply the exercises to a variety of circumstances, seeing that indeed, the many faces of your anxieties, problems, and upsets all boil down to one core fear and one chief defense.[3]

EXERCISE FOR FINDING YOUR CORE FEAR: DIGGING FOR GOLD

This exercise and the next are best done by writing in a journal, though they will soon become so familiar that you'll be able to do them in your head. Begin by picking a problem, any problem, big or small. It doesn't matter which one. All problems, as we will demonstrate with this exercise, lead to the core fear. As you conceive of the problem you want to work with, write it in a single short phrase at the top left of the page (see template below). On the same line at the top right of the page, write down one of these three questions in response to the problem:

1. Why is that upsetting to you?
2. What are you afraid will happen next?
3. What are you afraid you will miss or lose?

Each of these is a different form of the question "What is the fear underneath this problem?" The answer will get you one level "deeper," one step closer to your core fear.

It's important to state the problem in a short phrase (to circumvent any chance of making it too complex or losing the gist) and to state it in a way so you can ask one of the three questions. For example, you wouldn't want to say, "I need to be able to pay my bills" because this doesn't state an actual problem, or at least, one that you can ask these questions of. Rather, you would want to write, "I can't pay my bills."

Choose whichever of the three questions is most helpful for getting an answer. One is not better than another. You are simply looking for the one that helps define the fear underneath the first problem. Of course, if you need to change the wording slightly to facilitate an answer, by all means do so. [4] If you feel stuck with one of the questions, try another. With practice, you'll find that the question "Why is that upsetting to you?" being general and open, is usually more helpful for the first line or two of questioning. "What are you afraid will happen next?" because it lends itself to more specific answers, is often the best question throughout the middle of the process. And "What are you afraid you will miss or lose?" is frequently most effective at the end because it suggests a core fear, a statement about fundamental loss.

Having written down your problem and asked one of the questions, you'll write the answer on the second line of the left of the page, underneath the first. Again, make sure your answer is written in a short phrase without extraneous detail. Make sure as well that it describes a new problem that is one layer "deeper" than the first and of which you can ask another of the questions. You are looking for an answer that gets underneath the problem above it, explaining what the fear behind that problem is. An important point: watch out for a "repetitive loop" when the answer you come up with is actually a restatement of the problem above. For instance, "I can't pay my bills" and "I'll get behind in my payments" are really the same problem dressed differently. One doesn't explain the fear underneath the other . . . you haven't gotten a level deeper with that answer. Rather, if we say, "I can't pay my bills" and then ask, "Why is that upsetting to me?" the answer might be "The electricity will get turned off." This gets us closer to the core, to what's really going on under the surface.

Write whichever of the three questions is most helpful on the second line on the right side, answering with a third-level problem on the left side underneath the one before. Continue this process until you get to the core, and then summarize your core fear in, again, a short, succinct phrase.

Be careful not to skip steps as you go through the questions; it's important not to make any leaps in thinking but to fill in all the blanks. For instance, if your problem is that you don't have enough money, your answer to "What are you afraid will happen next?" might be "I'll end up on the streets." While the connection may seem obvious, it's important to fill in each missing step meticulously, such as "If I don't have enough money, I'm afraid what will happen next is that I won't be able to pay my bills," followed by "If I can't pay my bills, I'm afraid what will happen next is that I will get evicted," and then "If I get evicted, no one will take me in," and finally, "If no one will take me in, I'll be out on the street." Each of these intervening steps is full of meaning specific to your history and the development of your core fear, as we will see.

If one of the questions isn't yielding a ready answer, try a different one. If you feel stuck, it can be helpful to think how others might answer the question (your answer will still come from *your* core fear). It can also be helpful to visualize the process as if you were watching a movie. Begin the movie with your original problem and follow each step of what you are afraid will happen next. Make sure you watch the movie of your fear come true rather than a movie in which you are looking for solutions. Our goal at this point is to uncover our core fear. We don't want to use old strategies for escaping or resolving it before we fully appreciate what it is we want to escape or resolve. But watching your fear play out as if on a movie screen can make the process feel safer (providing detachment) and clearer as well. You simply watch what happens next on the movie screen. If you anticipate that you might become uncomfortable (which is, again, very unlikely), it can help to remember that you've already been living with the fear. Acknowledging it doesn't make it more real. By performing the exercise you are merely discovering what has been going on behind the scenes the whole time. This can actually be quite satisfying, instilling hope that you are on the trail of finding answers.

You will know you have arrived at the core fear when asking any of the three questions brings up the same answer over and over . . . you have already arrived at the deepest level and there is nowhere further to go. You'll also know you have arrived when you get an answer that has a universal, fundamental quality to it, some form of the five core fears we mentioned earlier: loss of love, identity, meaning, purpose, and the fear of death. Try to make a direct connection to one of these five—it will help clarify your thinking. The answer you get will explain the thought system at the very core of your personality, that which is behind *every* interpretation and decision you make. Be prepared to discover significant connections about why your life took the course it did, profound "Aha!" moments, as the puzzle pieces come together making sense out of the major, minor, and everyday choices you have made. This can bring a momentous, sometimes life-changing awareness of that which defines your personality, who you "are." It is often accompanied by powerful emotions, as well as the beginning realization that we are free to choose a different way of being.[5]

This exercise can sometimes evoke memories of the original incident that created your core fear as well as later occurrences that recapitulated it, with lots of spontaneous flashbacks. It's not necessary, however, to remember the original incident since "the past lives on in the present" (M. Pressman, 1999). The original incident is made plain in our present experiences because it is responsible for them. Each present moment, until free of fear, is a recapitulation of the original in disguise.

Here is a template for what the layout of this exercise looks like.

Digging for Gold: Finding Your Core Fear

The three questions:

1. Why is that upsetting to you?
2. What are you afraid will happen next?
3. What are you afraid you will miss or lose?

See figure 8.1.

TIPS FOR MASTERING THE TECHNIQUE

Defenses (and the resistance they inspire) can always arise to "protect" one from finding their core fear no matter how clear the technique. As simple and straightforward as it appears, this exercise can involve a good deal of finesse to negotiate through resistance. Still it is virtually

Problem: _____   Question: _____

Answer (new problem): _____   Question: _____

Answer (new problem): _____   Question: _____

Answer (new problem): _____   Question: _____

Answer (new problem): _____   Question: _____

Answer (new problem): _____   Question: _____

Answer (new problem): _____   Question: _____

Answer (new problem): _____   Question: _____

Core fear: _____

Figure 8.1.

foolproof, especially if the instructions are followed closely. Here are several troubleshooting points to become masterful with it.

- It doesn't matter what problem you start with, big or small, since all are manifestations of the core fear. You will therefore arrive at the same answer—your core fear—regardless of the problem you start with. Some people demonstrate resistance from the start by worrying about which problem to choose (in which case, you can start with the problem "I'm afraid I won't pick the right problem").
- Ask whichever of the three questions is most helpful or applicable to the problem written on the left. One may suggest an answer that makes it easier to see yourself in than another.
- Make sure the answer states a problem, one that you can ask one of the three questions of. This may seem unnecessary, but again, it's important to be meticulous in following these directions if we are to be skillful in avoiding resistance.
- As noted above, watch out for a "repetitive loop" when you actually restate the same level of the problem in a different form. The task is to get one level deeper, one level closer to the core fear.
- You don't want to skip steps even if you think you know where the exercise is going or are already sure of your core fear. In fact, the

more detailed you make it, recording each step in your thought process, the more effective it will be.

- Be very specific in your answers. Abstraction is a defense against looking at the fear. Describe what you think will *actually happen* (in real time), what you'll actually miss or lose. For example, rather than saying, "My head will explode," try "I'll feel overwhelmed and unable to move." Instead of "Everything will fall apart," you'd want to say, "I won't be able to keep up with daily responsibilities," or even more specifically, "I won't keep up with some particular responsibility."

- To help with specificity, you can visualize the problem as if it were happening on a movie screen. Make sure your answers to the questions describe what you see visually on the movie screen. This forces us to become literal and concrete about what is upsetting us, what we are afraid will happen next, or what we are afraid we'll miss or lose. Rather than vague emotional descriptions, we describe what we imagine would actually happen in real time and space, as seen on the movie screen.

- *Don't be limited in your answers by thinking rationally.* Our fears are, by definition, distortions and may seem ridiculous, but we believe them nevertheless. One person who went through the exercise couldn't think of what she was afraid would happen next after getting vulnerable with her partner. All she could see was that she would "feel badly." I invited her to watch the movie of her fear, visualizing a specific scene where she was vulnerable, and not to worry if it was realistic. She then described a scene where her husband would stare into her eyes, looking for connection. In the next scene, she described her fear that he would "swallow me up, sucking the life out of me until I was like a limp rag on the floor." I asked then, "What are you afraid you'll miss or lose?" and she replied, "The chance to do what I want; I'd be too drained and would end up living a meaningless life." With this, she found her core fear—a loss of meaning. She further realized that she had been defending against this her whole life ever since seeing her mother go through exactly the same thing.

- If there are two or more possible answers at any level in this process (i.e., two or more possible fears), pick either one. It doesn't matter which one because, again, they will all end up in the same place . . . at the core.

- Another device to help if you get stuck at any point is to imagine this is someone else's problem. Our resistance, of course, is heightened when thinking about our own fear versus someone else's.

- This process is actually quite simple, the answers to the questions, obvious—there are usually only a handful of options in any situation. But resistance can get sticky and our defenses can obscure the obvious. If, for example, you can't think of the answer to one of the questions, the problem may be a defense of perfectionism (hiding the fear of not having the perfect answer). In response, you can simply make your best guess. If you are a therapist working with a client, you can guess for them. The only proviso, and this is important, is that you not impose your interpretation upon your client when making such a guess. Doing so runs the risk of projecting your own core fear onto their experience. It's crucial to remember that the client's core fear might be making a very different interpretation than your own. As therapists, we have experience with the variety of usual interpretations people make so it can be helpful to *offer* suggestions. But you never want to assume you know unless you have prior experience with the client and really understand their background.[6]

- Another possible solution if stuck in answering the questions is to go to the extreme (as our fear inevitably does). Ask yourself, "What's the worst-case scenario, what would eventually happen in the end if the whole thing fell apart, if I could never get out of the situation, if I lost all control over it, etc.?" Sometimes we get caught up with the concrete details of a situation and need this approach to globalize, again, as our fear is wont to do. For instance, if someone begins the process with an anxiety that they have not kept in shape, he may answer the question "Why is that upsetting to you?" by saying, "If I go up to a woman, she might reject me." Asking "What are you afraid will happen next?" might then lead to "I'll be in pain," and he won't be able to go further than that. To get to the core fear, he would want to generalize from rejection by a specific woman to rejection by *all* women . . . forever. He would then be able to answer "What are you afraid will happen next?" by saying, "I'll always be alone and never find love." Similarly, the woman mentioned above who was afraid she would be left "like a limp rag on the floor" had to imagine that she would be there forever, with no chance of escape, before she was able to see her core fear of losing meaning.

- If our fear is about the well-being of someone we love or care about, we still ask the same questions because it is *our* fear about what might happen to them that will reveal the next layer of the process. At some point in the chain, it will become clear that our fear about what might happen to them speaks about something *we* are afraid to lose. When we are afraid for others, it is because we see them as extensions of ourselves. So if, for example, we are afraid our child will fail at something important, it scares us because we take it as our own failure as a parent, a threat to our fulfillment. It becomes easy at that point to see that our fear of their suffering reflects a fear of how we could suffer.

- Remember, one's core fear is one of the five universal themes of loss mentioned earlier: (1) abandonment, or loss of love; (2) loss of identity; (3) loss of meaning; (4) loss of purpose, or of the chance to express oneself; (5) loss of life, or fear of death, including fear of sickness or pain. Again, don't become preoccupied with these labels. They are meant to be guidelines for what to look for, but your own wording may better capture the essence of your core fear.

- You'll recognize the core fear when you can't go any further with the questions. And you'll want to keep asking the questions for a bit even after you think you've reached the core fear. Only when you come up with the same answer each time can you be sure you've arrived. You'll also recognize the core when you have an "Aha!" moment, understanding that you have found a secret at the root of things. This is often accompanied by powerful memories and flashbacks of how the core fear led to significant moments in your life. You may become aware of the connections between your present circumstances and earlier life experiences, decisions, associations, and learning. You may even remember the origin of your core fear.[7] All this can sometimes evoke powerful emotions, but in a most meaningful way.

- It's also important to understand that our core fear, when activated, can stimulate one or more of the other core fears, even if on a subtle level. Remember, we all have some of each of the five and they can be closely linked in our mind. For instance, if one is confronted with their core fear of death, they are, of course, going to be afraid of losing meaning, identity, purpose, and love. Death threatens to take all of these away. Less obviously, a core fear of losing love can also trigger other fears: we don't know who we are and can feel all is meaningless and without purpose when we lose love. It can also trigger, at least in the back of our mind, the sociobiological fear of dying . . . if we are cut off from our "tribe," it can be difficult to survive. Because the five core fears are so linked, you may have trouble choosing the one core fear that predominates over the rest. But if you continue asking the three questions until you can't come up with a new answer, it will become clear. As an example, one client I worked with had a core fear of losing his identity. He had always been treated as the "golden boy" so losing this identity meant for him that others wouldn't love him in the same way. He had also built up a chief defense of making sure others saw him as the golden boy and had all sorts of plans for becoming famous and "special." Without that identity, he felt his value (meaning) would be lost, as would his opportunity to fulfill his plans (purpose). In the end, he also saw the connection to a fear of dying, for it was the overprotectiveness of his mother that had built his identity as someone special. Since his core fear started when he was very young, he interpreted being special as necessary for survival. Otherwise, he felt, his mother might no longer adore him and he could lose her protection.

As you become practiced with the technique, it's exciting to see that all problems lead to the same core fear. If you are a clinician, it's equally exciting to discover that if two people start out with precisely the same problem, they may well end up arriving at different core fears. This is because the core fear is shaped in response to the unique circumstances of our childhood. It gets adapted to the many situations we all encounter throughout life, but each of us interprets those situations through our own distinctive lens. Someone, for example, who has a fear of acquiring a medical condition might interpret it to mean they could be abandoned by those who love them at a time of vulnerability. Someone else with the same fear may have this concern about abandonment as well, but it could be embedded in a primary fear of dying. Another person might feel that their very reason for being on the planet is to help others, and if they are laid low by a medical condition, their purpose is sabotaged. And yet someone else may feel their identity would be at stake if the medical condition should interfere with their ability to be who they previously imagined themselves to be.[8]

The more often you perform this exercise, the more powerful an agent of change it can become in your life. As you go through it with a variety of different circumstances, your confidence that there is always and only one core fear underneath all problems will grow. This gives enormous reassurance that you know the problem and can work on a real solution. It cuts through all the confusion and "lostness" we suffer when confronted with a situation that sends us reeling once again, our usual equilibrium shown to be a thin disguise over a basic insecurity. Seeing the core fear clearly builds mastery so that in any circumstance we can more quickly and thoroughly understand our reaction. It also makes it possible, as we will find with later exercises, to discover more helpful responses.

CASE STUDIES

Let's look at an example. Jake, a forty-two-year-old man, came to see me because he wanted to be "happier." He had significant social anxiety and had also recently been laid off. His social anxiety made him terrified at the prospect of going to job interviews. Because he was afraid of social situations, his life had become very "small," especially since losing his job. He had his own house but his mother lived with him, and he was filling his time going to the mall with her or staying home. This is how he went through the exercise:

Problem: I have to go on a job interview.

Question: Why is that upsetting to you?

Answer: I could make a fool of myself.

Question: What are you afraid will happen next?

Answer: I'll be rejected.

Question: Why is that upsetting to you?

Answer: I'll never be able to get a job.

Question: What are you afraid you'll miss or lose?

Answer: I'll lose my home and my security.

Question: Why is that upsetting to you?

Answer: I'll be out on the street.

Question: What are you afraid will happen next?

Answer: I'll be alone without protection.

Question: What are you afraid will happen next?

Core fear: It feels like I'll be exposed, alone, unsafe . . . that I'll die.

We had already discussed the fact that when Jake was one year old, his father "kidnapped" his older brother and disappeared with him, leaving Jake and his mother alone. His mother, a very anxious person herself, hovered over Jake and told him throughout his childhood that his father might come and take him away, too. Going through this exercise, he was struck with a deep awareness that he was replaying the fear of that time over and over in his life. The insight into his social anxiety was profound and revelatory: he felt basically unsafe with people, stripped of any security he may have known before he was one year old and constantly afraid that he would be "taken away" in various forms. When he reached the core fear, he spontaneously began making all sorts of associations to scenes from his past. He hadn't thought about most of these in many years, but suddenly, he said, they all "made sense." He remembered looking longingly at his group of cousins, all of whom played together. He felt outcast both because he wasn't allowed to see them often and because when he did, they would go home afterward to a loving family while he had to go home alone with his mother. He also understood why his relationship with his mother was so strained. Each time she expressed her own anxiety and helplessness, Jake was reminded that she had never really been able to make him feel secure. This would inflame his fear of being left alone all the more. He also realized why he always sought out older male mentors; he was looking for a brother or father figure to restore what he had lost. And he understood why he was so anxious about job interviews: not only was he afraid of possible rejection at the interview, he was even more anxious about getting the job only to have it "taken away."

This exercise also gave Jake the insight that he was projecting the face of his father onto potential employers. Each job interview would trigger the entire sequence of thoughts listed in his flow chart. Seeing this, he spontaneously laughed and realized how arbitrary the association was. His social anxiety didn't clear up automatically at this point . . . he simply lost his fear of interviewers. But he did understand the core fear and, later, the ways he was defending against it, unwittingly keeping it alive. Throughout the rest of our work (which included the exercises to come in this book), he succeeded in getting a job, joining a tai chi group where he established new friendships, and joining a dating service to find a girlfriend. In his own words, "I've come a long way from where I used to be. My world was so small before and I was afraid all the time. I really don't feel anxious anymore and am looking forward to getting some of my long-term goals like a new car, house, and, hopefully, more friends and a great relationship with a woman."

Martin was a fifty-three-year-old real estate broker who came to see me because of "itchy palms." He was an imposing figure who seemed unusually confident and gregarious. But we quickly recognized that his itchy palms were the result of anxiety, expressed in a way that was "acceptable" to him. Here's how he went through the exercise:

Problem: I'm depressed by the economy.

Question: Why is that upsetting to you?

Answer: I can't close any real estate deals.

Question: Why is that upsetting to you?

Answer: I've had a dream all my life to make lots of money, and now I'm broke.

Question: What are you afraid will happen next?

Answer: I won't get the retirement I've worked so hard for.

Question: What are you afraid will happen next?

Answer: I'll have to keep working too hard the rest of my life.

Question: What are you afraid will happen next?

Answer: I'll be old, tired, and depressed.

Question: What are you afraid you'll miss or lose?

Answer: The chance to be happy like when I was a kid, with my family.

Core fear: Life will be pointless if I'm just working hard, never reaching my goals, and I'm never happy.

At this point, he seemed mesmerized and had a distant look on his face. When I inquired about this, he said he was remembering a time in childhood when he was ten years old. His father, whom he idolized, came home from work looking severely depressed and deflated. Martin didn't remember what exactly had happened to cause this but said it was something about his father taking abuse from his boss and having no escape from his very unhappy job. It was at this moment, Martin realized, that his core fear took hold. He loved his father and had always wanted to be "just like him." But seeing his father so beaten down by his job, Martin became afraid for him and also for himself. At that moment, he made his vow: He would make a fortune in life, helping his father out of this predicament and ensuring that he himself never got caught in the same trap. In fact, he recalled going out shortly after this episode, knocking on his neighbors' doors and asking if he could paint fresh addresses on their sidewalks for a fee. From that moment on, he poured himself into the "purpose" of making money. He did, in fact, make millions through his real estate transactions. But when the economy turned, he found himself with lots of money on paper that was essentially meaningless. Still he held on to his dream and was wheeling and dealing as fast as he could, trying to negotiate with banks, employers, and clients to win at "the game." When one day he came into session confessing he was in a significant depression (along with his anxiety), I found the right timing and offered, "You must feel like Sisyphus."[9] With this, he let out a very heavy sigh and said, "I've gotten caught in exactly the same situation as my father"—the one thing he had been defending against his entire life. This, in fact, was the pivotal moment for him to realize he had taken the means (making money) for the end, endlessly postponing his fulfillment for the idea that someday he would "have it all." With this, he made a rather radical change, deciding he would get a "regular job," one that paid enough to meet his needs. This freed up time to pursue more of what was truly fulfilling for him, including asking his girlfriend to marry him. Interestingly, he didn't give up his real estate deals. He simply let go of the anxiety that drove him so hard. And yes, his palms stopped itching as well.

If the instructions are followed, this exercise works every time and very quickly. But don't mistake its speed for superficiality or lack of potency. This process is designed to bring insight at the deepest level. The *only* time one can hit a roadblock with it is if one's chief defense is at work. This makes sense since the chief defense is designed to protect us from facing fear. So while it is a relatively rare occurrence, it is possible the chief defense will try to sabotage our efforts in subtle ways.

Still there is a ready fix to this problem. If you get stuck while going through the exercise because your chief defense (or a secondary spin-off) is at work, simply perform the exercise on the fear that the defense is protecting you from. For example, one person I worked with kept qualifying her answers to the three questions by saying, "I think it's such and such but I'm not 100 percent sure." When this happened repeatedly, I recognized the signs of a chief defense at work. Despite my reminders that it wasn't crucial to get the wording exactly right, she was still struggling to give a definitive answer to the questions. I then asked, "What are you afraid will happen next if you don't give quite the right answer?" This question released the entire blockade as she instantly saw a defense of perfectionism at work (manifested as a secondary defense of intellectualization, trying to "figure out" the perfect answer). In a matter of thirty seconds, she saw the core fear that had been running her life, what she was afraid she'd miss or lose if she gave up this quest for perfection and precision.

Another client of mine was afraid to start the exercise, imagining that she would discover something frightening she wasn't already aware of. I began by encouraging her with the thought that if she found such a fear, she would have already been carrying it around anyhow and it would be healing to bring it out into the open. Still she was unwilling, so we then started the exercise with the question "If you go through this exercise, what are you afraid will happen next?" This gave her the necessary detachment from her problems to get the ball rolling and ultimately led to the same core fear she would have found regardless of the problem she started with. And another woman I worked with stopped the process when she was almost at the end of it. She had already realized that her upset with her mother and God (as a surrogate for her mother) was causing great distress, and she was ready to see the core fear underneath this defense. She suddenly said, "If I go any further, I'll have to let go of my anger at them." We then worked the process through successfully by asking, "What are you afraid you'll miss or lose if you let go of your anger at them?" She lit up with the insight of a core fear of losing her identity—her anger gave her a distinct identity from a mother who, she realized, had always used her as a "trophy" to show off to her friends.

So if you get stuck during the exercise, you can be sure there is a defense at work and that the defense is hiding a fear about the process. Simply ask, "What am I afraid will happen next if I go through the rest of the exercise?" or some version of "What am I afraid I'll miss or lose if I face the fear that I'm defending against?" and you will unlock the process quickly and easily.

PROOF THAT THE CORE FEAR IS UNDER EVERY PROBLEM

We have said there is one core fear under every problem we have, and now you can prove this to yourself. Whatever problem you start with in the exercise, it will always reduce to the same core fear at the end. A seventy-two-year-old woman started sessions with me for trouble urinating. Having already consulted with her physicians, it became quickly apparent this was an anxiety symptom. Going through the Digging for Gold exercise, she saw that her fear of not being able to urinate led to a fear of losing her purpose in life—she was afraid she would become confined to her house, never free to do what she wanted. At a later point, she was being harassed by local teenagers for being transgendered. Going through the exercise again, she saw that her anxiety for her safety (which might have been mistaken for a core fear of death) amounted to, again, the fear that she would always be looking over her shoulder, never able to go out of her house freely to live her life. And yet another time, she was afraid of retirement, fearing she would have nothing to do with her time. This began to look like a core fear of losing meaning, feeling empty without a job to go to. But underneath this, she discovered the deeper fear that she would not be able to express her potential once she retired, losing the chance to do what she loved. Three different problems, each interpreted through the same core fear lens.

I recently had a twenty-nine-year-old client with heavy anxiety (including OCD) ask me to demonstrate that every problem led to the same core fear. We had just gone through the Digging for Gold exercise and discovered a core fear of death (lack of security). It was closely tied to a fear of losing love. I already knew something of his background and that it had left him terribly anxious about not having enough "love and security." I also knew that the one time he had had a girlfriend, the feeling of love gave him a sense of security (and identity, meaning, and purpose) he had never known otherwise. To demonstrate the principle that all problems lead to the same core fear, I invited him to pick something that seemed innocuous or completely unrelated to what he thought his difficulties were about. He chose the problem of not wanting to brush his teeth at night. His first interpretation was that he "just didn't feel like being bothered sometimes." We went through the exercise again, this time asking, "Why is the idea of brushing your teeth upsetting to you?" At one level in the chain, he realized he was afraid that he would find a piece of food on his tooth. When asked, "What are you afraid will happen next?" he replied that he might brush his teeth with the piece of food under the brush and damage the enamel. Next he was afraid he would have to go the dentist, that the dentist might give him medication, and the medication would make him "foggy and unclear." He then had a flashback to the time he had to take antidepressant medication because his girlfriend left him. His association of feeling foggy and unclear from medication left him feeling exposed to the pain (the lack of security) he felt then. When I began the process with him, I had no idea how a reluctance to brush his teeth would lead to this same core fear.

Once again, it's vitally important that we find our core fear. Doing so, along with finding our chief defense, not only gives insight into the foundation of our personality but explains comprehensively why we suffer. And when we realize that the core fear and chief defense are the basic forces that drive behavior, we are given a profound understanding of the human condition—how we choose our projections, build a consensual reality, and respond to it as if true. Of course, these projections are not, by and large, making us happy. Knowing their source, we have hope for real change in our life and in the world, resolving the fears that gave rise to our problems in the first place.

NOTES

1. I'd like to give some background on the development of this technique. The technique first started taking shape in my late adolescence when I composed a poem about the power of asking "Why?" The poem visually laid out a process of deconstructing experience by asking the question "Why?" in serial fashion. Starting at the top left of the page, it described some existential problem (I no longer recall the details of exactly what the problem was). On the right side of the same line was simply the question "Why?" as in "Why is this so?" The answer to that question was written on the left of the page underneath the first problem, to which the reply was, again, "Why?" on the right. The end of the poem concluded that if one kept going with this process, extrapolating far enough to the original source, one could reveal important truths about the nature of the universe. Several years later, I attended a seminar by David Burns, who briefly mentioned a little exercise he had developed called the Downward Arrow or sometimes the Vertical Arrow. It took a psychological problem and asked the question "If this were true, what is causing me to be upset?" repeating the question again and again, writing the answers below each other with a vertical arrow pointing down between each. I immediately recognized the similarity to my poem and was excited about its potential. But as it turns out, the two processes had very different purposes. In the Vertical Arrow, the objective is to identify negative thoughts to then apply traditional CBT techniques of disputing these thoughts, seeing them as irra-

tional. I was searching for the ultimate source of a problem, the singular "irrational belief" under all others. The CBT model that Dr. Burns was coming
from doesn't propose such a singular source. Instead, it talks about our *many*
irrational beliefs. In the deconstructing anxiety model, these all spin off from
an ultimate "core fear." With the Vertical Arrow, it is possible that one could
reach this ultimate level, but they will usually stop short of it once they find an
irrational belief to dispute. Furthermore, if one did happen to reach the ultimate level, they wouldn't think of it as the cause of all problems, as the reason
they bought into irrational beliefs in the first place. They wouldn't be seeing it
as an explanation for the structure of their personality, their first and primary
interpretation of life that gave rise to all the rest. As per his stated goal, Dr.
Burns's technique might replace or dispute particular irrational beliefs, handling particular problems, but it doesn't attempt to get at the root of them all. I
was looking for a process that would get at this root so it could be dug up
completely, preventing it from generating new forms of the same problem.
Nevertheless, I found Dr. Burns's question "If this were true, what is causing
me to be upset?" more helpful than simply asking "Why?" and I tweaked it a
bit to apply to my own exercise. I also added two more variations of the
question that helped maximize the process. I was my own first subject to
undergo the exercise and was excited to find what clearly represented an original, fundamental belief—a true core fear. As I repeated the process with different problems, I found that at the bottom of each was the same core fear,
confirming my hypothesis that if we deconstruct any problem *all the way*,
extrapolating back to the beginning, we will find the ultimate source of our
entire worldview. In working with clients over the years, I discovered it was
true for them as well, eventually discerning the five general categories of core
fears described earlier.

2. This claim is made based on my work with clients and seminar participants over the past thirty-three years. A research project is also underway.

3. Some may wonder if facing one's fear in this and the exercises to come
can feel threatening or anxiety-producing, and it is a valid question. The wisdom of taking someone at their level of readiness is all-important; we don't
want to add fear to fear. However, in many years of working with these exercises and performing them with thousands of people, I've rarely found someone too anxious to go through with them. (In fact, in each case where I did,
their anxiety was too great to actually start the exercises. The solution, as will
be discussed later, was to help them discharge the physical energy of the
anxiety with a Gestalt-type abreaction. One might also begin with a relaxation
exercise to help create enough calm to begin.) Virtually everyone seems to find
the exercises relatively comfortable, with little or no undue stress. I believe this
is for two reasons. First, when someone buys into the exercises, they become

excited about the possibility of insight and healing. This is an important antidote to any discomfort that may arise from facing fear. Second, all of these
exercises give one a sense of control, as you will see, along with an intellectual
reason for examining one's fear. This creates a safe "distance" from the fear,
evoking an objective, "observer's" perspective.

4. A helpful alternative to "What are you afraid will happen next?" is often
"What are you afraid that will lead to?"

5. This exercise is designed to give insight into, more than provide release
from, the core fear. Other exercises to come will work specifically on its release. Still, a deep insight, if one sees the true root of things, can effect this
release, as we walk fully through the Doorway of the Mind.

6. As an example, I had a client who was afraid to tell his boss he wouldn't
take on extra work for fear he might get fired. Going through the exercise, he
realized that if he got fired, he was afraid he wouldn't be able to pay his bills. I
assumed that this would lead to a core fear of being out on the street and
dying, as it would for many people. When I suggested something to the effect,
I saw that my interpretation didn't exactly light him up with understanding. I
then followed the exercise without interfering, asking what he was afraid would
happen next if he couldn't pay his bills. His answer was that he would lose
others' respect. This eventually led to a core fear of losing his identity as
someone who always took care of his responsibilities. Growing up, he was
shamed by his father for not being responsible, and this became his preoccupation.

7. But again, it's not necessary to be able to trace back to the origin of the
core fear. Doing so can be helpful in gaining insight. But because any problem
leads to the same root, we can access the core fear just as readily by seeing how
it informs a present problem. Still the further back we can go in our history the
better because defenses accumulate over time. Therefore, exploring an early
incident of the core fear can make it easier to see it in its more pure (less
defended) form.

8. This is why it's so important that the clinician not impose his or her
interpretation of what a client's answer will be in advance of letting them
discover it on their own.

9. Sisyphus was a tragic figure in Greek mythology, destined for eternity by
the gods to push a boulder up a hill, only to have it roll back down each time.

9

"WHO ARE YOU REALLY?"

Finding Your Chief Defense

If I defend myself I am attacked. . . . Who would defend himself unless he thought he were attacked, that the attack were real, and that his own defense could save himself? And herein lies the folly of defense; it gives illusions full reality, and then attempts to handle them as real.

—Foundation for Inner Peace, *A Course in Miracles* (1975)

Now on to finding the chief defense. It is time to uncover the way we first responded to the core fear, the primary strategy we adopted for handling challenges, and the way we have been responding ever since. Dismantling the chief defense is the key to freedom and requires that we understand it through and through. If, as we said earlier, a therapeutic intervention is successful, it is because it has in some way short-circuited our use of the chief defense, exposing the core fear and showing us it is not real in the way we previously believed. In CBT, thought replacement is designed to chip away at the beliefs that fuel one's core fear and chief defense. In psychodynamic therapy, insight is attempted to see through the illusion of these beliefs. In a Gestalt-type abreaction, one discharges the emotional energy generated by the core fear, held in by the chief defense. And so on.

Something in us does not want to see the chief defense (this is fear's second deception). It is so completely "who we are," so fundamental to our personality, that it can be difficult to pull it out from the background. For us it's just the way things are, our only understanding of how to operate in life. Our spouse complains about a flaw in our personality that we just don't "get." A friend disagrees with our take on a situation when it all seems so obvious to us. A coworker proposes a plan for accomplishing a task but we're sure our plan would be better. We don't want to admit that our way is not the only way, having become convinced it is essential for getting us where we want to go. After all, we made a vow early on to respond that way always. This is why we react so automatically in almost every circumstance. If only we could train ourselves to take a moment before doing so! But rather than look for alternative responses, we go on autopilot and use a well-worn set of behaviors born of the chief defense. We are so tired from the futility of it, yet we still insist on the strategy, not willing to see any alternative. But while it can be hard to see the chief defense, we now have a new tool. Understanding the core fear means we only have to ask, "How have I protected myself from it?" And that is what our next exercise will do.

EXERCISE FOR FINDING YOUR CHIEF DEFENSE: "WHO ARE YOU REALLY?"

We could describe our chief defense as that which protects us from whatever core fear we have chosen. If, for example, one's core fear is loss of identity, we could say their chief defense is to find their identity or prevent circumstances from stealing it. But that doesn't give much helpful information. Instead, we want to specify *how* one tries to prevent their core fear from coming true. To demonstrate, I had a sixty-eight-year-old client whom we'll call David. He had a very severe father who would only give his approval if David were "interesting" to him. This, understandably, ignited a core fear of losing love. We could say that David's chief defense was to make sure he was loved and approved of, but again, that wouldn't be very useful. When I asked David for his earliest memory of wanting to please his father, he described a favorite book in childhood, Dr. Seuss's *Circus McGurkus*. David remembered walking home from school trying desperately to think up "a good *Circus McGurkus* story," something his father would approve of. He then recalled a time in boarding school when his father wrote him a letter saying he considered his son a "poor investment." David responded by joining every school group he could, especially if they were "interesting," eager to report back to his father on his improvement. And as an adult, he felt compelled to busy himself with one interesting activity after another, becoming highly anxious if he couldn't fill his schedule. In fact, this was the anxiety that brought him into treatment. Putting all these together, he understood his chief defense was to secure love and approval by "being interesting."

There are five ways to reveal the chief defense:

1. Look at your response to the original core fear.
2. Look at your response to fears today.
3. Look at your goals, large and small, and how you are trying to achieve them.
4. Consider how others would describe your personality style.
5. Think of what you could not imagine doing (that other people might do) to handle a particular challenge, problem, threat, or goal.

I. Looking at Your Response to the Original Core Fear

Of course our chief defense first appeared in response to our original exposure to the core fear. If you are able to remember that first exposure, finding the chief defense will be very straightforward. It is simply the strategy you discovered—what you did that worked—to keep yourself safe from the fear at that time. However, we have also said that the first exposure can happen in utero, is shaped in childhood, and is sealed by our encounters in adolescence. So as we look for that "original" exposure to fear, we are looking for whatever stands out from any of these periods as that which precipitates our chief defense.

We may or may not be able to remember when our chief defense first arrived. It might come from a time before memory was available or we may have repressed it. If that is the case, we have other ways of discovering the chief defense, described below. But as mentioned previously, the farther back we can go to look at our basic response to fear, the easier it will be to distinguish the chief defense because there will be fewer secondary defenses to weed through. So if you can remember an early incident of your core fear,[1] then immerse yourself in the memory. Bring forth the sights, sounds, smells, and feelings of it. Really "be" there and let the emotions of the situation come forth. Understand the ways in which you felt truly threatened, perhaps through abandonment, a challenge to your identity, or some physical threat. Now study carefully the way you responded to the situation—how you decided to deal with the problem, protect yourself from it, get control over it, or otherwise attempt to restore your previous state of relative ease. We're looking for some decision you made and action you took that was deeply important to you, with a powerful commitment to make things right and regain control. It's helpful to write all this down in detail. Then try to write the essence of your response in a short phrase or sentence that characterizes your chief defense.

As an example, Troy remembered being twelve years old when he won first place at a science fair. His award was a radio that he treasured. Of course, he took pride in his achievement and was building an identity on his intellectual talents. When his father came home, he told Troy to share the radio with his sister. Troy got angry—an attempt at a defense—insisting it wasn't fair. A fight broke out between the siblings, and the radio broke. Troy felt a good degree of upset over this (enough that the memory had persisted all these years) but not enough to stimulate a chief defense. Not long after, however, his mother announced she was leaving the family because "the kids were too difficult." At that moment, Troy gave up his emerging identity as a "star" to devote himself utterly to "being good." He had to prove to his mother that he would behave in order to get her back. His core fear of being abandoned and his chief defense of being good were set. Secondary adaptations came along as he used his intelligence to show people just how "good" he was. His grooming was immaculate, he prided himself on being articulate, and he continually practiced his ability to out-argue anyone! His entire orientation was to present himself as someone beyond reproach.

2. Looking at Your Response to Fears Today

It's not necessary to remember your original core fear to find your chief defense. Because, as we have said, "the past lives on in the present," it is the same chief defense operating today that we landed upon in the beginning, the vow we made to use our strategy each time we were confronted with a fear. Another way to find your chief defense, then, is to look at present-day situations that cause you anxiety and determine how you typically respond to them. Remember, it may not always look like anxiety, so ask yourself how you respond to threats, challenges, and problems. And since so much of our fear is instigated by other people, you can also ask yourself how you respond to threats, challenges, or problems with others. In addition, it can be helpful to look at the big-ticket items that most of us worry about like money, health, approval, success, etc. How do you try to handle these things when they present challenges?

The answer to these questions won't necessarily reveal a chief defense. Most will be secondary defenses, adaptations of the chief defense to the variety of circumstances we encounter. The whole panoply of human behavior is possible when we are talking about secondary defenses. As you ask yourself, then, how you respond to threats or problems today, try to summarize your responses with a single descriptor that characterizes them all. For example, my client who had trouble urinating developed a set of rituals, in OCD fashion, hoping to ensure a successful trip to the bathroom. She also insisted on being factual, resisting when I would want to discuss her feelings. As a third defense, she would sometimes talk over me to make her point heard in a conversation. All three of these were adaptations of a chief defense of being rigid and in control over her emotions. If the bathroom rituals went just right, she could obtain control over that which was creating her upset. If she stuck to facts only, there was no room for emotional ambiguity. And if she talked over someone, she could be sure to win the argument, with a rigid insistence intended to quell her anxiety.

You can also use the Digging for Gold exercise to see how you respond to fears today. Take your answers to each of the questions in the chain and ask, "What do I typically do to prevent that fear from coming true?" The answers will yield secondary defenses, but as you go down the chain, you will see a common theme emerging from all of them until they converge as the chief defense in response to the core fear at the bottom. Let's look once more at how Jake, my client with social anxiety, filled out the template in that exercise.

Problem: I have to go on a job interview.

Question: Why is that upsetting to you?

Answer: I could make a fool of myself.

Question: What are you afraid will happen next?

Answer: I'll be rejected.

Question: Why is that upsetting to you?

Answer: I'll never be able to get a job.

Question: What are you afraid you'll miss or lose?

Answer: I'll lose my home and my security.

Question: Why is that upsetting to you?

Answer: I'll be out on the street.

Question: What are you afraid will happen next?

Answer: I'll be alone without protection.

Question: What are you afraid will happen next?

Core fear: It feels like I'll be exposed, alone, unsafe . . . that I'll die.

When I asked him, "What do you typically do to protect yourself from the fear of job interviews?" he answered, "I avoid them." When I asked, "What do you do to ensure you won't make a fool of yourself or be rejected?" he said, "I hide from people." If he never got a job, he would "hide out at home." And if he lost his home, he would move in with his uncle, with whom he felt safe, "going into denial." Putting these together, he described his chief defense as "hiding from people and life."

3. Looking at Your Goals, Large and Small, and How You Are Trying to Achieve Them

Our goals can reveal much about our chief defense. They are usually driven, at least in part, by a desire to master some challenge or get control over some fear. Making more money than one needs for fulfillment is a common example. We use our defenses to try to ensure that we succeed in meeting the goal. Let's not mistake this for over-pathologizing . . . of course, goal-setting can be a wonderful thing. After all, we are in search of fulfillment, the ultimate goal. It's certainly possible that our motives when creating a goal can be "pure." Usually, however, they contain at least the seeds of fear. Until we have fully resolved our core fear, there will be some degree to which our goals are defense-based. It's the difference, for example, between a truly altruistic gift and a gift given for subtle or obvious personal gain. Remember that fulfillment and fear work in inverse proportion to each other: the more fear, the less fulfillment, and the less fear, the more fulfillment.

So, looking at our goals, we want to see if they in fact hide a measure of fear. You might use the Digging for Gold exercise to ask what would happen next if you didn't reach your goals. If they do hide fear, you have an opportunity to understand how you are defending against the fear. For instance, if someone has a goal to live a quiet, simple life, it might be driven by a wish to escape from too many problems and too much complexity. If someone hoards food or objects, there is often a fear of deprivation behind the scenes. If someone's ambition is to have a great social life, that could hide a fear of loneliness, of being unloved, of not belonging, and so forth. Again, in and of themselves, these goals are perfectly worthy; we're merely looking for any fears they may contain to then discover the defense used for protection against them.

4. Considering How Others Would Describe Your Personality Style

Other people can see our chief defense quite readily. They likely think of it simply as your personality style and may or may not be able to articulate it clearly. Asking yourself (or trusted others) how they would describe this personality style can be helpful in seeing your chief defense. Would they say you are controlling, perfectionistic, caretaking, passive, pessimistic, optimistic, ambitious? Each of these can be defenses and possibly chief defenses. To get more insight, you can ask them how they observe you handling challenges, problems, threats, and goals or how they would describe your personality when interacting with others.

Of course you'll want to be judicious in considering this feedback. If someone is upset with you, for instance, or has a difficult time with certain aspects of your personality, be careful not to assume their perception is untainted. On the other hand, many have a defense against telling the truth if they think it might be hurtful so you'll need to read between the lines to get useful information. Look for people you can trust in this regard, people who know you well enough but who also wouldn't want to use the opportunity for their own agenda. Of course, a psychotherapist is trained to see this sort of thing while being as neutral and objective as possible.

5. Thinking of What You Could Not Imagine Doing (That Other People Might Do) to Handle a Particular Challenge, Problem, Threat, or Goal

Finally, consider those responses you could not possibly see yourself making when confronted with a challenge, problem, threat, or goal. We're not talking about unreasonable things; make sure it is something that other people are sometimes perfectly comfortable doing. For you, however, it would be so out of character that just thinking of doing it brings up shame, embarrassment, guilt, or another negative emotion (some form of fear). Because thinking of this brings up a fear, it can shed light on the defense you use to prevent exposure to that fear. It highlights what you think you must do instead. For instance, if you are very shy, to imagine going into a crowded room and drawing attention to yourself might feel highly uncomfortable. You are convinced it's better to remain anonymous. This can reveal a chief defense of "being invisible." Or if the idea of taking a leadership role at work brings up heavy anxiety, it might point to a chief defense of being passive and dependent. And how many people in our society are trained to be embarrassed about crying or showing other emotions? If they imagine doing so, they can get in touch with a chief defense of appearing stoic and invulnerable.

Another form of the same question would be to ask yourself, "What am I afraid *not* to do if faced with a challenge, threat, problem, or goal?" This is really the same as looking at how we respond to fears today in its inverse, showing us what defense we feel we must use to protect ourselves from the fear of not doing so.

HELPFUL GUIDELINES

Finding our chief defense is simply a matter of looking at how we habitually respond to life any time we are not completely fulfilled in the moment. As you consider your own response style, ask, "How do I handle difficulties; how do I try to get control over my situations?" Then ask, "How is this response different from the response of others?" If you come up with several kinds of answers, ask yourself, "What am I trying to achieve in all of these?" You are looking for the general description of how you manage problems, challenges, threats, and goals. The chief defense is our attempt to ensure that things turn out the way we wish, on the way toward our fulfillment.

We can look at the five core fears to explore some common chief defenses. Those with a core fear of losing love might become dependent, cautious around others, people-pleasing, attention-seeking, or attention-avoidant. Those with a core fear of losing identity might become narcissistic or chauvinistic, or they might seek power and prestige. A core fear of loss of meaning might lead to distracting oneself with busyness and stimulation, bitterness, altruism, addiction in any form, or spiritual or religious pursuits.[2] Those with a core fear of losing purpose might become highly ambitious, depressed, philosophic, intellectualized, driven to make money, etc. And those with a core fear of death can become preoccupied with making the most of their time; overly careful; focused on safety and health, on leaving a legacy, on preserving their youth, etc. Of course this list is far from comprehensive, considering that any and all behaviors from the human repertoire can be used as a defense.

Notice also that the same defensive behavior can be found in the service of different core fears. One person may use philanthropy to cover a fear of meaninglessness while another gains a sense of identity from it (becoming a "philanthropist"). Someone who finds that caring for others gives them a sense of purpose is different from the people-pleaser who "caretakes" to secure love. Furthermore, you'll want to make sure you are not confusing a secondary defense with your chief defense, the umbrella description that captures all of your behavior. For example, I have a twenty-five-year-old client with body dysmorphic disorder. He is obsessed with his physical appearance and worries about becoming disfigured. He has a daily exercise regimen that is extreme.

But even though this occupies almost all of his thinking, it is not his chief defense. Before he attached his obsessions to his body, he was equally consumed with being a star basketball player and, before that, with being a top athlete in various other sports. In going through the Digging for Gold exercise, we discovered his core fear of losing love. All of these various secondary defenses were attempts to get the love he wanted. When he received attention from women for his physical appearance, he found his current preoccupation with working out. But the drive to be "the best," as a way to secure love, was the description of his chief defense that captured all of these behaviors.

In looking for your own chief defense then, make sure you have accounted for why you do what you do in every circumstance. At the same time, don't get hung up on details or minor discrepancies. You are looking for the "big picture" that describes your *chief* defense, your overall response style. When a situation inspires very little or very great fear, we can respond in uncharacteristic ways, taking risks we wouldn't otherwise be willing to take. For instance, if we feel secure with our family, we might become playful, loud, and boisterous, even obstreperous, when our personality style is otherwise shy and retiring. Also, if you get confused because you seem to have conflicting behaviors, then understand these behaviors as secondary defenses and not as the chief defense. For example, you might see yourself as a people-pleaser but know that, if cornered, you can lash out. You'll want to look for a chief defense, an overarching theme that ties both of these behaviors together, such as the effort to make sure no one thinks poorly of you.[3] Think also of borderline personality disorder when someone may cling to their love object at times and reject them at others, testing to see if they'll stick around. The underlying drive behind both behaviors is to secure that love.

And don't forget that we can also have tertiary defenses (and more) to complicate the picture further. Still it is always a matter of finding the theme that connects them all in an encompassing description of the chief defense. Here's a case in point: Caroline's chief defense was captured in the thought "I shouldn't have to." Her parents divorced when she was ten years old. Each of them neglected or abandoned her in their own way and she was forced to take care of herself. In adopting the thought "I shouldn't have to," she was trying to demand that they take care of her. As she grew older, she generalized the response to others. This manifested as a secondary defense of entitlement as well as anger when no one would take care of her. In turn, she developed a tertiary defense of being unwilling to be vulnerable (for if she were vulnerable, she couldn't maintain her anger). All of this hid a core fear of loss of love, the pain of having lost her parents.

Because we know that all defenses backfire, you can see your chief defense as that which protects you from fear in the moment but ultimately creates more trouble. The continuous vigilance required by the defense leaves us anxious and exhausted. It becomes the very thing that blocks fulfillment. I'm currently working with a forty-three-year-old woman whose chief defense is to be hyper-responsible, trying to be all things to all people. Going through the Digging for Gold exercise, she found her core fear to be a loss of purpose; she lives to take care of her family and is preoccupied with thoughts of something bad happening to them. To protect herself from this fear, she compensates by anxiously running around, checking and double-checking that everyone is okay. She is also a mentor to many girls at a local college and has directed her defense to worry about each of them as well. The backfiring effect is readily apparent at this point—she is truly exhausted, unable to sleep, grinding her teeth to the point where they are breaking, and having regular panic attacks. The more she tries to take care of others, the more depleted she becomes. This in turn makes her more anxious that she won't have the resources to take care of everyone sufficiently.

You'll recognize your chief defense, then, in two ways: it is the behavior that makes you feel better in the moment but leaves you anxious overall, never giving you the guarantee of the security you seek. It's also that which leaves you exhausted as you try harder and harder to achieve that guarantee. Use any or all of the five approaches above to find your unique chief defense. Write down your answers to each and look for that which connects them. Come up with a single phrase or sentence that captures the underlying drive behind them all. You may well want to include in your sentence a secondary defense or two if it helps describe the distinct flavor of your personality style. Instead of saying, for instance, "My chief defense is to be perfect," you might say, "My chief defense is to be perfectly happy and kind to everyone all the time" or "My chief defense is to run my life in a perfectly ordered way." Instead of simply labeling your chief defense as "specialness," you would want to describe the basic manner in which you try to be special such as "being especially good at sports" or "being especially nice." The task is to achieve as much clarity as possible in understanding why you do the things you do, seeing that the chief defense is making your decisions for you.

CONTROL: THE CORE DEFENSE UNDERNEATH ALL CHIEF DEFENSES

It may be obvious by now, but all defenses, including chief defenses, really boil down to what we may call the core defense—the attempt to get *control*. Because fear is ubiquitous, we are always trying to get control over it. We work to make sure obligations are taken care of, our environment is set up to protect us, and we are on track to reach our goals . . . that everything is under control. We are engaged in a never-ending search to get what we want and avoid what we don't want. As we saw in chapter 6, all the sensory data we receive is organized by the mind to coalesce a picture of reality that makes sense, something that holds together and that we know how to interpret. This is our first step in control. We then perceive that which agrees with our interpretation and disregard that which does not—our next step in control. We continually cross-reference new sense data with old to make sure everything in our picture fits together, checking and double-checking that our worldview holds up, that nothing gets out of control.[4] And we make decisions for action accordingly, using our body to exercise control, grabbing hold of what we want and pushing away what we do not. All of our behaviors, when not released from fear, are attempts at control in some form. Anger's intent is to scare someone into submission. Blame is designed to guilt someone into doing what we want. Ambition hides a wish to master something. Even kindness, when not free of attachment, would ask another to return the favor. All this is sourced by a core fear and chief defense whose aim is to control all threats and reach fulfillment. And each of our thoughts has been drawn along the lines of one question: "Am I getting closer to or further from this goal?"

This causes constant anxiety in the background as we use fear to keep up the effort and never let our guard down. We live in perpetual "fight" mode, always driving to get things the way we wish instead of relaxing into how they are. Any time we are not completely fulfilled, there is still some unmet need, no matter how subtle, no matter how repressed. And the need is always accompanied by a fear (no matter how subtle or repressed) that we might not be able to meet it. We set up a tension inside as our motivation to take care of the need, to get control, unwilling to release the tension until we have succeeded. You might recognize this tension as worry about how to pay a bill, pressure to get chores done, or stress about beating a deadline. But it can also be more subtle than that. Whenever we engage with people (unless we are completely comfortable with them), we create the same tension, using it to keep us on our toes. If the control we seek is to have others think well of us, we might use the tension to make sure we are being socially appropriate, kind, or worthy of approval. If the control we seek is to manipulate them, we might use aggression or deception, tensing up to make sure we deliver on our strategy. In either case, we are trying to get control over the situation, to get what we want and avoid what we do not. Our facial expressions, body language, and eye contact, the modulation of our voice, the maintenance of personal space, and so forth all attest to the pervasive ways in which we try to exercise control. If any of these things are out of place, our fear is triggered and we prepare our defense. Until then, we carry all the tension of making sure we execute these details in just the right manner. Once they are executed properly, we can relax, enjoying our fulfillment for the moment. But because it is driven by control, it is a fulfillment that cannot last. Invariably the next moment brings another call for tension. We are constantly driving to get control over the forces of entropy, meet the requirements of daily life, or keep things from falling into chaos and disrepair.

We can see this drive for control on the macro level as well. It is behind every human endeavor. Medicine seeks to get control over disease and physical dysfunction. Science strives to understand and gain control over the laws of nature. Governments are established to get control over our relationships (ensuring civility) and basic survival needs. Children's games are about winning control in various situations, while adults like to overcome challenges and feel masterful. As before, all of these can be pursued in the name of pure fulfillment, without fear, when we simply enjoy creating our reality and keeping it well-ordered. The question is always in our motivation: are we trying to get control over a fear or threat, or are we genuinely pursuing our good?

This is true for all of us. People with clinical anxiety are those whose core fear includes the thought "I must be *extra* careful that fear doesn't get me." While the core fear demands we all be vigilant, the anxious person believes they must be hypervigilant. It is seen as necessary insurance, as a measure for making certain their defenses are always prepared and they are not taken by surprise. They remain on high alert with a heightened startle response. Imagining the first sight or sound is a call to action, they are immediately ready to deploy their defenses. When all these preparations still don't give a guarantee of safety, they become even more anxious, beginning the cycle again with renewed intensity. Each time they do, they fill their mind with more fear, projecting a picture of a more threatening world than most. Those with clinical anxiety also have a greater sense of vulnerability. This, I believe, comes from an increased sensitivity to our existential aloneness. Anxious people often demonstrate more concern about being alone than others. Their anxiety puts them more in touch with the experience of separation (something they share with those who suffer from depression).[5] This creates a feeling that they cannot truly get enough comfort from others. They may try in earnest but feel their safety is up to them alone. This too requires extra vigilance in being ready to defend themselves. The end result is like quicksand: the more they struggle to gain control with their defenses, the deeper in they get.

But again, this description is true for all of us. It's only a matter of degree. All of our defenses are geared toward getting control over anxiety. And they always backfire, creating the anxiety they were meant to protect us from. In Richard Bach's beautiful little book *Illusions* (2001), he opens with a parable about certain underwater creatures who spend their life clinging to the face of a rock wall. Each is focused on its personal effort to make sure the current doesn't sweep it away as it hangs on to the rock wall with all its might. One day, one of the creatures decides he is tired of living this way and announces his intentions to let go. All of the others cry out, "You'll be swept away to your doom!" Undaunted, he lets go. Everyone watches, amazed, as he "flies" past them, safely taken by the current to wonderful adventures.

Until we get wise to the suffering it creates, it never occurs to us to let go of control. Instead of allowing things to be as they are, we impose ourselves upon reality in order to create and maintain control. We don't usually even inquire whether a situation needs to be controlled. Believing in fear as the best strategy for securing fulfillment, we use our defenses as the agent of control to try to reach this goal.

PERFORMING A LIFE REVIEW

Performing a life review from the perspective of the core fear–chief defense dynamic can be especially powerful. It shows us how this dynamic has directed all of our major and minor decisions, shaping the course of our life. The process starts with writing down in a box at the top of a page our earliest memory of a significant problem, challenge, or success.[6] Include in your description how you interpreted the situation (according to your core fear) and what you did to get control over it (i.e., your chief defense in some form). Then draw an arrow from that box to another box underneath. This box contains a description of your next significant encounter with a problem, challenge, or success, as well as how you interpreted it and what you did to handle it. Continue in this fashion until you get to the present day. Then, with this map of your life laid out before you, track how the core fear and chief defense in the first box influenced how you responded in the second box, and how the core fear and chief defense in the second box influenced how you responded in the third, and so on. Each time you exercised your core fear interpretation and chief defense behavior, the direction of your life shifted. You can actually trace your course to the present day, recognizing how the decisions you made at each point along the way opened certain doors and closed others. Making a different choice at any stage would have created an entirely new set of circumstances causing a very different response—a very different "you"—at the next stage. Follow the theme of your core fear and chief defense in this way through all the boxes to discover the thread that ties them all together.[7] This process can reveal essential and sometimes astonishing insights into how you got where you are today as well as how you might redirect your future course with greater awareness.

LIVING IN THE HERE AND NOW, LOSING
THE SEPARATE SELF

Vowing to fixate on the core fear and chief defense locks us into the past where these things were set. As a result, we fail to see that the world before us is not, in fact, as threatening as we had imagined. But we believe it is too dangerous to let go of these controls, hypnotized by projections of fear dancing before our eyes. In this way, we fill our mind with what happened in the past, using it to project our fantasies of the future. This is why so many psychological and spiritual traditions advise that we live in the "here and now."

The peak experience (Maslow, 2014), sometimes called "being in the zone" or a state of "flow" (Csikszentmihalyi, 2008), is an experience of absorption in the present moment. The sense of a separate self dissolves as it arrives in its fulfillment, no longer cut off from what it needs. Our separate selves are built from thoughts about past and future, thoughts about getting what we want (in the future) and avoiding what we have learned in the past that we don't want. Absorption in the moment, therefore, enables a selfless experience. With all needs met, we can let go of the defenses usually used to get control. We discover a new way of being, "flowing" with our situations instead of pushing against them. Separating boundaries dissolve as we expand in a natural movement toward wholeness (Flaws & Wolfe, 1985). Consider the experience of lovemaking. We can become fully absorbed in the moment, feeling joined with our partner and perhaps something much larger, losing our separate sense of self. Any time we enter the present moment, our narrow, constricted focus softens and then enlarges into a more encompassing view. Our awareness swells as the fears and defenses that blocked this awareness—the walls we hid behind for safety—drop away. By relaxing our previous definitions of self and nature, we recognize a much vaster picture of reality and can open to greater human capacities as well (see for example Krippner [1992]; Kornfield [2014]; and Young [2016]). [8]

Stephen and Ondrea Levine in their wonderful book *Who Dies?* (1989) give an example of how fear and defensiveness create the sense of a separate self. In their work with terminally ill patients, they met a pediatric surgeon who believed he could operate on children with almost no anesthesia.

"They have so little identification with their body, so little resistance to pain, that it is as if the sensations have more space to float in." It wasn't that they didn't feel the sensations but they didn't close around them so quickly. "The pain threshold seems to tighten as the child gets older. The longer he is in the body, the less the area of acceptability, the more the identification with that body. As children get older, the same stimuli require more pain reliever. For instance, a one-year-old can get what might be hypothetically called a number-three stimulus and it doesn't bother them too much. A rub on the belly and a few soft words might be sufficient to alleviate the tension. But by the time that child is two or three an aspirin might be required. And by the time they are five or six or seven, that stimulus becomes yet more bothersome. By the time they are ten, there is yet more resistance and it necessitates stronger pain relief. By adolescence the pain has become an emergency and necessitates opiates and the like."

In short, children do not seem to experience pain as adults do because they don't generate the same tension around it—they don't defend against it as strongly. We may say the many layers of defense have not accumulated to solidify as a sense of "self" that will contract around the pain. As before, only resistance causes suffering, and only a separate "self" can resist.

The chief defense is the source of such resistance. It breaks up the wholeness by resisting that which we fear. In so doing, it creates the boundaries of division between what is acceptable and what is not. It has us push against the unacceptable. This projects the idea that reality is opposing us . . . that it is pushing back. And this is how the world of separation is established. It is how we reify our suffering, believing there is something that must be defended against. Just as much as the core fear, it is imperative that we understand our chief defense thoroughly, seeing not only that it is responsible for our troubles but also that it is a fabrication. Taken together, the exercises for finding one's core fear and finding one's chief defense give crucial insight into the foundation of personality, its organizing principle. This gives a sweeping and panoramic view of what moves our world, illuminating the source of our perception and the character of our experience. Once this is seen, we have a way to understand why we suffer, individually and as a collective. We also know where we must direct our attention for the resolution of such suffering. In the end, deconstructing the core fear and chief defense makes it possible to *reconstruct* our life in a new way.

NOTES

1. Sometimes it can help to find these early incidents by asking parents or siblings about that which you can't remember directly.

2. Of course spirituality and religion, like anything on our list, can be pursued for good or bad reasons. It depends on whether one uses them as a defense against their core fear; as a true expression of the search for meaning, love, purpose, or identity; or as a resolution of the question of death.

3. Lashing out, in this example, would be a way to convince the other they are wrong about you.

4. Notice our compulsion to make sure we have our facts straight and how quick we are to correct someone when they do not. Notice, too, the satisfaction of reviewing our to-do lists and realizing everything has been checked off as completed. In the extreme, this can turn into OCD but it speaks to the drive for control we all share.

5. This can actually become an advantage once the fear is resolved, giving greater awareness of this existential truth and allowing them to see the essential problem more clearly than most.

6. Successes can help set our interpretation and response to life as well if they make us feel we must hold on to the experience and ensure we get it again and again. The fear behind the scenes, in this case, is the fear of losing the experience.

7. For further instructions and examples, see *Radical Joy* (T. Pressman, 1999).

8. As discussed earlier, there can be great resistance to the idea of expanded states of consciousness, higher realities, and alternate ways of knowing them. We cling to the view that only what our senses show us is real despite all evidence of their lack of reliability. But we must consider the possibility that this is the result of defensiveness and the quest for control. Other ways of knowing might not give as much control or as great an ability to manipulate the environment as when we are working with sense data. This doesn't mean, however, that the picture given by this data is more valid or that other epistemologies might not "work" better for fulfillment.

10

THE MASTER KEY TO RESOLVING FEAR

"Doing the Opposite" of the Chief Defense

> When a resolute young fellow steps up to the great bully, the world, and takes him boldly by the beard, he is often surprised to find it comes off in his hand, and that it was only tied on to scare away the timid adventurers.
>
> —Ralph Waldo Emerson

Now that we've found the core fear at the root of anxiety and the chief defense that preserves and amplifies it, it's finally time to ask the only real question that matters: What to do about it?

If our defenses give validity to our anxiety, making it seem as if there is something real to defend against, then we must remove, dissolve, or otherwise "undo" our defenses. Again, this is really the aim of most forms of therapy, as the therapist works to first challenge and then renegotiate the client's maladaptive (i.e., defensive) responses to life. But it's not enough to simply advocate that we "dismantle" the defenses, "resolve resistance," or "restructure personality." Nor is it sufficient to recommend we "replace" the irrational beliefs behind the defenses. Instead, we must use our insight into the mechanics of defenses, the details of exactly how they protect us from fear, in order to accomplish the goal effectively. Understanding the process that got us into trouble in the first place, we may see how to reverse it. And what we find is that this reversal is a matter of "doing the opposite" of what the defenses would have us do. We reject defensiveness as a strategy to protect ourselves from fear and preserve our fulfillment. We pinpoint the precise moment where we would otherwise apply our defense, pushing or running away from the fear, and turn around instead to confront it.

This is the master key to unlocking any and all of our three doorways. We said earlier that fear is preserved by our refusal to look at it. Since the inception of our core fear, we have assumed that it is truly threatening. We have spent a lifetime defending against it, certain of the danger it poses. Our defenses are meant to cover the fear, keeping it under wraps so that it cannot escape to attack. But if we are to find out whether it truly carries the threat it promises, we must look at it directly. And in order to look at it, we must lift the cloak of our defenses. "Doing the opposite" is to be our method. It gives us the opportunity to address the problem in a real way. The moment we do, we break out of our hypnotic trance, dispersing the mirage of what we imagined the fear to be. Seeing it in the plain light of day, we find it is always something quite ordinary and manageable—if there is anything there at all.

The idea of "doing the opposite" can be found in many traditions. Tai chi's dictum is "Strength through softness," suggesting that the tension of defensiveness is the opposite of real strength. Jiu Jitsu and Aikido, similarly, transform an opponent's "attack" (defensive action) by allowing it rather than resisting it. Instead of meeting force with force, we "do the opposite"—the opponent's force becomes usable energy. A Course in Miracles (Foundation for Inner Peace, 1975) proposes the same idea when it states, "In my defenselessness my safety lies," while Christian teachings encourage us to "offer the other cheek." In the therapy world, exposure and response prevention would have us "do the opposite" by failing to respond with defensiveness in the face of fear. Psychodynamic therapy, once finding an insight into its source, suggests we "invade" our anxiety. And mindfulness trains us to bring our attention back to the breath every time it wanders off to follow a thought.

In fact, the principle of "doing the opposite" is found any time there is a transformation or healing. If avoidance is the hallmark of anxious behavior, we must, as we have said, look at and face fear to get free of it. Without this, the best we can hope for is an illusion of freedom, picturing ourselves as we would like to be while the fear lives on in another part of our mind, body, or spirit. As one of my clients has said, "It's like putting frosting on garbage."

I once co-facilitated a weekend workshop where one of the attendees was adamant that she should only allow happy, loving thoughts into her consciousness. She had brought in a large crayon drawing of hearts and arrows bursting in every direction. It looked very positive indeed. But another facilitator, who had training as an art therapist, noticed a detail in the drawing: one of the arrows had a kink in it. She offered that perhaps it indicated a kink in the woman's view, that perhaps everything was not as happy as she indicated. At first the woman defended her position in a pleasant way, insisting that the kink in the drawing was the result of a crack in the floor she was drawing on. When someone else in the seminar challenged her gently on this, she protested somewhat fiercely. No one else said anything and her protest hung in the air, the intensity with which she spoke it echoing in the silence. Finally she said, "I guess that wasn't very loving, was it?" With this she had a rather huge catharsis, breaking down in tears and admitting how terrified she was of anything that wasn't loving and sweet. She flashed back to a time in childhood when her parents were fighting and remembered the origin of her core fear. After she quieted down, she announced that she hadn't let herself cry in many years and that she felt a lightness and energy that was far more satisfying than "pretending" everything was wonderful.

Here's another example of "doing the opposite": in Victor Hugo's *Les Misérables* (2012), a single moment near the beginning sets the rest of the entire story in motion. The protagonist, Jean Valjean, has just been released from jail after many years. He steals some silverware from a kindly bishop, intending to sell it as a means of survival. As he is fleeing the scene, he is caught by the inspector, Javert. Just then the bishop comes out from his house to interrupt the expected course of events. "Doing the opposite" of what his own defenses might have suggested, the bishop says that, in fact, he gave the silverware as a gift to Valjean. To take the point further, he tells Valjean he forgot to take the best part of the gift and hands him his silver candlesticks. This begins Valjean's transformation as he determines to live by the same principle of kindness and defenselessness demonstrated by the bishop. The story goes on to portray the many lives he affects as a result of that decision, precipitated by the bishop's healing influence.

When we discussed the manipulations of fear in chapter 2, we defined various defenses used to keep us from looking at and facing the correct fear. For instance, fear's hypnotizing effect prevents us from looking through it to the other side, where we would discover that the fear passes and is not the catastrophic thing we imagined. In "doing the opposite," we move through this wall of defense. Similarly, when we face the lie of fear, we discover there is only one problem (at most) to deal with at a time, and if the problem exists at all, it is manageable when confronted in real time. "Doing the opposite" of these manipulations is how we look at and face the correct fear, putting it to the test to find out what it is really all about. This is invariably healing as we watch the fear transform into something quite different from what we had imagined.

"Doing the opposite," of course, challenges all our defenses. Meeting fear without defenses is like undergoing a rite of passage. In fact, rites of passage have been understood by many cultures as critical for learning how to face fear and develop competency in a world of potential dangers. In this way, they mark a child's journey into adulthood. In the Cherokee tradition, when a boy comes of age, he is taken by his father into the forest at night, blindfolded. He is told he must sit on a rock, alone, without moving the entire night. He is also instructed that he must not take off the blindfold until he can see the sun's rays peeking through in the morning. And as a test of manhood, he is forbidden to cry out for help.

Understandably, the boy is terrified, hearing the sounds of the night and not being able to look at the source or run away. Howling coyotes, the rustling of the wind in the trees, and the possibility of bears or snakes are all around him. His fantasies run wild with thoughts of danger. But this is the only way he will become a man. He must face these fears and not run. In the morning, when he is allowed to remove the blindfold, he finds to his surprise that his father has been sitting next to him the entire night, keeping him safe and watching over him.

THREE WAYS TO "DO THE OPPOSITE"

There are three ways to "do the opposite" of our defenses:

1. Move directly into your fear.
2. Do nothing.
3. Do something completely unrelated to the fear.

1. Move Directly Into Your Fear

In the first approach, we move directly into our fear, doing exactly what our defenses tell us not to do. If they would have us run away from a situation, we move straight toward it instead. If they tell us to fight and push against something, we welcome and embrace it. For example, if we are having an argument, rather than defending ourselves we might empathize with our opponent's view or even apologize for whatever they are complaining about. Or if we have OCD about touching door-knobs, we touch them repeatedly on purpose. This is where traditional exposure therapy has done us a great service: we perform those positive actions that are counter to the negative actions anxiety would dictate, demonstrating to ourselves that nothing happens when we give up our defense and let the worst take over. Gandhi was a master at this. On one of the many occasions when he was arrested for his cause, he was asked by the judge if he was conducting his own defense. He replied that he had no defense (the double meaning of the word is not insignificant), then beseeched the judge to impose the harshest penalty possible! In response, the judge "cooperated" but made it clear that his admiration for Gandhi was such that if he could, he would have done the opposite himself. Similarly, when Muslims and Hindus were fighting bitterly over who would rule the newly independent India, Gandhi, rather than defend his Hindu faith, said, "I am a Hindu and a Muslim and a Christian and a Jew."

2. Do Nothing

The second way to "do the opposite" is to literally do nothing.[1] With this step, we get the message that fear doesn't have the power to force a reaction. Of course, something is only frightening (upsetting, disturbing) when we make it real with a defensive response. By our doing nothing, it loses its meaning as a source of fear. A simple example would be when a child is having a tantrum and says to their parent, "I hate you." The parent (hopefully) knows not to take it personally and gives no defensive response. Similarly, in the TV series *West Wing*, President Bartlett is walking out of the White House with his chief of staff. Deep in conversation, he notices a group of protestors angry about one of his policies. Looking up for a moment, he simply tells his chief of staff, "Those people don't seem to like me very much," and then resumes his conversation. There is also a story about a monk who lived at the edge of a village. A young woman in the village had gotten pregnant out of wedlock and the villagers demanded to know who the father was. The girl falsely accused the monk. When the villagers confronted the monk with his "crime," they demanded he raise the child by himself. The monk said nothing but took the child. He fed him, clothed him, and took care of his needs as if he were his own child. Years later, the mother revealed the truth about who the father was. The villagers returned to the monk, apologizing and taking the child back. Again the monk accepted this without saying anything.

3. Do Something Completely Unrelated to the Fear

When we do something completely unrelated to the fear, we prove to ourselves that not only is the fear powerless to make us react, it can't even hold our attention. Of course we have to be honest about this; it's no use going through the motions of something unrelated to the fear while filled with anxiety. And we're also not talking about repressing the fear by distracting ourselves with activity. Distraction, as we have said, rarely has the potency to truly resolve anxiety. Rather, we are talking about finding something that is compelling enough to draw our attention away from the fear, freeing it up to become absorbed in our new activity. We no longer energize the fear with our attention, and our perception shifts accordingly. This is essentially the purpose of meditation. By training our attention on the breath, a mantra, or whatever the object of focus, we tell ourselves that our usual thoughts, largely based on fear, don't have the ability to hold our attention. We want the rewards of the practice more than we want to focus on fear and defense.

In our third approach to "doing the opposite," any activity will do as long as it is captivating enough that we can invest our attention in it more than in the fear. Choosing something that is rewarding makes the job easier. The more rewarding, the easier it is to shift our attention. In the final chapter of this book, we will discuss the power of the Vision

Quest, where we find a purpose so compelling that fears drop away easily as we keep our eye on the goal. An interesting example comes from the James Cameron movie *Avatar*. On a mission to save the planet Pandora, the character played by Sigourney Weaver gets shot. She is too busy, however, with the mission and seems almost to ignore the bullet wound, simply saying, "This is going to ruin my day." Making the same point in a comical way, Captain America in one of the Avenger movies, tells his team as they prepare for a mission, "If you get hurt, wait for help. If you get killed, walk it off!"

Gandhi's movement of nonviolent noncooperation was a perfect demonstration of all three approaches to "doing the opposite." He would not cooperate with violence or even self-protection as a defense, convinced that it would only breed more of the same. The power of his conviction was such that he moved an entire people to practice this kind of defenselessness. At times they would move toward their fear, doing precisely what their defenses told them not to. In one instance, they marched straight into a line of British soldiers and their batons. One row of Indians followed another, each receiving severe beatings as they did. At the end of the day, as a reporter wrote, they won a moral victory; even though badly bruised, through their actions they garnered the sympathies and support of the rest of the world. This proved a turning point in the fight for independence.

Gandhi used the principle of doing nothing as well. We have already described his response in the courtroom. But the same courage was demonstrated by countless of his followers as they allowed themselves to be taken to jail without resistance, filling the cells until there was no more room. On another occasion, when about to be trampled by British soldiers on horseback, they lay motionless on the ground. Doing nothing, it turned out, was the best strategy for protection . . . the horses would not step on them if they were lying down.

And they used the principle of doing something completely unrelated to their fear as well. While the British were waging war upon them, they began spinning their own clothing and making their own salt, both in defiance of British rule. Their joy in these acts was profound as they asserted their independence, free from the fear they had been living under. Even though they knew they could go to jail for such actions, they were focused on something greater instead.

Again, any form of therapy or healing involves "doing the opposite" in some fashion. Guided imagery, for instance, entrains the mind to stay with a visualization rather than following thoughts of fear and defense. It is an example of our third approach, "doing the opposite" by focusing on something unrelated to the fear. The same is true, as we have said, of meditation on the breath but also of chanting, davening, or whirling (as the dervishes do in the Sufi tradition)—drawing attention away from the problem and to the physical sensations of the breath, the vibration of the vocal cords, the rocking motion in davening, and the spinning experience of whirling. These and many other techniques counter the pull, the mesmerizing effect, of fear and defense. Distraction, too, is an attempt at this kind of approach but can only work if one successfully trains their attention on that which they are using for distraction. Snapping a rubber band, for instance, or even focusing on one's here-and-now surroundings, will only work for the instant that the distraction is powerful enough to steal attention away from fear. Faith and prayer can also work, but again, only when the inspiration they provide can sustain one's focus.

I once learned a little technique that is surprisingly powerful given its simplicity.[2] It's an effective way to practice placing our attention on something other than fear and defense. With both hands in front of you, repeat an upsetting thought out loud and imagine putting it in your left hand. Then repeat a thought that is pleasant or uplifting, imagining it in your right hand. It doesn't matter what the thought is; it doesn't even have to be related to the upsetting thought. We are simply placing our attention on anything different from the first thought, discovering our ability to choose freely. Concretizing the experience by looking at the appropriate hand helps with focus and makes the experience seem more real. If the upsetting thought bothers you enough, your mind will quickly snap back to the left hand, making all sorts of protest to the thought in the right hand such as "That's not going to help" or "This is a serious problem." Repeat one of these protest thoughts out loud, placing it in the left hand. Then follow this with another uplifting thought in the right hand. You might want to add after each thought, "I am free to choose that thought (there's nothing wrong with it)" or "I can choose this thought instead" and move to the other hand. Keep going back and forth in this manner until something starts to shift. After a while, we see that, indeed, we are choosing these thoughts; they are not independently generated, forcing us to think them. The negative thoughts then become a little bit boring, losing their luster and their ability to compel us quite so much, while the thoughts in the right hand gain in momentum, occurring to us as real alternatives. It's not that the thoughts in the right hand are more valid than those in the left—both are neutral until we attach meaning to them. But since we are free to choose, we find the meaning we attach to the positive thoughts more fulfilling. This exercise is a great way to see the projections of our positive view forming and solidifying as the thoughts in the right hand feed each other and grow in strength. We can watch them build a perceptual reality as it becomes easier and easier to choose new positive thoughts, the whole process taking on a life of its own.[3]

Think of a time when you were verbally attacked. Assuming you responded with some degree of defensiveness, imagine what would have happened if you admitted to the other person that what they said hurt or upset you. This kind of vulnerability is an instance of our first approach, "doing the opposite" by moving directly into the fear that warns you not to be vulnerable. Or you can "do the opposite" by putting your attention on something completely unrelated to your fear, such as the other person's needs. In that case you might say, "I'm sorry if what I did hurt or upset you" or even, if appropriate, "You're right!" St. Francis, when becoming somewhat renowned for his work, was accused by a jealous friend of seeking fame and personal glory. He was on his way to visit the pope at the time, and he simply replied that if what his friend said was true, the pope would no doubt point it out. His friend was left speechless by this, having nothing to continue fighting against. Similarly, I once attended a conference where someone was criticizing the organizer for a choice he had made in the conference schedule. I knew this man and also knew that he had put his heart and soul into creating the best conference possible. After beginning to react defensively, he stopped himself mid-sentence. His shoulders visibly dropped, as did his tension, when he said, "I just wanted everyone to have a great experience." The other person was completely disarmed and apologized appropriately. The next time you find yourself in the middle of an argument, whether the accused or the accuser, you might try converting your defensive reaction into the phrases "I'm afraid that . . ." and "I'm asking for . . ." This can be a really helpful application of "doing the

opposite," expressing the fear behind your upset and inviting understanding in a defenseless way.

In the following chapters, we present the three primary techniques
for resolving anxiety in the deconstructing anxiety model. These are the
most powerful tools I know, targeting the precise moment when defenses arise and providing effective strategies for "doing the opposite."
They are designed to help us see through fear's deceptions and manipulations, breaking out of its bubble and finding it to be an illusion. These
techniques involve "doing the opposite" of the chief defense in each of
our three ways: moving into the fear, doing nothing at all, or doing
something completely unrelated to the fear. Without the distorting filter of the chief defense, our perception of the core fear shifts and
reveals the deeper truth it was hiding. These techniques, therefore,
promise a complete resolution of anxiety, moving through it all the way
until there is nothing left to resolve.

NOTES

1. This is the meaning of "response prevention" in "exposure and response
prevention." We are distinguishing it as a separate way of doing the opposite
from exposure.

2. I'd like to credit Angela Fisher and "Lou" for the development of this
technique.

3. This is a very different practice from positive thinking. Because positive
thinking doesn't address so-called negative thoughts, it runs the risk of repressing them. Here we are practicing our freedom to choose what we think, fully
acknowledging the negative but withdrawing our investment in it.

11

THE ALCHEMIST

Asking "What Happens Next?"

Listen—perhaps you catch a hint of an ancient state not quite forgotten; dim, perhaps, and yet not altogether unfamiliar, like a song whose name is long forgotten, and the circumstances in which you heard completely unremembered. . . . Not the whole song has stayed with you, but just a little wisp of melody, attached not to a person or a place or anything particular. But you remember, from just this little part, how lovely was the song, how wonderful the setting where you heard it, and how you loved those who were there and listened with you. . . . Listen, and see if you remember an ancient song you knew so long ago and held more dear than any melody you taught yourself to cherish since.

—Foundation for Inner Peace, *A Course in Miracles* (1975)

Welcome to the first of our three exercises for resolving anxiety. I call it the Alchemist because it involves turning a base experience (fear) into something higher and finer. In this exercise, entering through the Doorway of the Mind, we will "do the opposite" of what our defenses would have us do by moving directly into and through the core fear (in imagination). And as promised, we will do so all the way until there is no more fear left to move through. We will actually be moving through the wall that has been erected by the hypnosis of fear, the wall that warned us of dire consequences if ever we should approach it. But riding on the faith that fear is never what it promises to be, or at least on the hope of finding a less anxious way of living, we determine to test out the all-important question we have always avoided: Is the fear real?

As you go through the exercise, you will find it is actually not that threatening to examine fear in this way. As we said earlier, we are simply admitting what we are already feeling and doing so with a detachment and intellectual curiosity. In fact, because fear has hypnotized us to stare at the wall of our projections, in moving toward that wall we can feel as though we are taking back some of the control the fear has stolen from us. We are choosing what to think and how to respond rather than feeling victimized by the automatic response of our defense.

Our technique is simple to describe. Don't be deceived by its apparent simplicity—this exercise has the power to radically transform your fear as you watch the projections of a lifetime dissolve. We will begin as we did with the Digging for Gold exercise, starting with a problem and piercing through its many levels to find the core fear waiting underneath. This time, we will use only one form of our three questions: "What happens next?" But we will not stop once we arrive at the core fear. In this exercise we will continue to ask, "What happens next?" moving through all the way to resolution. Our objective is to find out what the core fear is actually composed of, what happens when we live through it in imagination, and ultimately what is on the other side of it. We will be meticulous in this, skipping no steps. Otherwise, aspects of the fear can remain in hiding, ready to scare us at another time or in another disguise.

This exercise is to be done as a meditation and requires full concentration, so you want to make sure you won't be disturbed. Expect it to take between approximately a half hour to forty-five minutes. With practice, one can shorten this time immeasurably.

We begin by choosing any problem, big or small, significant or seemingly inconsequential. As we know, they will all arrive at the same core fear. Alternatively, we can begin by choosing the core fear directly. Then, as we also suggested in the Digging for Gold exercise, we will want to visualize the scene of our problem as if on a movie screen. This is especially important for the Alchemist. I often say to clients, "Tell me what is happening on the screen in a way that I can see it," redirecting with "I don't know how to see that" if they describe something abstract. This helps in moving through any defensive obstacles to stating what actually happens next as concrete actions in space and time. For example, instead of saying, "I'm depressed," we might say, "I am sitting on the bed without moving, everything looking gray and still around me." Without a concrete description, the exercise can devolve into vague ideas of what the fear threatens, and we won't be able to see clearly what happens after that. We will be playing out this movie of our fear, moment-by-moment, even frame-by-frame. We will watch the movie all the way through to the other side when the fear has done its worst and passed.[1] The crucial aspect of this exercise is to make sure you watch the movie of your *fear* unfold, not a movie about solutions to the fear, escaping or distracting from it, or in some other way avoiding a full confrontation with it. Remind yourself often to simply *watch* the movie of the fear playing out, without directing it in any way. You are not writing the script, merely looking passively as you keep waiting to see "what happens next."

Once you have pictured the scene of your problem, let it come to life by vividly noticing all the details—sights, sounds, internal and external feelings, smells, and, if applicable, tastes. Again, make sure you are picturing what is actually happening in space and time rather than being satisfied with abstract ideas about emotions. Then begin the process of asking, "What happens next?" (or alternatively, "What is happening now?").[2] You are asking about the very next moment in the movie, the scene that inevitably follows from what you have just seen. Again, this is a movie of your fear come true; you don't want to prematurely resolve the problem or make it better in any way. You want to find out what secrets your fear holds. It won't disclose these secrets if you try to fix it or escape too soon.

Once you have your answer to "What happens next?" making sure you can actually see it on the movie screen, settle in to this new scene for a few moments. Then when you are ready, ask again, "What happens next?" If you haven't already started there, you will soon arrive at the scene of your core fear, just as with the Digging for Gold exercise. You want to get very detailed in your picture of the core fear. Describe to yourself all the features you see, such as the physical environment, where you are in that environment, what you are doing, the look on your face, what you might be saying, and so forth. Try to describe the "mood" of this scene as well—the temperature, the quality of light, the stillness or movement in the air, and anything else having to do with the emotional atmosphere (but always in concrete terms).[3]

After settling in to the scene of your core fear, continue to ask, "What happens next?" There is a chance, at this point, that your initial response will be "Nothing is happening next; nothing is different." After all, fear has had you staring hypnotically at its wall of projections, never daring to approach it, let alone imagine what was on the other side. If it seems that nothing new is happening next, that nothing is changing, then that is your answer for the moment . . . that is what is happening next. Just keep watching the movie, staying with the process without forcing an answer, waiting until something spontaneously happens next.

This stage of the exercise is all-important. It is where defenses will try to exert themselves most vigorously. Many struggle at this point, ready to give up, thinking there's nothing more to the story, their situation hopeless. But in fact, this is our opportunity. We are at the wall and poised to move through it. This is exactly the point at which we are ripe for a breakthrough. Remind yourself that this is the scene of fear that has been chasing you all your life. You earnestly want to get to know it. All you need do is stay with this scene and wait for something to shift. You'll know it when it does. Just keep waiting and watching what happens next.

You may find that nothing happens for a long time. And you may continue to protest, "Nothing is happening next and nothing ever will happen next." These are defenses trying to assert themselves, to dissuade you from your goal. If your core fear is of abandonment, you may feel "just alone, completely alone, forever." Or if it is a core fear of death, you may assert, "There's nothing after death . . . that's it." Or if it is a core fear of meaninglessness, you may insist, "I'm in an empty place where there is no life and no joy and that's never going to change." In each case, you want to remind yourself that the exercise is to stay with what you are seeing on the movie screen, just watching it as you continue to ask, "What's happening now?" or "What happens next?" Determine to stay with it as long as it takes. You don't want to end this process too soon, assume it doesn't work, or find any other reason to quit. These reasons are part of fear's strategy, the tactic of its defenses, to lure you away from your purpose.

Eventually, if you have followed the guidelines and stayed with it, something will start to shift. When it does, your job will be to continue with the same protocol, waiting and watching to see what happens next. This process takes care of itself . . . it's important not to direct it in any way. If you abide with your moment-to-moment experience, this small shift will grow into a *profound* shift in perception and awareness. Eventually, you will have the wonderful realization, by virtue of sitting in your fear and experiencing all it has to offer, that you have come out the other side unscathed. Nothing terrible has happened after all. That which you had always imagined to be so threatening, after a long enough period, reveals itself to be completely benign, something quite acceptable, even peaceful. The great surprise is that when finally we give up the fight against fear, refusing to use our defenses to find a way out, we settle in to it and become comfortable. Only our fight created discomfort ("Resistance is suffering"). This is what causes the shift in perception, freeing us from the belief that the problem was scary, something requiring defensiveness. With this, as we said at the beginning, we will either discover new ways to handle the problem or, most often, find it was completely made up, left over from childhood beliefs that had never been challenged. Because we see it as illusory, nothing compels us to stay in the scene, and we are free to choose a new experience.

This discovery hits us like a revelation! It can literally bring freedom from the fear of a lifetime. Indeed, people often describe the experience as life-changing, which makes sense because the core fear has been darkening our experience and enslaving us in unfulfilling ways since its inception.

It is possible to speed up the process in the following way. After you have gotten a very clear picture of your core fear, you can imagine sitting in it for longer and longer periods of time, as per the script below. Again, it's most important to remind yourself not to try to change the picture, improve it, escape it, or make it more tolerable. People often look for something productive to do while sitting in it for an extended period, but this too will interfere with the experience. You simply remain in the scene exactly as it is without adding anything. Wait for a little while between each new time interval so you can really sense what it is like to be there for that period, and then imagine sitting in it for the next stretch of time. Between each interval, you will want to interject various thoughts to keep the experience fresh and help it feel real, especially reminding yourself of the "mood" of the experience (as above). Otherwise, there is nothing to do but keep waiting and watch-

ing, asking, "What happens next?" Here is a sample script to illustrate.
Move through it slowly, giving it your full concentration.[4]

> Now that you are clearly picturing the scene of your core fear, ima-
> gine that you will be here for the next hour, nothing changing. Just
> here, with things exactly as they are. (Pause for some time to absorb
> what that will be like). Next, imagine you will be in this scene for
> three hours. (Review the characteristics of the scene. Pause again).
> Three hours turns into six hours. You are settling in a bit more . . .
> the situation is not quite so new as it was. (Pause). And now imagine
> that you have been sitting in the scene for twelve hours. Nothing
> changing, nowhere to go, nothing to do. Just be there. (Pause).
> What's happening now? (Notice the mood of the scene in all its
> details. See yourself sitting in it. Pause). Now visualize that you have
> been there for a full day. Settle in to that possibility. Wait. Just be
> there. (Pause). One day turns into three days. You've been here for
> three full days. Nothing changing, nothing different. (Review the
> characteristics of the scene. Pause). Three days turns into five days.
> (Pause). And now you've been in this scene for a week. The sun has
> come up and gone down seven times and you're just here . . . same
> place, nothing different. Let yourself imagine what that's like and
> describe it to yourself. (Pause). One week turns into three weeks—
> you've been here for three weeks and have settled in perhaps, found
> some sort of routine. (Watch yourself moving through that routine).
> Things are becoming more familiar. (Pause). And now imagine that
> it's been a month. Really picture that. (Pause). Now three months
> have gone by. Again, the sun comes up and goes down each day and
> you are still here three months later, doing the same thing, day in
> and day out. Three months ago you were living your life but you
> haven't been part of that life for a long while now. (Pause). Imagine
> that six months have gone by. Same place, same experience, day in
> and day out. Describe to yourself what's happening now. Notice the
> quality of light, the passage of time, and the overall mood. (Pause).
> And now a year has gone by. Seasons have come and gone, and
> you've been here for a whole year. What's that like? What's happen-
> ing now? Just be there. (Pause). Three years have gone by . . . you've
> been here for three full years and this is your life now, this is where
> you are. Your old life is becoming more of a memory. (Pause). Three
> years turns into five years and you are quite settled in your routine
> now. (Pause). Ten years have passed . . . you have long ago gotten
> used to this place, your old dreams faded after so much time, and

you've been living in this place with your familiar routine for ten years. What's happening now? (Pause). Imagine that thirty years have passed. For thirty years this has been your life, your world. Thirty years ago you had a different life but it is becoming a distant memory. The people you loved have all moved on. This is where you are now, this is what you know. (Review the characteristics and mood of this place. Pause). Imagine that fifty years have passed (don't worry about whether you might realistically live that long, just imagine that you are in this scene for fifty years). The outside world has changed much (picture how different from when you were part of it) but you are just here. (Pause). One hundred years have gone by. Everyone you knew has disappeared; the life you were so invested in has gone. All traces of who you were have been dispersed . . . all that you worried about, your ambitions, hopes, and dreams, the struggle to keep up or get ahead . . . all of it has gone. Just be in this scene. This is where you live now. (Pause). Three hundred years have passed. Governments have come and gone, economies have changed, the world outside looks very different than when you lived in it. But you have no connection to that world . . . you remain just here. This is where you are. Just here. What is happening now? (Pause). Five hundred years have passed. (Pause). One thousand years have passed and you are still here. What looks different, if anything? (Pause). One thousand years turns into three thousand years . . . imagine what that's like. The universe itself has changed in three thousand years. Stars have been born and others have died. The galaxies have continued in their rotation, and you are still here, just here. (Pause). Five thousand years have passed. (Pause). Ten thousand years. Ten thousand years ago there was someone called "You" who had a life in the world with certain problems and circumstances. All that disappeared so very long ago. (Pause). Thirty thousand years have passed by. You're just here . . . watching . . . being. (Pause). Fifty thousand years. (Pause). One hundred thousand years. What is it like to simply be here for one hundred thousand years? What's happening now? (Pause). Three hundred thousand years go by—a short span of time in the existence of the universe. (Pause). Five hundred thousand years. (Pause). One million years have passed. You have been sitting here for one million years, just being, while the universe continues on undisturbed. (Pause). Three million years pass by. (Pause). Five million years. (Pause). Imagine ten million years pass by and you're still here, just here. (Pause). Thirty million years. (Pause). Fifty million years. Really imagine that. Fifty million years of evolution, of history, of expansion of the universe. And you are still here. (Pause). One hundred million years. (Pause). Three hundred million years. (Pause). Five hundred million years have gone by. (Pause). Imagine a billion years have passed. Just being. (Pause). Many billions of years. Just being. (Pause). Eons upon eons have passed by and you are . . . just here. Just here. What's happening now?[5]

What happens when you allow yourself the possibility of sitting in the scene of your core fear for 10,000 years? Or 10 million years? Of course, eventually the fear will evaporate; how can we continue worrying about it for millions or billions of years? Sooner or later, the fear becomes boring, uninteresting, and meaningless. It gets swallowed up in the fullness of time (and space too, as we will see in the next exercise). If you really stay with the exercise, you'll eventually wear down your resistance and "settle in." This is a life-transforming moment, and you will know it when it arrives. The projections of fear dissolve—as one client said, "They just drift away"—and your perception clears. Letting go of the fixation on trying to get out of it, you no longer see the situation as something to be afraid of. You have a clean slate, your attention now free to place where you choose. Finally released from a lifetime of fear, you feel an extraordinary lightness, energy, and joy as well as a natural impulse to pursue fulfillment. Some people become interested in looking around this "place" they have been living in for so long, as if for the first time, getting to know it and wanting to see what else is available here. While they were so busy trying to get away from the fear, they failed to see what it would be like to settle in and be present in it. Now that they have done so, they find infinite possibilities for how to explore, remain in, and enjoy the same circumstances that were previously so abhorrent. Often, because they realize that there was nothing real holding their attention on this place, they discover that they are free to "go" elsewhere, no longer imprisoned in this scene.[6]

Do not underestimate the power of this tool! Even in a single session, one can discover a complete freedom from the core fear. Of course, the experience usually needs to be repeated. The defenses of a lifetime will, like a long-lived habit, try to reassert themselves, causing us to forget that the projections of fear are arbitrary. Until you build a repertoire of experience with the exercise, you will want to remind yourself that the process is trustworthy and that fear really does give way to it. To further this goal, we can actively practice building a new association between the scene of our core fear and the release we have found. Each time we meet a new problem, we want to call forth the experience of our core fear as a place of safety, resting there before activating our defenses. We have already become relatively fluent in seeing that any problem has the core fear at its root. This means we can translate our understanding of the problem in terms of the core fear to then shift our association from the old experience of entrapment to the new experience of freedom. We more and more quickly remember that we have no need of defense because we have come to peace with the situation, no longer afraid of "losing" what the situation threatened to take away. This enables us to act in the most effective way possible, seeing the situation with clarity and objectivity. The action we choose may or may not be the same as that we would have chosen from defensiveness, but if it is the same, it will be a true choice, unburdened by the constraints of fear. Its meaning will, therefore, be completely different, and the consequences of the choice completely different as well.[7] This is the practice that will ultimately establish a new and permanent link to the core fear.

When you know that whatever happens in life your integrity and sense of self cannot be moved, when you trust in your ability to deal gracefully, effectively, and powerfully with whatever comes your way, when you have come fully to terms with that which you can't control but with an unshakeable belief that you can always choose your experience, then you become an unstoppable force. You tap into the wellspring of pure potential, the potential to make change in your life and in the world. *You* choose how you fill the blank canvas of space and time that has been given to you. No longer driven by primitive impulses and habits, you are free from the dictates of the core fear and chief defense and can design your life accordingly.

TIPS FOR MASTERING THE TECHNIQUE

- As tedious as the process may seem, it is necessary to go through it slowly and precisely to achieve the transformation we seek. We are mimicking the experience of living through fear in real time while condensing it as much as possible. The shift will occur—every time—

if the exercise is done properly. But this requires enough realistic exposure to the fear that one settles in to it and gives up resistance. The shift can happen at any point during the exercise.[8] But be prepared for it to take as long as necessary, staying in the experience and keeping it fresh.[9]

- Another way to speed up the process, as we mentioned with the Digging for Gold exercise, is to generalize, or globalize, the problem. This would occur eventually on its own since the core fear threatens complete ruin of whatever sort. But if you find yourself stuck in the process, unable to see that anything might happen next, you can ask yourself, "What would be the ultimate expression of this problem, the state where everything possible has gone wrong, where all has been lost forever?" Or to say it more simply, "What would this problem lead to in the long run, the extreme worst-case scenario?"

- In this and all our exercises, it's important to remind yourself that it may seem unpleasant to address your core fear in this manner, but our task is great—nothing less than freedom from the very source of suffering.[10] Remember, we are already carrying around this fear anyhow, day in and day out . . . a very heavy burden that saps us of our life force, vitality, and happiness. This is our opportunity to do something about it. Refusing to acknowledge fear simply keeps it alive and continuing to hurt our outside awareness. It can also be helpful to remind ourselves that we actually want to go to the full depth of our fear—whether it looks like the loss of love, complete and forever; loss of identity; loss of meaning; loss of purpose; or even loss of life—so we can be sure we are digging up the root of it and cleaning it out entirely. Once again, it's necessary to look at the fear directly if we are to find its cure. Doing so, we will see it is only a set of projections from the long-ago past keeping us chained to our imaginations that something awful is waiting.

- The most important task in this exercise is to make sure you are not changing the script of the movie. Defenses will show up in many subtle forms, but one need only keep their eye on the simple question "Am I attempting to fix, change, or somehow improve the situation rather than passively observing the story of the fear as it plays itself out?" There may be times when it's difficult to detect the difference. For instance, if we visualize that "what happens next" is our death, then we have to make sure that dying isn't seen as an escape or relief from the situation. This is readily solved by asking ourselves, "Which would be worse . . . to die or to stay in the scene?" If still unsure about the answer, you can simply play out one of the two scenarios to see if it leads to further revelation about your fear or if it results in more positive outcomes. If the latter, you'll want to go back to the moment before you changed the script.

- Another point to mention if the fear of dying comes up for you is this: since you want to keep asking, "What happens next?" even after you imagine dying, you may think, "Nothing happens next . . . I don't believe in an afterlife." This is fine; the exercise doesn't depend in any way on dogma. We are merely looking at the fear you hold about death. Even if it is an experience of nothing, something about it is upsetting you. Resistance can be high at this point, and you may insist that there's no more to say after an experience of "nothing." But as before, you want to simply stay with the process and understand that "nothing" *is* what's happening next. Try to describe the "nothing" to yourself. The initial answer will usually be "It's just nothing . . . all blackness" or something to that effect. But this description of blackness is helpful. "Blackness and nothingness" is what is happening next. Simply stay with the experience. Eventually something will shift as you settle in fully. You could, perhaps, ask yourself, "Where am I in this nothingness?" since you must be present in some form to be experiencing the nothingness. But it's usually better to find yourself in the scene spontaneously after sitting in it long enough. Again, we are looking at what is so upsetting to you about death. Some people continue to resist at this point, saying, "There won't be anything upsetting about death because I won't be there to experience it." In that case, remember, if that were true, you would be relieved of your problem. If not feeling that relief, there must still be some aspect of "you" in the scene that is experiencing the upset.

- As with Digging for Gold, if you have a fear of more than one thing happening next, choose whichever you prefer. It simply doesn't matter since all will come to the core fear. Once we are sitting in the scene of our core fear, the rest of the process takes care of itself.

- Interestingly, every time I work with a client (or myself) on this exercise, there's some form of darkness in the picture of fear, and when they (or I) get to the breakthrough, there is always some experience of light. This is a demonstration of projections creating perception. I've often wondered whether this has something to do with the etymology of the word "Enlightenment"!

• Remember not to be limited by rational thinking. Fear is never rational. Similarly, the visualization in this exercise can often be highly symbolic. Let your mind stretch as it looks for "What happens next?" watching the movie that depicts the full extent of your fear, no matter how irrational or symbolic.

• Finally, as we also said with the Digging for Gold exercise, the only obstacle to success with the Alchemist is if a chief defense keeps one from moving through the process as described. This bears repeating: if we are stuck at any point, we can be sure there is a chief defense at work, throwing up its blockade and trying to derail us from continuing with the exercise. The blockade is easily removed, however, by applying the exercise to the fear our defense is hiding. We ask ourselves, "What am I afraid will happen next if I continue with the process?" Remember the woman who kept stalling with the Digging for Gold exercise, afraid that her answer to the questions might not be just right? I simply asked her to start by visualizing what would happen next if she gave an imperfect answer, following this movie all the way to its conclusion. She quickly discovered her core fear of abandonment—no one would love her if she weren't perfect. Once settled in to this possibility, she saw the whole idea of being perfect as both "painful" and "silly," realizing that after millions of years, no one would care. Remember, too, the woman who was afraid that if she kept going with the exercise she might have to let go of her anger at her mother and God. In her case, we restarted the process with "What happens next if you let go of the anger at your mother or God?" Since her core fear was a loss of identity (her mother having made her a prize to be shown off), she went through the experience of "disappearing." Coming out the other side, she described a most beatific experience of (in her words) "disappearing into God."

TWO CASE STUDIES

I once worked with a forty-year-old woman who had, by her report, a highly narcissistic mother. She described her mother as being extremely overbearing, using her children as "servants" to do her bidding. In addition, her mother continually disparaged her children's needs, always drawing the attention to herself. In recent years, she had had a stroke and was confined to a wheelchair. This increased her demands upon the children, especially my client who lived close by. My client was constantly anxious whenever the phone would ring, anticipating that her mother would have another complaint about some minor detail. Several times a week at least she would have to drop everything and run to her mother's house. Ultimately, she was afraid her mother would "squash" her chance to be who she wanted to be and do what she wanted to do in life. As she visualized this scene in the Alchemist, her mother took the symbolic form of a huge boulder, keeping her "squashed" against a wall with no way out. She felt she was sentenced to be there forever. Settling into this picture, she eventually gave up the fight to get out from under the boulder. With this, she spontaneously felt herself become what she described as a "sprite," a little fairy of light with a touch of mischief, someone who could easily slip out from behind the rock and fly wherever she wanted. In fact, she landed right on top of the boulder and sat there for a while, enjoying the view before flying off to other adventures.

A thirty-four-year-old man came to me for help with severe social anxiety. When performing the Alchemist, he arrived at the scene of his core fear, a scene where he had died and was floating in space, complete darkness and emptiness all around. I asked him if he had a body and he said, "No"; he felt like a free-floating awareness that couldn't rest anywhere. As he stayed with this scene, imagining that nothing would change for longer and longer periods of time, he eventually settled in and gave up the resistance to being there. Slowly he noticed his "eyes" were adjusting to the place as the scene began to light up bit by bit and he could see what it looked like. He now felt himself to be sitting on a rock (presumably in some sort of body), and this gave him an orientation. Next he explored his environment further and was surprised to discover new features in the landscape where before there was "nothingness." He saw that in addition to the large rock he was sitting on, there were many small stones forming a rectangle around him. These represented, he said, the space within which he had always been confined because of his social anxiety, afraid to go outside the protected area of the rocks. But now he was actually enjoying this space, finding it to be comfortable and "homey." He began setting it up according to his wishes and saw it as a place he would choose to be. A little later, however, he had the (for him) remarkable realization that the rocks didn't actually hold him to this space; he could easily step over them to explore beyond their territory. At that point, he spontaneously described a wish to connect with other people and left the area to go find them, without his former anxiety.

There is a story called "The Bound Man" that really captures the essence of the exercise. This man has been accused of a crime he did not commit and is chained to a prison wall as punishment. At first, he strains against the shackles until his feet and ankles bleed, outraged at being confined unjustly. Eventually his strength leaves him and he falls into a deep depression. After some years it is discovered that he did not, in fact, commit the crime. The townspeople rush to his cell to set him free. Once the chains are taken off, they watch with great anticipation, expecting him to celebrate his release. But instead, he quietly stays where he is, without moving, for he long ago found his peace within.

And finally, this joke, understood in the context of the Alchemist, has a poignant message. A man asked God, "How long, in terms I can understand, is a million years to you, God?" God replied, perhaps a little boastfully, "A million years to you is like a second to me." The man next asked, "God, how much, in terms I can understand, is a million dollars to you?" And God replied, "A million dollars to you is like a penny to me." The man finally asked, "God, do you think you could spare one of those pennies?" Whereupon God said, "Sure . . . give me just a second!" Our fulfillment comes when we settle in. Again, "infinite patience yields immediate results" (Foundation for Inner Peace, 1975).

NOTES

1. Because of the manipulations of fear, we usually don't even consider that a situation will pass when we are anxious.

2. If you are a therapist taking a client through this process, you'll want to ask the question for them. It's not necessary that they answer each time, but it's a good idea to check in this way every now and then. Verbalizing their picture helps make it "real" for the client while giving you, the therapist, a chance to make sure they are describing something concrete. It will also let you know if and when they might get stuck.

3. Therapists might want to repeat their client's descriptions of what they are seeing from time to time, letting them know they are "with them," followed by a gentle but firm reminder to "just be there" or "stay with it" before asking, "What happens next?"

4. The time intervals used in this script, or some close approximation, have been found to be the most effective for moving through the process. They make it possible to imagine stretching to the next interval because it is not too distant from the one before, but at the same time these intervals cover enough ground to speed the process up.

5. It's best to simply follow the script and keep asking, "What happens next?" staying with the process as long as necessary. Near the end of the script, however, if you want to help things along, you can remind yourself how very tired you are of fighting against this scene after all this time, pushing against the inevitable, always struggling, straining, and worrying. Then imagine what it would be like to relax, to finally let go and settle in to where you are. What would it be like to give up the fight and rest, letting go of those old, worn-out hopes and dreams? Encourage yourself in this, relaxing and settling in . . . relaxing and settling in . . . relaxing and settling in. When I present this technique at a seminar, I show the following magnificent video by the American Museum of Natural History at the end to enhance the experience: www.youtube.com/watch?v=17jymDn0W6U.

6. This is an important illustration of discovering a greater truth behind the distortion of fear.

7. It's important to remember that any behavior can be used in the service of fear and defense or freedom. The meaning of the behavior is completely determined by our motive.

8. This is another reason why the therapist, taking their client through the process, will want to check in regularly on their status. Asking them, "What's happening now?" or "What happens next?" gives the client an opportunity to let you know when the shift has occurred.

9. I actually had one client who resisted all the way through until I offered the line at the end of the script about "eons and eons of time."

10. The therapist must be convinced of this too, demonstrating to the client they are unafraid of their fear, knowing the process will expose it as illusory. We have to be willing to go wherever our clients' fear takes them, even through a visualization of their death or any of the other scenes that the core fears can project. If we help them avoid it, we are reinforcing the idea that there is something to be truly afraid of.

12

THE WITNESS

Enhanced Vipassana (Mindfulness) Technique

The wind and the sun argued one day over which one was the stronger. Spotting a man traveling on the road, they decided on a challenge to see who could remove the coat from the man's back the quickest. The wind began. It blew strong gusts of air, so strong that the man could barely walk against them. But the man clutched his coat tightly against him. The wind blew harder and longer, and the harder the wind blew, the tighter the man held his coat against him. The wind blew until he was exhausted, but he could not remove the coat from the man's back.

It was now the sun's turn. He gently sent his beams upon the traveler. The sun did very little but quietly shone upon the traveler's head and back until the man became so warm that he took off his coat and headed for the nearest shade tree.

—Aesop's Fables

Our next exercise for "doing the opposite" is called the Witness. It starts with the Doorway of the Body then moves into the Doorway of the Mind and finally opens the Doorway of the Spirit. I call it the Witness because instead of defending against the world of our projections, we simply abide with it as it is, witnessing rather than aggressing upon it. We thereby remove its power to frighten us, becoming free to choose our perception of it and free to choose whatever action we then wish to pursue. This exercise starts with certain principles from Vipassana Buddhism[1] and extends them for our purposes. We will join these principles with our understanding that all problems are different disguises of the same core fear, maintained by our chief defense. By identifying with the witness, we take ourselves outside the hologram of projected perceptions, assuming our true identity as the one who created these perceptions in the first place.[2]

In the Witness we will locate the exact moment and mechanism of resistance, the precise point at which we apply our defenses. Our purpose is to become exceptionally aware of and skillful at working with this moment to then "do the opposite" by disengaging and relaxing out of it. As such, we reverse our way of relating to anxiety, changing the meaning we assign to it. It is no longer seen as something to defend against and, therefore, no longer as something threatening.

Again, this exercise starts with the Doorway of the Body. It works with the physical manifestations of our emotions, recognizing them as expressions of anxiety at the root of a problem.[3] By concentrating on these physical sensations, we may practice "embracing" or welcoming them. Our task is to reverse the habit of pushing away unpleasant sensations, removing the judgment that they are "bad," something to be fixed or changed. Instead we let them be just as they are, even inviting them in.[4]

This exercise is to be done as a meditation, so find a time and place where you won't be disturbed and can fully concentrate. Recognizing that every emotion has a physical aspect (along with its mental and spiritual aspects), we will think of a problem and place our attention on the physical sensations attached to the emotions of it. The first part of "doing the opposite" is simply to look at these sensations, as our defense is to look away from them. To facilitate this, we will ask a series of questions about the sensations, training our mind to stay on them. If you find your mind wandering or otherwise resisting, gently bring it back to the questions. We will then enhance the experience by working with the projections that make these sensations something to be defended against in the first place until we arrive at a point where the projections have been withdrawn, revealing a greater truth behind the distortions.

We begin, once again, by thinking of some problem or upset (any situation will do) or perhaps the scene of our core fear. As with the Alchemist, we want to spend a moment bringing this picture to life in our mind, noting all the details, hearing the sounds, seeing the sights, feeling the feelings, etc. Once we've put ourselves in the scene well enough that we are feeling a bit of its discomfort, we focus only on the physical sensations of that discomfort.

Start by asking yourself, "What is the shape of the discomfort, the outline of these sensations inside my body?" Give it as detailed a form as possible, mentally tracing every nook and cranny of its surface. Make the edges clear and sharp in your mind's eye and stay with it until you can really bring that shape out from the background in three dimensions. Study its details for a little while.

Next ask yourself, "What is the color of this sensation?" Obviously there's no right answer to this, but it can help capture the feeling of the sensation. And it's another way to keep your attention on the sensation, letting it come into your awareness a little bit more. Whatever color suggests itself to you is fine. Visualize that color clearly.

Now we ask, "What is the weight of this sensation?" Imagine holding it in your hands and feeling the heft of it. If it helps, you can imagine comparing the weight of it to other objects you are familiar with, getting a good sense of how heavy or light it is. As before, stay with it for a few moments until it becomes real to you.

Next, "What is the texture on the surface of this shape?" Imagine running your hand over it and discovering whether it is rough or smooth, grainy, porous, or whatever else you might notice. Does it have sharp points, peaks and valleys, bumps and ridges? Is it silky, polished, or more like sandpaper? Again, stay with this for a few moments until the texture becomes very clear in your awareness.

Now ask yourself, "What is the texture inside this shape?" Does it feel smoky, airy, like cobwebs, or like something denser than that? Is it stringy, spongy, or more like a gelatinous mass? Spend some time noticing the details of the texture inside the sensation.

As you continue with this practice, be aware of any intruding thoughts that would have you look away from the sensation or somehow push against it, pay attention to something else, get distracted, or even become bored with this exercise and find a reason to end it too soon. All these responses are defenses in disguise, our old habit of avoiding fear or trying to "make it go away." Gently but firmly bring your attention back to the sensation. Stay with it.

Our sensation now has a discrete shape, color, weight, and texture, inside and out. Next we ask, "What is its flavor, metaphorically speaking?" That is to say, "What is the character of it?"

"What is the smell of this sensation?" Again, this may be more metaphorical.

"What is the temperature of this sensation, both on the surface and inside?"

Finally, ask yourself, "What is the movement of this sensation?" "Is it solid and frozen, like a lead weight, or does it perhaps move in waves? Does it pulse and throb? Does it undulate like a jellyfish? Or does it spread out fingers that touch different points inside your body, stimulating the experience of sensation?" Spend some time observing the movement of the sensation.

Now notice, if you've been staying with the exercise, that you have gotten much quieter inside than when you started. At first, you probably felt some agitation as you tried to manipulate or get rid of the sensation. But now you are able to sit with it a little more quietly. Let's continue this by taking away any judgment that the sensation is "bad" or "wrong" and must be pushed away. In fact, we will allow it to come a little closer in our awareness and will allow ourselves to feel it a little bit more poignantly and a little more fully. Feel the sensation on purpose, with its various qualities of shape, color, texture, and so on. Hold at this distance for a moment. Now let it come a little bit closer again. Hold for a moment and feel it even more vividly. Let it come a little closer still so that it is right before you, looming large. And now let it engulf you completely so that you are surrounded by it in every direction. Feel the sensation wash over and through you. Let it drench you thoroughly. It's safe to do so . . . it's only sensation. Let yourself relax any resistance to feeling all of the sensation. Relax into it, feeling it fully. Remain here for a few minutes and explore what the sensation is actually like without the overlay of projections that would color it as something "bad," something to be pushed away.

To continue with this form of "doing the opposite," we now enter into the sensation another way. Focus on one of the points at which the sensation touches the inside of your body, one of the points at which it actually triggers sensation. Picture this as a spark of light accompanied by a tingling—a tiny burst of sensation. Notice the precise location where it touches the inside of your body and watch it sparkle, feel it tingle. Slowly begin to zoom in on this spot as if looking at it under a microscope. If your mind wanders, keep bringing it back to this pinpoint of light. Immerse your attention more and more in the light's center. Let it absorb your concentration. Visualize that you are traveling toward it as you do so. See it getting a little closer and a little closer . . . a little bigger and a little bigger. Continue immersing your attention in the very center of the light until, finally, you feel as though you *are* inside it. It surrounds you now in every direction. See the light sparkling brilliantly all around. Feel yourself bathed in its tingling, with a warmth that penetrates you through and through. It is now just energy, no longer labeled as "unpleasant" or "uncomfortable." Rather, you are surprised to discover that it holds a healing quality that soothes and nurtures or perhaps invigorates your being. This is life-giving energy. Rest in this a little while, enjoying the energy of a sensation you once tried to push away, like massaging waves of warmth flowing throughout your being.

For the final stage of this exercise, we once again become aware of the sensation with its various qualities of shape, color, weight, texture (inside and out), flavor, smell, temperature, and movement. Instead of being located in our body, this time we visualize the sensation floating in a room with us beside it. It's very cramped in this room because the sensation takes up most of the space, literally bumping into the walls. Visualize as well that an invisible hand is squeezing the sensation, its grip increasing the experience of constriction and tightness. Settle in to as comfortable a spot as possible in this room, resting beside the floating sensation. Settle in especially with the understanding that you may be here a long time. There's nowhere you have to go and nothing you have to do. Now pay careful attention to your thoughts of resistance, those that would label the situation "bad," objectionable, unacceptable. Notice too the thoughts that say, "I must do something to change it or make it 'go away.'" The moment you generate these thoughts is the precise moment at which you assign meaning to what is otherwise a neutral sensation. It is accompanied by a subtle push against the sensation, a tiny movement of consciousness to press against it. This movement is the mechanism of resistance, the source of your strain and discomfort. Spend some time sharpening your awareness of these impulses.

Then, when you can see these thoughts and this movement clearly, gently, very gently, pull back from them. Instead of pushing, release, soften, and relax out of the movement. Instead of labeling the sensation "bad," say to yourself, "It's okay for it to just float there quietly. It doesn't have to go away." Repeat these words a few times, slowly and in a relaxed manner, while continuing to gently pull back from the impulse to press against the sensation. Soften. Relax. Release. Settle in some more and remind yourself again, "It's fine for this sensation to float there quietly, just as it is. It doesn't have to change or go away." After a few moments, notice that the room seems to have opened up ever so slightly and the hand has softened its grip the tiniest bit as you continue to settle in. The sensation feels a little less squeezed and has a little more space in which to float, making it just a little easier for you to breathe. Again, relax. Settle in. Keep reminding yourself, "It's okay for this sensation to float there quietly. It doesn't have to go away." You are just abiding with things as they are, reversing the tendency to push against them. Nothing needs to change. After some time has passed, you'll notice the room has opened up a little bit more, the hand relaxing its grip a bit more as well. The whole thing softens, loosens, settles. Continue to abide with the sensation, reminding yourself, "The sensation is fine just as it is. There's nothing I need to do about it." Keep settling in, getting quiet. Now you feel a noticeable release as the room opens up twice as much, the hand relaxing twice as much, too. It is significantly easier to breathe, with more space for the sensation to just float there quietly. Stay with it. Just softening, relaxing, resting. Letting things be exactly as they are. And now the space opens up twice as much more once again, the hand loosening its grip twice as much also. Lots of room to breathe. Lots of space for the sensation to float there quietly. Continue repeating to yourself, "It's just fine for this sensation to be as it is; it doesn't have to change or go away." Nice and soft, easy, relaxed. Just resting. Just abiding.

And now you feel something deep inside let go, as the walls, floor, and ceiling of the room disappear altogether. The hand disappears, too, as the sensation floats freely in infinite space . . . an infinite cosmos within. You float freely as well, your attention available to place where you wish. There's nothing that calls you to fixate on the sensation any longer. Looking around, you notice an almost infinite array of other floating sensations. These are all the experiences of your past and present, existing in your internal universe. Each sensation is neutral, just floating, bobbing gently up and down in its own place. None of them draws you to it more than another. A so-called negative sensation doesn't compel your attention more than a positive one. It does not have the power to require that you attend to it; neither is it forbidden. It is simply a matter of free choice. Let's practice this now. Over there is a sensation associated with the experience of playing with a baby. Shine the spotlight of your awareness on it and immerse yourself in its qualities. Feel the sensation and bring out its shape, texture, color, weight, temperature, flavor, smell, and movement. Let it come alive in your consciousness as you energize that reality. Explore this for a few minutes, just abiding with it, not pushing against or clinging to it, not trying to change it in any way. And now gently withdraw your attention from here and place it on a different sensation, floating over there. This one holds the memory of the death of a loved one. Once again, immerse yourself inside the sensation, noticing its various qualities. Be aware of any thoughts that would try to attach to these qualities, labeling them "good" or "bad," inspiring a defensive response of any sort. Recognize that these are just projections *you* are generating, meanings you are assigning to the qualities of the sensation. You are the witness, no longer taking these projections as "real." You are free to attach these thoughts or not—it is neither required nor forbidden—but either way you know it is a choice. After a few moments, withdraw your attention once again and place it on a sensation associated with being on the beach. Feel the unique texture, flavor, and "mood" of that sensation. And finally, set your attention back on the original sensation we started with, floating now in some faraway corner of this internal universe. You remember the thoughts you originally attached to it, causing resistance and discomfort. What previously mesmerized you, compelling your attention and creating your upset, is now seen as "just sensation," a composite of qualities without any meaning beyond what you wish to assign them. It is simply an experience of energy, just floating, just being. And so it is with this entire universe of perception, a great playground of sensations for you to experience as you choose.

And that's the paradox in this exercise: when we stop trying to push away the sensation of fear, when we sit with it quietly instead of resisting it, we free our attention to land on whichever world of perception we prefer. And the number of possible worlds in this inner universe is limitless, each brought to life as we energize it with our awareness. We are not forced to look only at what fear tells us to look at in the way fear tells us to look at it. It is *always* a choice. This is how we break the hypnosis of fear. Continue to spend a few moments playing with this, focusing your attention on various experiences from your past or present—the wedding of a dear friend, the loss of a job you liked, the comfort of being at home on a quiet night, and again, the sensation we started with that you once called a fear, floating among countless others in the universe within.

When ready to end this exercise, come back to your immediate surroundings slowly, bringing your discoveries back with you. Just because we are returning to the everyday mind doesn't mean we can't hold on to this perspective at the same time. In fact, it is essential that we learn to do so. Otherwise, the thought that we must hurriedly get back to the details of our life will begin the anxiety cycle again. We want to extend this peace for longer and longer periods and practice checking in with it often throughout the day so it can become the new lens through which we view our life rather than returning to the lens of anxiety and stress. Very slowly, then, return to the here and now, watching your mind closely so it doesn't race away into old habits.

Still, we will forget this perspective. But once we become skillful at identifying the precise moment and movement of resistance, we can let go of our defenses more quickly and reliably. We practice with this moment, watching the resistance arise and then letting it relax, sinking back into the undifferentiated ground of being. We want to become very aware of the subtle, internal movement when resistance starts to form, the tiny "push" against a sensation we don't like. So too we want to become aware of the judgment that labels a sensation "bad." Eventually we become aware of the almost instantaneous decision to try to change it, distract from it, brace against it. But catching the resistance, we invite the sensation in instead, feeling it on purpose, relaxing around it, softening around it. We give it lots of space and patience to just float there quietly. Keep playing with this moment, noticing the tension of resistance then relaxing, tensing and relaxing, tensing and relaxing once again.

Here's a way to practice the Witness quickly, in the midst of everyday circumstances. Whenever you notice some upset, stress, or strain, try repeating to yourself the word "feel" several times, bringing your attention to the Nexus point.[5] This evokes the physical sensation of the experience, pulling it out from the confusion of thoughts and emotions in the background. It's a way of focusing your attention inside the sensation on purpose. Each time you repeat the word "feel," let the sensation come a little bit closer . . . and a little bit closer . . . and a little bit closer. You can, as above, concentrate on the centermost point of it where the sensation is most intense, fully immersing your attention there. Notice any resistance that arises, the squeezing effect of clamping down upon or pushing against the sensation. Then invite the sensation in again by repeating the word "feel." Go back and forth, letting yourself first squeeze and resist, watching the reality that tries to coalesce around the idea that this sensation is something "bad." But before getting caught up in it, remember that you have already discovered you have a choice. Then relax around the sensation once again, softening, slowing down, settling in. Remind yourself, "It doesn't have to go away" and let it float there quietly. In this way, as with the Alchemist, we build a new habit, replacing our old association to the circumstance with our new interpretation and response.

Over time we can train our attention to stay in the Nexus point. As we enter the physical sensations there, we walk through the Doorway of the Body to open the Doorway of the Mind and the Doorway of the Spirit as well. Ultimately, we rest in the place of witness, identifying ourselves as the creator of our perception rather than as a figure caught in it. We are no longer victimized by our circumstances. This is what it means to be "in" but not "of" the world. We see the three-dimensional hologram projecting out all around us and we play with different perceptions as we choose our experience. By joining with rather than resisting these perceptions, we break down the illusion of separation and build a world that more closely approximates original Oneness.

NOTES

1. *Vipassana* is a Pali word that can be translated as "inward vision" or "insight." For those who don't know, the popular use of the term "mindfulness" is taken from and built upon the ideals of Vipassana Buddhism.

2. The devoted meditator can arrive at this same realization, where fear gives way to a higher truth as we step outside our projections. In meditation, all problems are understood as the result of thoughts we have attachments to.

These attachments are a form of defense. Allowing (witnessing) our thoughts without attaching to them frees us from their influence. Eventually we see all thoughts as equally "unreal"—and we are no longer compelled to attach to them. As such, they lose their meaning as something fearful. Where this can take many years in meditation, our approach is designed to hasten the awareness. By knowing all fears are products of one core fear, we move through the source of attachment in one fell swoop and can come to the same realization very quickly.

3. Every emotion has a physical sensation associated with it. It's important to not confuse this with the physical sensation of an injury, tense muscles, or other medical problems. This is exclusively the physical sensation of our *emotions*, which are always felt in and around the Nexus point.

4. Letting them be just as they are reflects our second approach to doing the opposite (doing nothing), while inviting them in is our first approach (moving into the fear). Because of its focus on the physical sensations of anxiety, this exercise works very well with physical pain or discomfort as well (see for example Levine & Levine [1989]).

5. You can also hold your breath for a few moments or even press down on your diaphragm to increase the effect.

13

THE WARRIOR'S STANCE

I refuse to be intimidated by reality.
—Trudy the Bag Lady in *Search for Sings of Intelligence in the Universe* by Jane Wagner

Our next exercise, called the Warrior's Stance, unlocks the Doorway of the Spirit to expand beyond the limits of fear. We commit, with a warrior's resolve, to a purpose so powerful that nothing can move us off our stand. Our stand is for truth. Our commitment is to restore our authority over fear. We are like Don Quixote in search of a glorious quest. The windmills we fight are the projections of fear, creating exaggerated illusions that would frighten us into submission. In this exercise, we use our spiritual determination to "do the opposite," choosing a different response in body and mind than fear would choose for us. Specifically, we practice the second way of "doing the opposite" by doing nothing at all. We take a spiritual stand and refuse to let ourselves be moved, physically, by fear. In so doing, we tame our anxious thoughts as well, those that would compel us to step off our mark and abandon our cause. With mind, body, and spirit fully engaged, our perception begins to shift. No longer seeing ourselves as small and vulnerable, we grow into our true magnanimity, creators of our reality and masters over fear.

By refusing to let the body move in defensive ways, this exercise can be understood as a simple, behavioral technique. In truth, it is a sophisticated tool that gives deep and dynamic insight into the layers of fear that compel us to act as we do. This insight shows that every fearful thought begins with some form of "I have to" or "I must." This is what compels our defensive response as we to try to "fix" the problem or "make sure" we get the outcome we want. It is the third type of manipulation in fear's arsenal . . . what we have called the "demand of fear." When fear strikes, we feel we *must* do something about it. The problem here is in the compulsion. There's nothing wrong with trying to fix a problem, but a compulsion to do so actually reinforces the fear. It tells us there is something about the problem that is so scary, so intolerable that we simply have to find a way out—we must do something. As always, when we "do the opposite," the fear disappears. In this case, doing the opposite means physically doing nothing. In the Warrior's Stance, we enlarge our perspective beyond the fear instead of shrinking and running from it. As the spirit grows, we feel ourselves to be "bigger" than the fear. Ultimately, our perspective becomes so vast that the fear gets swallowed up in its expanse.

The compulsive thoughts of "I have to" and "I must" form the constant background noise that is the ubiquity of fear. Whenever we are not wholly free to choose our way, experiencing a deep fulfillment in the moment, some version of these thoughts is at play. It may take place on a subtle, almost undetectable level, or it may be in the front of our mind, the mantra we repeat to ourselves throughout the day. In the West, we are especially driven by thoughts of "I must get this done and that done." Such thoughts act like obsessions, causing us to defend ourselves by making sure things do get done in a compulsive way.[1] Examples include "I must finish my chores," "I have to meet a deadline," "I must please others," and "I have to put on a persona." It can also show up in the negative form of "I have to avoid challenges" or "I must stay away from fear."

In the Warrior's Stance, we will do the opposite by refusing to act on these compulsions. When we "have to" look, for instance, at a text every time the phone pings, we are acting on fear-based conditioning, obeying the compulsion to get control. It's a bit like Pavlov's dogs salivating at the promise of satisfaction. In the Warrior's Stance, we recognize that this can never provide real fulfillment and make a commitment to choose our response freely. Unlike the other exercises, this one is primarily meant to be performed while we are moving through our daily activities. It is therefore an especially useful way to integrate our practice into everyday life. With the Warrior's Stance, we are to catch ourselves in the middle of some defensive response, some action we feel compelled to perform, and practice doing the opposite right then and there. We refuse to move in the way our defense is driving us to move. We have taken our stand and will not budge. Our goal with this practice is to become more and more aware of our compulsive reactions to fear, interrupting the process and taking back our freedom to choose our way.

Here, too, the process is simple enough to describe. We begin by noticing our many thoughts that start with "I have to" or "I must" and the actions that follow to satisfy the demand. These can be any actions that have a compulsive quality to them. We are looking for those actions that are driven by a subtle or not-so-subtle fear, threatening some negative consequence if left unattended. The negative consequence is thought of as "I have to . . . or else . . . !" It is that which pushes us to "make sure" something is taken care of. Any action we perform to get or keep things under control, no matter how seemingly insignificant, will work.

Then in the middle of the action, we simply stop. We literally freeze, becoming immobilized. With the courage of a warrior, we refuse to continue to move. Our objective is to leave the task incomplete. We simply stand there, refusing to move *until we no longer have to finish the action.*

Next we watch as, very predictably, an army of fear's voices comes rushing in to threaten us. At first, they merely poke and prod to move us off our mark, threatening in irrational but convincing ways that this is not a good idea. As we continue our stand, they begin cajoling or coercing, with all kinds of negative predictions if we continue with this "nonsense." The longer we hold our stand, the louder and more threatening the voices of fear become, now with warnings of catastrophe, doom, and gloom. They try to convince us that everything will fall apart, that our safeties will fail and our fortress will be stormed if we don't resurrect our defenses. Without fear's strategy of self-protection, they say, we will forever lose our chance for fulfillment.

When we still refuse to move, something starts to shift. As with the other exercises, we have the realization that nothing terrible is happening. Once again, we begin to settle in. We have disobeyed the demand of fear to act and countered the impatience of fear to act now. The lie of fear begins to break up as well, no longer able to forecast a disastrous future because we are living that future now and realize that things look very different than we had imagined they would. This breaks up the hypnosis of fear, and we start to remember a truer perspective, relaxing and settling in to the moment more and more. The structure of our fear starts falling apart, like a glacier dropping off huge chunks of ice into the ocean. Having thrown their full fury at us, the screaming voices fade and the racing heart calms as we arrive on the other side of our fear unscathed. We did precisely the opposite of what fear told us to do. We dared to disobey its orders, to discover that it could not carry out its threat. The world did not end, our life did not fall apart. Now we are free and anxiety has gone. Our mind is once again our own as we see the truth of things that had been so distorted a moment ago. [2]

While we have to be willing to stand there as long as necessary, the whole process usually takes very little time—perhaps an average of three to five minutes. But it must be repeated that the key to success in this exercise is to refuse to move, standing there resolutely and immovably, until we no longer have to move. We must be willing to stay where we are, frozen to our spot, as long as it takes. [3] The resistance dissolves when all hint of wanting to escape is released. Once again, "infinite patience yields immediate results" (Foundation for Inner Peace, 1975).

Our objective in this is to refuse to move until we no longer have to finish what we were doing. This is what sets us free from any fear that would compel our actions. As our second postulate states, we are then able to see the objective "truth" of what best serves our higher purpose. It may be to continue what we were doing before, this time without fear's dictates. Or we may discover we have been acting on automatic pilot and that our interests are better served another way.

We can practice the Warrior's Stance any time we catch ourselves with a compulsion to get something done. It begins by recognizing the ubiquity of the thought "I must" or "I have to." We can also recognize the discomfort, perhaps very subtle, of something "clutching" inside, bracing to do battle. This is the tension to exert our will, our way of making certain that things turn out as we wish. If it is something we would find difficult to leave unfinished, it is an opportunity to listen for the thought "I must" or "I have to." If it is something we are eager to master, we can look for that clutch inside. Any activity we would find difficult to leave unfinished is a call to practice the Warrior's Stance. [4] What would it be like to freeze in the middle of multitasking or answering a phone call? What if we disobeyed fear's command to rush toward a deadline? Notice the stress that can happen when we are late for work, unable to find an important email, or laboring through a burdensome task. What if we refused to cooperate with fear's threats and stood stubbornly still in the face of such compulsions? These examples highlight that the pressure driving us most of the time comes from the power of our investment in fear. It robs us of our freedom to choose. The Warrior's Stance is a way to take that freedom back physically, mentally, and spiritually. It directly challenges our defenses, including our chief defense, forcing a confrontation with the core fear and all of its derivatives.

We can also practice this exercise with any ordinary action, even if it is not experienced as stressful or anxiety-producing. Notice, for instance, how challenging it would be to freeze in the middle of typing a sentence or while walking to the next room, brushing your teeth, or doing the laundry. Try closing your eyes in the middle of a TV show. Become aware of the obligatory smile you make when passing another person in the hall or the urge to fill in gaps during a conversation. Observe what comes up if you resist scratching an itch, pause before putting that next bite into your mouth, or even, once you have begun chewing, resist swallowing. Upon reading this, it may not seem like doing so would be important, but try it. You will be surprised at the intensity of the compulsion to finish what you are doing. If you stay with it, you will be even more surprised at the degree of anxiety that can come up, projecting all of the pictures of catastrophe threatened by the core fear. Because we are bypassing the core defense, surrendering all control, these seemingly innocuous practices can confront us with the full measure of our fear of losing love, identity, meaning, purpose, or life.

But like a warrior, we are ready for this challenge and resolve to hold our stance. We are called to freedom more than compulsion, to fulfillment more than fear. And we derive strength from the "revelation" we have already discovered that all anxious projections, no matter how threatening, *will* dissipate . . . every time. Bit by bit, as we stand strong in the face of fear, its thunderclouds break up and ultimately disperse. Because we have such an immediate and embodied experience with the Warrior's Stance, the release from fear it gives can be unusually powerful, leaving us both peaceful and exhilarated. We feel a profound sense of freedom, now seeing the truth of things that has for so long been distorted. And no longer compelled to move in one direction more than any other, we can clearly see what our next move should be: that which best promotes the cause of fulfillment and serves our higher purposes. We may find that it is to continue doing what we were doing before, but this time with freedom and peace. Or we may choose to do something completely different, no longer afraid not to.

This practice is not for the faint-hearted! Obviously it requires a great deal of determination. Of course we can start with easier challenges, situations where the investment is not so great and we can more easily let go. Otherwise, if you find the exercise brings up resistance, it may help to remind yourself that your fear is "unreal," a set of neutral sensations joined with arbitrary assumptions made long ago. The fact that the instructions are so easy to follow ("Simply freeze") would seem to minimize the chance for resistance. But fear will find its way if we let it, using its deceptions and manipulations. People often "forget" to practice the exercise or get confused about the instructions, taking a moment out here or there but not freezing until they no longer have to move at all. Some people interpret the instructions as an opportunity merely to "take a break" from what they are doing. Others forget that we are "doing nothing" and they look for a different action to handle the same problem. Still others hold their position for a while and then convince themselves they've done enough but before the real benefits are realized. In this exercise, the two key points to remember are, first, we freeze, refusing to take *any* action, and second, we do so until the compulsion to move disappears altogether.

Even if we follow the instructions explicitly, our fear will still project all sorts of fantasies to throw us off our commitment. Thoughts such as "It would be irresponsible of me not to do such and such," "People will think I'm crazy," and "How do you function in the world if you're not making sure you take care of things?" are common. The power of this exercise is that it is capable of answering all these questions with one sweeping blow: Nothing matters as much as getting free of anxiety. Nothing matters as much as getting out from under the tyranny of fear. Any rebuttal you can make must, itself, be a form of fear no matter how rational, no matter how convincing. Until we resolve the fear in the way, all our efforts will be limited at best, misguided or harmful at worst. What's more, we find that fear can be handled very quickly with our exercises. Again, the Warrior's Stance averages about three to five minutes at first and less as we gain experience. In the end, it actually saves time as we accomplish our true purposes much more effectively and without fear.

So we bring the full force of our commitment to this exercise, remembering that above all else we want to be free to choose our course, moving steadily toward fulfillment and the realization of our higher goals. We are no longer content to simply manage the threat of the moment with a compulsive defense, one that leaves us chained to fear for a lifetime. If we are to find our freedom, we must become willing to face *all* of our fear and move through it *all* the way. Only this will dissolve its effects and prove to us it has no power. In the Warrior's Stance, we do this by refusing to react with our habitual defenses. This exposes us to the core fear and shows it to be illusory. Our anxious compulsions to secure love, identity, meaning, and purpose are all equally denied. We can even stand calmly in the face of death, discovering, as one spiritual teacher said, "the one thing about death . . . it's perfectly safe!" (Rodegast & Stanton, 1987).

When properly performed, this exercise can bring a radical shift in our understanding of all five core fears. We see that most of what we had taken to be all-important, what we just had to defend, doesn't really matter in the end. Once we've lived through what we thought would ruin us, literally or metaphorically, we get profoundly in touch with what does matter, as our spirit moves into its naturally expansive view.

APPLYING THE WARRIOR'S STANCE TO OUR THOUGHTS

This exercise can also be applied to those "actions" called thoughts. This can be harder than freezing physically because our thoughts occur so quickly and fleetingly. A large part of what makes freezing so effective is that we use concrete actions; there is no ambiguity about "what to do." If we are to apply the exercise to our thoughts, then, we must first catch ourselves in the middle of "moving" our mind with defensive strategies, noticing the compulsions of "I have to" and "I must." Instead of making plans and figuring out solutions, we remain in the moment and tolerate "not knowing." Instead of ticking off items on a mental to-do list, we trust that we have remembered sufficiently or can handle what happens if something was forgotten. We resist the impulse to follow the trail of our thoughts to a successful conclusion and leave them unresolved. This will bring up the fear, or at least the agitation, of not ensuring we have a path to control. But it also leaves us available to see things in a fresh, more accurate way when the time arrives.

So we break the chain of our habitual thoughts, refusing to let our mind finish its usual sequence. No matter how powerful the compulsion, no matter how much we want solid ground under our feet once again (Chodron, 2002), we resist the urge to solve a problem, find an answer, come to a conclusion, or organize our thinking in a neat and tidy way. We surrender the attempt to get control through understanding. This brings up the same fears that freezing in the middle of a physical action does. We imagine we will "lose" an essential insight, be unprepared for an important presentation, or miss some new idea for how best to reach our goals. The urge to use thinking as a defense can be powerful. But if, like a warrior, we hold our resolve, we find that nothing terrible happens after all and we can think just as well without defensiveness.

Sometimes our defensive thoughts are merely attempts to make sense of a situation, to see that everything fits into our interpretation of how things should be. These are our judgments and opinions. They are intended to keep our world orderly and sensible, to stave off fear. We can feel the security it gives when we have formulated our opinion and stamped it with our certainty. What would happen if we were not so certain? What if we didn't insist that things look the way we say they should? What if we became open to seeing things in a new way instead? Similarly, we can question our goals and aspirations, understanding they too are often by-products of a need to order reality. Challenging our assumptions about what is so or the "proper" way to respond to life can be very threatening. But if we are to see through the distortions of fear, we must be willing to be wrong in how we have thought about things. As *A Course in Miracles* says, "Do you prefer that you be right or happy?" (Foundation for Inner Peace, 1975).

Of course, it can be difficult even to notice, let alone change, these assumptions. Our mind is unruly and likes to wander off, making such awareness elusive. This is where a meditation practice can be helpful. Meditation can be seen as one version of the Warrior's Stance applied to thoughts. We gently but firmly catch the mind wandering and bring it back either to stillness or one-pointed attention. If we find it too difficult to tame our thoughts with the Warrior's Stance, we can still "do the opposite" in our two other ways. We can move directly into the fear, thinking of a problem on purpose and imagining that it will not work out. Or we can think about something totally unrelated to a problem. We focus on some distraction that can hold our attention, tolerating the anxiety that we won't find a solution to the problem. We refuse to let our thoughts go back to the problem until its "pull" weakens and disappears.

It can be especially effective to apply the Warrior's Stance to the thoughts we have upon first waking. Before getting out of bed in the morning to start our routine, we check the compulsion to "rush into" our day, meeting deadlines and the other demands of fear. Even before that moment, we can watch our first thoughts of waking consciousness come into focus, pausing before they project the experience of the perceptual world and holding on to the stillness of mind we had in the sleep state. We can practice the same thing when coming out of a meditation or relaxation exercise. These are excellent opportunities to watch, as if in slow motion, exactly what we are doing with our mind. These moments make it especially easy to see that, indeed, we have a choice and that, indeed, we are projecting our perception. Seeing this makes it more possible to withdraw the projection. We simply rest in the experience before the projection arises, refusing to move our mind at all. Then from this state of equipoise we can choose a perception and response that will better serve our fulfillment.

APPLYING THE WARRIOR'S STANCE IN PUBLIC

Of course, it won't usually be possible to stop in the middle of some action, or pause to work with our thoughts, when others are around. But if the situation permits it, doing so can be especially powerful. If you freeze in the middle of a conversation, for instance, you could say that you are waiting until you get clear on exactly how best to respond. If you pause in the middle of an action, you can explain you are thinking about the best way to proceed. This can be a wonderful tool for breaking the compulsion to defend oneself, to conform to others' expectations, to react habitually, or to behave according to protocols you don't really subscribe to. These compulsions represent a major driving force in most of our lives so our exercise has tremendous potential if it can be performed with others.[5]

There is also an application of this technique for couples or groups. Imagine stopping mid-sentence in an argument or in the middle of some other action designed to defend, manipulate, or attack. Obviously it's not appropriate to stand there mute and immobilized. Again, you interrupt yourself and say, "Give me a moment" or something to that effect. As well as you are able (and "Fake it until you make it" is permissible here), break the momentum of the course you were on and see what other actions would be more helpful for the situation. If nothing else occurs to you, you might offer, "I'm trying to find a better way of responding so we can come together on this" and maybe add, "Will you help me?" The words aren't as important as the attitude of defenselessness. In fact, you may end up saying or doing the same thing you were going to say or do before. But without the attack that usually accompanies a defensive response, your expressions and intonations will change and the other person will receive it in a very different way. What if you were the generous one to break the cycle of defense and attack first? The other person or people are likely to respond very well, more willing to hear and understand once they feel heard and understood. Imagine the potential of this for healing our relationships. Imagine, if applied on a grand scale, the potential for healing our global conflicts as well.[6]

In group therapy, this practice can be structured in the following way. One person on the "hot seat" instructs the others about an upsetting situation, extracting a few key sentences that are especially triggering. These are sentences that make the person feel misunderstood, wrongly accused, thwarted, or in some other way upset about the situation. The others are to repeat these sentences, trying to elicit a reaction. If, for example, the person on the hot seat had a fight with their partner, the others would repeat a few lines the partner might have used in the argument.[7] They goad the person on, trying to provoke them on purpose. But instead, he or she freezes, refusing to respond at all. The therapist and perhaps select others in the group can offer encouragement to hold to their commitment, reminding them of their purpose, how tired they are of the same old merry-go-round, and how much they want to be free. To amp up the effect even more, the person on the hot seat can wrestle with the process out loud, verbally fighting the impulse to defend with sentences such as "I don't care anymore about being right or understood. I just want to be free from being so reactive, free to choose my own response," etc. Saying all this with much force helps even more. Again, the therapist can support and encourage the effort, reminding them of the importance of their goal.

TIPS FOR MASTERING THE TECHNIQUE

As in the Alchemist and the Witness, any time something interferes with one's success in this exercise, you can be sure there is a chief defense operating. Some people even find it difficult to figure out what actions to practice with. The answer to that problem should be obvious by now: *any* action we feel compelled to finish, any action that would be difficult to freeze in the middle of, is appropriate. If one's defense is strong, however, they might take this answer and think about it, still confused. But that would be a defense as well . . . this is not an exercise in thinking! Instead, we want to use the Doorway of the Body to actually freeze in the middle of different behaviors, or the Doorway of the Mind to stop our runaway thoughts. Most of what we think or do has at least a component of fear so there is never a shortage of opportunities to practice.

If you still find it difficult to think of situations to practice with, try looking at a problem that you currently have. Think about how you plan to handle the problem. Unless you have resolved any compulsive need to act on it, this plan is a defense, a strategy to manage the problem or keep it from hurting you. When the opportunity to deploy your plan arises, so does your opportunity to practice freezing. For example, if you know you are going to get a new project at work tomorrow and are worried about the demand, decide that when you see the pile on your desk you will freeze, for as long as it takes, before looking through it.[8] If your plan involves some interaction with others that would make it inappropriate to freeze, then you can do the Warrior's Stance with your thoughts, simply *imagining* what it would be like to move through the situation without using your defenses. Say you want to ask your boss for a raise or speak to your spouse about last night's argument. Instead of using your plan to follow a certain script, visualize yourself saying just the opposite or saying nothing at all. If necessary, it's okay to start with situations that are not too challenging or overwhelming, building confidence with each successful interruption of a defense. Then you will be able to apply the practice to "bigger" problems, learning they are all handled with the same shift in perception.

I see a similar defense when working with clients who report they haven't had any need to practice the Warrior's Stance since their last session. Again, our thoughts and actions are almost always, at least in part, compulsive, fueled by a fear of what will happen if we do not stay in control. In fact, our entire life has, for the most part, been dictated by choices we made long ago that are more about avoiding fear (such as loss of security, being alone, the disapproval of others, or feeling insignificant) than they are about a real freedom to choose our way and create the life we want. We don't want to settle for a mediocre fulfillment that leaves so many defenses intact.

Other defenses too can try to interfere with this exercise, and you'll want to see them coming to ensure maximal success. They may tell you the exercise is "silly" or that you have done it long enough. They may try to convince you that you get the point of the exercise before you have truly let go of the defense, becoming willing to leave it forever. Some people will postpone the practice until a more convenient time. But doing the exercise properly is supposed to feel "inconvenient." We *want* to feel this. It signals our opportunity to assert our authority over fear's compulsion to "just get things done." If this defense shows up in its related form of "I don't have time for the exercise," know once again that this reveals the very compulsion we are working with. We earnestly want to discover that there is nothing real chasing us in our race to "stay ahead." We are free, at any moment, to stop and choose a different perception and a different response. And since all defenses backfire, we actually save time when we do. No longer frittering time away with anxious rumination and haphazard actions, we move instead with a new clarity about how best to reach our goals and with a targeted efficiency in doing so.

Another defense that can show up is a worry that we will become irresponsible, throwing caution to the wind and letting come what may. There is nothing about this exercise that asks you to renege on obligations that actually need to be taken care of. It may alter your perception of just what those are, according to a higher truth that *you* discover.

Otherwise, we will continue to act as we always have, but without the fear that drove us previously. Remember, this is not an exercise in deciding never to do a thing again. Rather, it is an exercise in *being willing* to make that decision. If we try to make such a decision before finishing the exercise, we will scare ourselves with the belief that we are letting go of something truly essential. We may try to muscle our way through this fear, but it will be of no use. It must be genuinely transformed by our moving through it all the way.

Consider the drive to make money. Pausing in the middle of some money-making activity, we might confront a core fear of starving to death. As the voices of this fear die down, our perception shifts to a very different picture. Most of the time we discover that it simply won't make a difference in our overall financial picture or, at worst, will require that we scale back our lifestyle. Or we may realize we don't need that much money. If money will, in fact, help us reach our goals, we usually find that there are other ways to make up for the loss or that the loss doesn't really change our plans. Even if a lack of money necessitates a significant change, we have lived through that change in our mind and become quietly accepting of it. This can be hard to trust until you have experience in the Warrior's Stance (though you can already refer back to similar experiences with the Alchemist and the Witness). If reading these words brings up resistance before trying the exercise, look for the fear that is coming up. Remember that our defenses are supposed to stimulate this feeling. Until we go through the exercise, they will interpret these words as an invitation to disaster. But once we are on the other side of the exercise, living through the fear all the way in our imagination, we find that our perception cannot help but shift. And with this comes a vast, new outlook on what is actually meaningful, what fulfills our identity, what serves our purposes and promotes greater love. We realize we are free to pursue money to our heart's content but our interest in doing so is determined by this greater context. Whereas before we may have pursued more money for its own sake, we now ask whether or not it will actually be helpful in reaching our goals. What's more, we become aware of countless new ways to reach our goals that don't require money at all. Limited to the options dictated by our chief defense, we couldn't see these possibilities before. We are equally free to choose any of these paths as much as we are the path of making money. And we will have a new understanding of which path leads most directly to fulfillment.

Because of the depth of commitment required for this exercise, these and other defenses can try to shake us loose from our warrior's stance. We therefore want to remind ourselves often of the enormous healing potential if we hold our position. We can also perform the Alchemist or the Witness on the fears that come up when we attempt the exercise. That is to say, we can ask ourselves, "What happens next?" as we visualize stopping in the middle of some activity, then asking what happens after that and what happens after that. Or we can practice allowing the sensations that arise when we think of the same scene, letting the sensations float without resistance, as in the Witness.[9] Otherwise, because the instructions in the Warrior's Stance are so straightforward, we will either freeze in the middle of some activity or not. This makes it much harder for defenses to interfere, but again, they can still find a way. If this happens to you, review the instructions and follow them closely, making sure you actually start the practice rather than merely think about it.

If you are a clinician, here are some strategies for practicing the Warrior's Stance during a therapy session.[10] Pointing out some defensive behavior you notice, invite the client to resist the compulsion to use it. You may observe an affectation in their voice or an overly dramatic facial expression that covers their true feelings. You may notice their attempt to evoke a certain response from you, whether it is approval, empathy, or distance. You may point out that they are apologizing unnecessarily, trying to sound witty, hiding themselves in a sunken posture, or exaggerating their inflections, for example.[11] Invite them to continue talking while trying to resist these defenses or even going overboard in the other direction, "doing the opposite" in a more literal way. If your interpretation of their defenses was on target, they will quickly show signs of restlessness or compulsion. Remind them to stay with the exercise and tolerate the discomfort. Tell them that this is for therapeutic purposes so they don't have to worry about appearing inappropriate. It will still be plenty challenging for them. You can also directly ask them to freeze in the middle of a sentence, waiting until the urgency to finish the sentence dies down and disappears altogether. Then ask what fears came up for them and, more importantly, what happened to those fears in the end. In the concentrated atmosphere of a therapy session, this practice can bring up—and resolve—fears of not being heard, of being misunderstood, of being uncared for, of being unable to take control, of wasting time, of not getting the wanted results in therapy and therefore in life, and so forth. And you can take whatever insights arise to create further practices they can use throughout the week for discussion at the next session.

Ideally, the Warrior's Stance should be done regularly throughout the day to break the compulsion of the chief defense. We might want to start with committing to a practice of three times a day. This forces us to be on the lookout for the defense, knowing we have to find three opportunities to practice breaking free. We can build up from there as needed, performing the exercise any time we notice a compulsion driving us. The goal is to release the tension of fear before it builds significantly, working toward a state of continual freedom from such tension. In fact, tension can be our cue for recognizing a defense at work. Eventually we can become skillful enough that we simply notice the tension and relax out of defenses without having to go through any of the exercises.[12] Only make sure that your relaxation is not a defense in itself, an avoidance of fear.[13] If it is, you'll feel more tense as you compulsively try to relax!

Once again, as with the Alchemist and the Witness, we are building an association between situations that previously scared us and our newfound freedom. The Warrior's Stance will give deep release each time we do it, but we must integrate the experience in a lasting way, rearranging the structure of our personality without the core fear and chief defense. So we practice building the association as before, reminding ourselves each time we become afraid that the cause of fear has been vanquished.

As we develop the facility with this tool and take it to its extreme, we discover not only its extraordinary power for change but its applicability to every moment of our lives. This is how we become aware of the ubiquity of fear, realizing that all of our time, except for moments of true fulfillment, is spent in the pursuit of defensiveness and control. But this is very good news! It means that we can practice these exercises and find freedom in *any* situation—consistently so—to find a true and enduring peace in this world. It reveals that all our difficult experiences are amenable to change; they are the result of arbitrary projections we have chosen to energize and take as "real." We now have the tools to take back these projections and thereby reclaim our rightful place as the master of our experiences and our lives.

CASE HISTORIES

Frank was a sixty-five-year-old man with a chief defense of being "the world's nicest guy," someone who would always take care of others. In fact, he had been a physician all his life and prided himself on his ability to make people "feel better." During our work together, he came to clearly understand that this was, in part, his chief defense, hiding a core fear of being thought unworthy. In going through the Digging for Gold exercise, he remembered a time when he was five years old. His sister and father were dancing to music when his fathered invited Frank to join them. Frank declined, whereupon his father teasingly said, "You're no fun." In that moment, Frank's core fear was launched as he interpreted what his father said in an extreme way. His chief defense arose to resolve the upset; he would make sure of his worth by being forever helpful, good, and kind.

These many years later, he entered treatment to resolve an obsessional guilt over the death of one of his patients. He had just retired from a very successful career as a gynecologist. In all his years of practice, this was the only time one of his patients had died. Even though he knew he had done everything correctly and that the patient died from an unavoidable reaction to anesthesia, his guilt was overwhelming. He would wake up with it each morning, tortured by it. We began working with the Warrior's Stance, finding opportunities to combat Frank's compulsion to make others feel better. During this time, his daughter was going through a difficult divorce. He ran to her rescue, flying in from another state to stay with her. He helped her emotionally and financially, taking care of the children and helping her find and buy a new house, prepare for the move, etc. He then received a call from his wife back home that she was having a medical problem. He had already been running around rather frantically, taking care of his daughter and grandchildren. With the news of his wife, he became completely overwhelmed, his obsessions out of control. Just then, he remembered his practice. Freezing in the middle of the living room, he refused to move and refused to let his mind continue thinking about all he had to do.

While standing there steadfastly, he resisted the temptation to review his mental checklist. He reported a significant amount of fear—that he might "forget" one of his responsibilities and somebody would be upset with him—but he continued to stand resolutely. Finally, his mind let go and he saw clearly that his fears were "only" (his word) made up . . . everyone would be fine if he didn't rush in to fix things. He further discovered that he had been enabling his daughter to stay regressed in her grief. As soon as he withdrew to an appropriate degree, she rallied, recognizing the need to take care of her children, move into her new house, etc. And finally, with the help of the Alchemist, his obsession about the patient who had died resolved as well. Not only did he understand her death was "not his fault," but he described a peaceful compassion for her and her family, detached from any guilt or undue responsibility. His release from this obsession, which had consumed him for decades, accompanied his release from his core fear, and he described a dramatically new sense of peace in his life as a result.

Angela was a fifty-three-year-old woman with multiple personalities—seventy-two to be exact. At one point in our therapy, she visualized a situation of childhood abuse as a furious tornado whirling beside her. In an adaptation of the Warrior's Stance, she bravely stood beside the tornado without running away. After a few moments, she felt courageous enough to stick a finger into the rushing winds. To her great surprise, she reported, "it died down a little." This gave her the incentive to put her hand into the tornado, which responded by dying down a bit more. Next her whole arm went in and the winds died down even more. When eventually she placed her whole body inside the tornado, it (and the emotional charge of the associated memory) disappeared completely. This was but one aspect of her trauma that resolved. Using the same principles we have been discussing, she eventually integrated all her personalities into one, becoming one of the most peaceful and spiritual people I have ever met. (For a full description of Angela's therapeutic journey, see Fisher & Pressman, 2008.)

David was a forty-five-year-old man whose core fear was of losing his identity as provider and protector. He built a chief defense of working hard, suffering silently, and always making sure everything got done for his "loved ones." One day he came into session saying he didn't practice the Warrior's Stance as we had discussed because he didn't want to "waste the time." He already knew his core fear but I wanted him to see it driving this defense. We went through the Digging for Gold exercise again, starting with the fear of wasting time. At the bottom of the chain of questions, he saw that if he took the time to do the Warrior's Stance, he would be taking time away from other things that needed to get done—specifically, filing the necessary paperwork for his son to come live with him. Because David was still resistant to doing the Warrior's Stance, we performed the Witness instead, focusing on the sensations associated with the fear of losing his son. He emerged from the session and confessed something he hadn't told me before: the fear of losing his son had paralyzed him to the point that he was unable to file the paperwork. [14] Each time he would sit down to do it, he became highly anxious, afraid that he wouldn't fill it out "just right," that the judge would not approve it, and he would "blow [his] chances." But as he went through the exercise, his fear lost its influence. That night when he sat down to do his paperwork, the habitual compulsion to get up from the desk and distract himself came forth. However, it was so weakened by what he experienced in the Witness that he easily resisted it. Committing to the Warrior's Stance, he spontaneously visualized himself tied to the chair, unable to leave until the paperwork was done. He described sitting with his core fear—not being able to take care of his loved ones. But he remembered too what had happened in the Witness and allowed the sensations to float there. The next time I saw him, the paperwork had been filled out and he had a quiet joy that I had not seen before.

NOTES

1. In the Buddhist tradition, thinking is considered a form of action. Our fearful obsessions and defensive compulsions can therefore be seen as different aspects of one process.

2. Eventually we learn to watch all this with detachment and can become almost amused by these voices of fear, so predictable in their tirade, trying to fool us yet again into believing them. But it's important to distinguish between this practice and what is ordinarily meant by "response prevention." We are not simply avoiding a particular response, as in traditional exposure therapy, but avoiding all responses. When we completely freeze with the Warrior's Stance, we are facing all possible fears at once, risking the loss of control over everything. In short, we are moving through our core fear and resolving it at its root.

3. As in the Alchemist, we must be willing to stay with the exercise, giving up our defensive maneuvers, for "eons upon eons."

4. This is true for things we deem positive as well, for example finishing preparations for a party. We still want to resolve any fear of not finishing that comes up along the way. Even though it is joined with excitement, this fear hurts us, giving life to anxiety and stress. We can accomplish just as much, and enjoy the fulfillment more, without this anxiety.

5. One of my favorite quotes comes from the Zen tradition: "You know you are enlightened when ten thousand people call your name and you don't have to turn your head."

6. Be aware, too, that relational problems can manifest as avoidance behaviors such as people-pleasing, shutting down, manipulating, passive-aggressive behaviors, etc. All of these, of course, are defenses and the same principle applies: do the opposite in the middle of some interaction when these behaviors show up.

7. Or if, in a couples session, the other person *is* the partner, the therapist can moderate a structured re-enactment of the argument between them.

8. Remember, it should only take a few minutes to complete the exercise, and doing so will likely save you time in the end as you proceed with the task more calmly and efficiently (as well as more joyfully). Still, your primary motivation is that nothing is more important to you than freedom from anxiety.

9. We can also use the abreaction technique of Gestalt therapy to help us if stuck. Abreaction is defined as the expression or release of a repressed emotion. In Gestalt therapy, it is a powerful instrument that employs the Doorway of the Body. It is a way of discharging the physical energy (pounding out our pain, roaring out our anger, or shaking out our fear, for example) that builds from negative emotions. This approach only sometimes leads to resolution because it doesn't always foster the insight necessary to integrate the results. That is to say, it doesn't always open the Doorway of the Mind, although in my experience, it usually opens the Doorway of the Spirit. Therefore the results, while impressive, are often temporary. So even though it is not discussed as one of our primary tools for transformation, it can give one at least a taste of freedom as well as helping to clear out obstacles when performing our exercises. By overwhelming our defenses with the abreaction, perception shifts. It invokes a great sense of power because our fear seems inconsequential compared to the force of our expression. If stuck in the Warrior's Stance, you can try discharging the fear and draining the tension of the defenses in the way.

10. The motivated reader can try these suggestions on their own as well, though a therapist is trained to recognize our defenses and can make the job easier. But this is also why stopping in the middle of various behaviors is so helpful; it makes it easier to see our own defenses, bringing them out from the

background as we feel the urge to employ them. And as we do, we can pay attention to our "personality style" as manifested in our facial expressions, use of language, posture, vocal inflections, etc. We can also ask others who know us well to give feedback about what they see as unique characteristics in our self-expression. And we can use the exercises for finding our chief defense (and secondary defenses) in chapter 9 as well.

11. Of course, you will want to ask permission to point these things out in advance.

12. See chapter 14 for more on this.

13. Remember, sometimes a defense has us avoid an action, in which case we "freeze" by not running away from the behavior.

14. This is an illustration that all defenses backfire. David's chief defense was to make sure everything got done for his loved ones, but he found himself paralyzed with fear when it came time to do just that.

14

RESISTING RESISTANCE

The Final Defense

Break the legs of what I want to happen. Humiliate my desire. Eat
me like candy. It's spring, and finally I have no will.

—Jelaludin Rumi

We have come far in our work of "doing the opposite," countering our
defenses, and resolving the anxiety they were hiding. In the Alchemist,
we accomplished this by living through, in imagination, each moment of
our core fear. We saw the importance of not skipping any steps, secretly
protecting some aspect of it. This is how we would ensure moving
through our fear *all the way* to finally reach its other side. In the Witness, we accomplished the same goal by pinpointing the exact moment
when we applied our defenses. We recognized this as the physical sensation that is resistance, and we released the resistance by allowing a
problem to be just as it is. And in the Warrior's Stance, we forced a
confrontation with our defenses to expose the fear they were hiding,
letting that fear move through us completely until, once again, we
found ourselves on the other side of it.

But at this late stage in our journey, we can encounter a final defense. To understand this defense, we must make one last deconstruction. Because any defense is a manifestation of the core defense of
control, that will be the focus of our attention now.

The moment we conceived of a separate self, control came into
existence.[1] The reason defenses backfire is that the separate self uses

control to "forget" that it is part of a larger whole. Since fulfillment lies in identification with the whole—without it we feel cut off from our source—we have sabotaged ourselves from the start. Nevertheless, we wanted to be a separate, autonomous self. So we denied that fulfillment comes by participating in the whole and projected a world where we could find fulfillment "on our own." This made us afraid of the whole, imagining that it would take away our separate existence and swallow us up. Denial of the whole, what we have called Oneness, was our first defense . . . the first moment of control. Ever since, we have been elaborating more and more complex defenses in the attempt to fully establish our individual existence. We narrow our focus with the blinders of these defenses so that we will see only what we wish to see: that which supports our idea of being in control. Knowing that reality can intrude on our illusions at any time, we become anxious. We then try to defend ourselves against this anxiety, looking for more control. Fear becomes the harbinger of that which could threaten our intentions. We scuttle about as a separate self, alone and vulnerable, hiding in dark corners from imagined attacks, plotting our coups and retaliations in response. All this gives rise to the perception of a dangerous and frightening world, one that can wipe us out unless we are ever on guard, ready to take control.

In order to maintain the illusion of control, we must repress our awareness of just how vulnerable we are. We don't want to admit that we live in an infinite universe that can, indeed, swallow us up or wipe us out at a moment's notice. This accounts for the five deceptions of fear—we repress awareness of the ubiquity of fear; we hide our fear under the disguise of many emotions; we avoid looking at fear; we avoid facing fear; and we avoid looking at or facing the correct fear. Once we have repressed these awarenesses, we then imagine we are safe from them, free to go about the business of pursuing what we want. This too is an attempt to deny our vulnerability, for what we really want is to get control over all possible threats, immortalizing the separate self. We spend so much of our life trying to attain this kind of control. Making money, manipulating our relationships, and acquiring prestige, authority, power, or fame are just a few examples. Once again, our plans inevitably backfire. Most often, we fail to achieve these things to our satisfaction. Even if we do, we find they don't provide the fulfillment we had hoped for. Sooner or later, the realization dawns that we are still vulnerable to abandonment, loss of purpose, meaning, or identity and that we can still get "swallowed up" by death.

The mechanism of control is resistance.[2] When confronted with a threat, we brace against it, press against it, push it away, or tense up around it in an attempt to gain control. Anger is an obvious example: when something or someone thwarts our ambitions or attacks our integrity, we throw up a powerful wall of resistance while trying to push back against the threat. This, once again, makes the threat seem real; by resisting it, we give ourselves the impression that there is something "really there" to resist. Resistance creates a clash of energies, one force pushing against another and creating pressure, "stuckness," lack of flow, a stalemate. In this way, it creates the very vulnerability we want to get control over.

We learn to resist from the very beginning, as soon as we buy into fear as a strategy for securing what we want. Our superego forms around injunctions to "watch out" and "be good." These are the seeds of resistance, accompanied by a physical tension as well. I remember my own experience with this at the age of about seven. My brothers and I were about to be picked up by the mother of one of our friends, and our mother told us to thank Mrs. So-and-So for driving. She must have said similar things many times before but I distinctly recall this event because it was the first time I was determined not to forget. Throughout the ride, my mind would slip away, flowing freely and peacefully with whatever was happening in the moment. With a slight jolt, I would then snap back to my focus, creating a tension inside that would serve as the reminder to stay on task. It was this use of tension-as-a-reminder that was key . . . I trained my mind to resist (defend against) its natural flow by tensing up inside. Because the tension was subtly uncomfortable, it begged for resolution. Fear's strategy for such a resolution was to keep me on my toes, unwilling to relax, until I had delivered my thank-you message.

This is the tension of resistance. As we age, it can leave us in a chronic state of stress or anxiety, always on the alert to make sure everything is under control. If, for example, we learn of a problem at work, we brace inside until the situation is taken care of. If something breaks down in our house, we hold a tension until it is fixed. This happens even on the most subtle level as well. If we have a pang of hunger, if the volume of the TV is too low, if the temperature in the room is not quite right, we are compelled to take action and resolve the tension we feel. Even if we are bored, lonely, depressed, or restless, we experience an agitation to rectify the problem and regain control. Our life is composed, for the most part, of an endless series of such moments; we never really feel that we have arrived at our goal and can rest, secure and certain of our security. Instead, we fill our mind with constant concern about the next moment, wondering if it will bring a new threat, a new challenge to our control. Even our "good" moments are usually tainted with the fear that such good won't last as we are all too aware of the ephemeral nature of such things. We are always standing at the ready, with one eye on danger. The pressure of trying to achieve control, resisting what is, causes our suffering. As we have said, it is the act of pushing against a problem that reifies and amplifies it, for in resisting a situation, trying to bend it to our will, we realize that it might not yield. Our response is to try all the harder, exacerbating the resistance, increasing our suffering. The entire effort is built on the idea that we will make ourselves safe from fear first and then find our fulfillment later. We continually postpone the day when we will enjoy the fruits of our efforts. And we can end up postponing it for a lifetime.

But now we have seen that this is the product of fear's projections and that such projections are capable of being recreated according to conscious choice. We have learned the wisdom of looking at and sometimes facing the correct fear. And we have our exercises for doing so. This gives us a new type of control, one that is truly invulnerable to fear. At this point, fear's ability to convince us it is our ally is severely shaken and it pulls out all the stops to win back our favor. Having seen the power of our exercises, it sneaks in once again by enticing us with a last form of control, our final defense. It tells us we must hold on tightly to these exercises, that we must be sure to use them to escape fear and find fulfillment . . . or else. Whereas our exercises are designed to help us let go of resistance, this can tempt us to *try too hard* to use them to let go of resistance. This shrewd defense has the appearance of supporting us in our effort to get free. But we must not be fooled. It is still an attempt to gain control by using fear.

Trying too hard to let go of resistance in itself creates resistance. It hides a subtle fear of not being able to get rid of the anxiety. And so it becomes another form of pushing against reality. This is the defense of "resisting resistance." In each of our exercises, we have practiced accepting our anxiety as the key to releasing it. We must not now use these same exercises as a tool to exert control over anxiety. If we unwittingly think, "I can use the exercises to let go of anxiety" with a subtle push to get the result we want, we set ourselves up for the fear of not succeeding in this task. Doing so creates a fear of fear, the self-generating quality of fear we spoke of in the eight manipulations. And this gives the fear its power, coaxing us to take its hand once again. Our response to this fear of fear is to resist resistance, trying too hard to let go of the resistance rather than genuinely releasing it.

We could say that the purpose of our exercises is to bring us to a point of "I don't have to": "I don't have to finish the task I was doing" (in the Warrior's Stance); "I don't have to escape the scene of my core fear" (in the Alchemist); or "I don't have to change the experience I'm having" (in the Witness). It would be ironic if we now added the pressure of "I have to" in our approach to the exercises themselves. Having understood that avoiding fear backfires, we don't want to start trying too hard to face fear. This would be a different kind of avoidance, the avoidance of accepting our fear. We must therefore become sensitive to this subtle defense of resisting resistance, trying too hard with our exercises (or any tool for healing). This is our new task . . . we succeed with the exercises by letting go of the need to succeed with them.

For example, we can try too hard with the Alchemist as we sit in the core fear, attempting to hurry up the experience of settling into it. Obviously one can't hurry up to settle in. With the Witness, the resistance to resistance can show up as a willful attempt to make, rather than let, the sensation float where it is. In trying too hard not to do anything with the sensation, we are still trying to do something with it . . . a subtle push to stop pushing. And with the Warrior's Stance, we can be too eager to freeze, holding a hidden expectation that doing so will get us free. Instead, we have to be willing for the exercise to take as long as it takes, with no such expectation.

We can also try too hard by thinking we have to hold on tightly to the *results* of our exercises. The problem in this case is the fear of losing the freedom we have achieved. But being afraid of losing it is a surefire way to lose it, as we fill our mind with such fear and try too hard to prevent the possibility. Instead, we want to let go of this resistance by imagining we might indeed lose the results we have gained and never get them back. We must live through that version of the core fear in our imagination . . . forever, if need be. Nor do we want to "try too often" to apply the exercises. If we feel a compulsion to perform them, we are defending again with a drive to ensure (get control over) our freedom. In that case, we want to relax such defensiveness and come to the practice with more patience.

The reason we are at risk of trying too hard is, of course, because we are afraid of the suffering caused by our fear and want to get rid of it. Or we could say we have become giddy with the feeling of release the exercises give and want more. If this defense arises after going through our exercises, it is because we still believe, to whatever degree, that fear is a better strategy for security and fulfillment. Going through any of the exercises all the way, opening up all three doorways completely, will show that fear is *only* an illusion . . . it can only hurt not help us. But if we hold back even a little bit in this, we will finish an exercise and return to the world of projections. It's at first glance quite a conundrum: our mission all along was to practice facing, not avoiding, fear. Now we find we can actually avoid fear by facing it! First, we had to apply effort, so to speak, to become defenseless. But now we learn there is such a thing as too much effort (or, really, the wrong kind of effort). We are at risk of using a defense to stay defenseless, tensing up in the effort to relax, controlling to let go of control. This is fear's ultimate survival tactic, generating anxiety about the possibility of not getting free of anxiety. Our solution, as always, is to "do the opposite," not trying too hard to get rid of anxiety, not *needing* to resolve our resistance. Only this, paradoxically, will release us from the problem. We let go of our resistance to resistance by accepting that we are resisting, accepting the anxiety such resistance is creating instead of trying to get rid of it.

THE MIDDLE WAY

It's not that we are to stop trying at all, of course. The distinction between trying and not trying too hard is all-important. We want to become aware of the subtle tension, the interruption of flow that comes with the belief that we must get control over fear. Of course we want to "try" to apply our exercises if we are to resolve our suffering, but only when we are free of the hidden motivation to get control over it. We ride the razor's edge, becoming aware of the almost imperceptible thought "I must succeed with the exercises." That's the thought we now "try" to let go of, the true fear at the root. Again, the final step in resolving fear is to let go of the need to resolve fear. Only this will take care of the resistance that energized the fear in the first place.[3]

When I present a lecture or seminar on deconstructing anxiety, I often hand out Chinese finger puzzles at this point in the presentation. For those who don't know, Chinese finger puzzles are little straw tubes just big enough to put an index finger in either end. Once the fingers are inside, any attempt to pull them out will only lock the fingers more tightly into place due to the action of the woven straw that knits the strands more closely together. To get out of the finger puzzle, one need only relax. The relaxation releases the tension of the tube and it opens up, making escape effortless. I hand this out at my presentations not only as a metaphor for the principle of resisting resistance but as an actual biofeedback tool. If one tries too hard to escape, the puzzle will lock. If one tries too hard *not* to escape (resisting resistance), their fingers will push in and the puzzle will be too loose. The objective is for the puzzle to lightly touch the fingers as we allow the sensations to float there quietly or otherwise come to acceptance. As in any meditation practice, we want to hold a mental posture of alert relaxation. We don't turn off our awareness of the problem, becoming "unconscious" and blindly bumping into it without any attempt to rise above. This would be a case of not trying hard enough, we might say. But we also don't try too hard to get out of the problem, making ourselves anxious about it. We follow what the Buddha called "the middle way."[4]

The principle of the middle way shows up throughout Buddhism. In mindfulness practice, for example, we have the dictum of "non-striving." This is distinguished from "not" striving. Non-striving is an attitude of applying oneself but without the strain of too much effort. We find this principle in Zen Buddhism as well, where one of the techniques for finding liberation is *koan* practice. A koan is a type of paradox, such as an unanswerable question, but one that the student must answer in order to progress. It forces the student to try too hard to answer the question until they surrender completely, floating in a higher level of awareness. At that point a new kind of answer spontaneously appears. The same thing happens with our exercises when we let go of "thinking" with the fear-defense dynamic. The shift in perception we achieve comes from surrendering control, no longer trying too hard.[5] Similarly, when one performs *zazen* (sitting meditation in the Zen tradition), the hands are held in what is called a "cosmic mudra." One palm rests on the other, both facing up, with thumbs lightly touching each other. If the thumbs push too hard, one is to become aware of this tension and release it. If there is not enough attention on the thumbs (and therefore the meditation), they will become too limp, as will the mind. And finally, the meditator can try too hard when attempting to keep attention on the breath. Again in the Zen tradition, they might be advised to practice what is called *shikantaza*, or "just sitting," holding a relaxed but alert state of attention, focusing more lightly on a general awareness of being.

In tai chi, too, there is a technique called "push hands." Here the backs of the opponents' hands make a moving point of contact. During training, a rose petal or butterfly wing will be placed between the hands. The opponents must not press too hard against each other or the petal or wing will be crushed. Nor must they press too lightly, allowing the petal or wing to fall. The purpose, as one teacher described it, is "to undo a person's natural instinct to resist force with force, teaching the body to yield to force and redirect it." In the martial arts in general, a student can try too hard by using tension to move their body in the correct manner. Of course, the goal is to hold an effortless attitude and fall into the flow of things. Making too much of an effort becomes counterproductive. My own experience as a tai chi student of many years included a time where I was working on letting go of the tension held in my left hip. This tension, I believed, was necessary to hold me up. At one point the teacher came around and helped me release the hip, whereupon I thought I was going to literally fall. Instead, I found myself shifting into a state of deep relaxation and felt as if I were floating, being held up by *chi* rather than muscular force.

This principle is important for the psychotherapist as well. Countertransference can show up as trying too hard to help one's client, wanting their release too much. Instead, healing is always better fostered with an attitude of acceptance—accepting the client's level of readiness with a patient willingness for the healing to take as long as it needs to.

It's essential that we recognize the subtle defense of "resisting resistance." It can interfere with progress as much as avoiding fear can. A defense is a defense, no matter how sophisticated it is, and will always maintain and aggravate our fear. Training our awareness of this final defense, we may practice doing its opposite. The paradox of trying too hard is that the harder we try, the less we advance. Instead, we accept our lack of acceptance, facing the fear of not facing fear, and short-circuit the whole problem. This is the "psychological jiu-jitsu" (M. Pressman, 1999) that brings resolution.

A NEW WAY TO LET GO OF RESISTANCE

Even though, when resisting resistance, the exercises have become the target of our defense, we can still use them to find our way out. Because a problem is always about resistance (defensiveness)—even if it is a resistance to resistance—we can "do the opposite" in the ways we have already learned. We simply apply any of our exercises to the fear of not getting free of anxiety. We might try the Witness, floating with the physical sensation of this fear. Or we could utilize the Alchemist, living through the movie in our mind of "what happens next" if we don't get rid of it. We could also refuse to move in any way against the fear with the Warrior's Stance, to see once again that nothing terrible happens if we let it wash over us.

And this will usually work. However, the defense of trying too hard is crafty and very subtle. We can even start trying too hard to let go of trying too hard! This is the defense of resisting the resistance to resistance, trying too hard to not try too hard to get rid of anxiety, fighting too hard not to fight it. All this hides the same anxiety of having anxiety. I've even seen people get caught in trying too hard to not try too hard to accept anxiety and then, realizing that mistake, trying too hard to not try too hard to not try too hard to accept it, and so on, creating a really nasty loop. When stuck in this rut, we might have to "do the opposite" by giving up our practices altogether until the knot of resistance releases.[6] But this, too, can bring up the deep fear of never getting free of fear. We have seen the power of our exercises and don't want to let them go. Even if we think we are up to the challenge, we must be wise to our motives . . . the resistance to resistance may show up again with the thought "I will give up my practices so that I can get back to them."

The reason it can be so difficult to let this go is because, once again, it confronts our basic strategy for survival as a separated self—the strategy of control. This core defense has hijacked our thoughts.[7] The resistance to resistance locks this in further, using control to try too hard to let go of control. As our most basic defense, the bedrock of the human experience, the wish for control is the mantra of the separate self seeking its autonomy and exerting its will. But we must remember that the idea of a separate self and its need for control is a projection of our own making. As we continue to deconstruct the core defense, instigator of all projections, we look for its essential components. Finding them would enable us to stop the projection before it starts. If it is already in progress, we will be able to see what keeps generating it, moment to moment, and interrupt the process. Because the projection of control is the source of all resistance, discovering its fundamental components will give us access to the levers and dials that operate it. Instead of being caught in a movie of fear, we will recognize it as a movie and simply step out of it. Or, sitting in the "control" booth, we can stop the movie and replace it with another one. So if trapped by resistance to resistance and unable to find our way out with the exercises, we want to work instead with the source of resistance itself—the impulse to take control—sidestepping the problem before it captures us. This will be a new way of letting go of resistance that can quickly and easily resolve fear at its source.

THE FIVE COMPONENT THOUGHTS OF CONTROL

So we continue our deconstruction of control, in search of its ultimate components. We will start with the Doorway of the Mind to find the thoughts underneath it. The first thing we discover when we do is, as we have already seen, that we are constantly asking the question "How do I feel right now?" This is how we assess whether or not our efforts at control are working—whether they are bringing us closer to security and fulfillment or threatening to take these things away. We ask this question incessantly. It is literally how we orient ourselves in any situation. It is the consequence of our separation from wholeness and the resultant ubiquity of fear. You might better understand it as the question we continually ask ourselves about whether or not things are going "well." It is why, for instance, we always ask each other, "How are you?"

Upon further deconstruction, we find there are five component thoughts that make up this question. As the essential ingredients of control, these five thoughts are the organizing principles for all our projections. It is these thoughts that fuel the impulse to exert our will, projecting the idea there is something we must take control over, stimulating and feeding our defenses. They are all, in some form, a way of convincing us that action is needed and that we (the separate self) are the ones to take that action. They entice us to resist, to impose our wishes upon reality and try to have it conform to our ideas. Exposing these makes it possible to "do the opposite" and disengage from resistance as well as the resistance to resistance.

The five component thoughts of control that motivate all resistance are:

1. "Something is wrong."
2. "I have to fix what is wrong."
3. "I must make sure I get the outcome I want."
4. "I alone must make sure problems are taken care of."
5. "I am capable of exercising control over reality."[8]

1. "Something Is Wrong"

First is the idea that something is wrong with what is going on "out there" in reality. Control, and therefore resistance, arises in response to the idea that we cannot accept things as they are. This creates the basic anxiety of the human condition, leaving us feeling as though we are not "at home" and cannot settle in or rest. We human beings seem wired to look for what is wrong.[9]

2. "I Have to Fix What Is Wrong"

Declaring that something is wrong—with reality, our life, other people, or ourselves—automatically leads to the next thought in our core defense: "I must fix what is wrong." This idea necessarily creates anxiety because it is immediately followed by "What if I don't succeed?" Saying "something is wrong," therefore, *makes* something wrong, as we have seen (resistance creates the problem). When we hold the thought that something is wrong, it becomes our reality—we are no longer at peace with things as they are.

3. "I Must Make Sure I Get the Outcome I Want"

The next component thought in the defense of control is "I must make sure I get the outcome I want" (or alternatively, "I have to arrange circumstances to be the way I wish"). Of course this is similar to "I have to fix what's wrong" but is more general, speaking to our overall goal of fulfillment. It comes from our question once again: "Is this situation fostering or threatening my purposes?" or simply "How is everything going?" We are hypervigilant about anything that can threaten our objective. Once we have assumed something is wrong and that we are to fix it, we lock our sights on the final picture of how we want things to look, vowing never to rest until we have succeeded in making them that way.

4. "I Alone Must Make Sure Problems Are Taken Care Of"

Even if we let others help us, we use the tension of resistance to make sure we get the outcome we want by assuming final responsibility for the job. After early childhood, we entrust our safety and fulfillment to no one more than ourselves. Again, we continually judge what's wrong, specifically and overall, to try to fix it, and only we can be the arbiter of how well that project is going. In truth, what is at stake is the entire idea of the separated self projecting the world it wants in order to affirm its own existence.

5. "I Am Capable of Exercising Control Over Reality"

Buried in the other four component thoughts of control is the assumption that it is possible to get control in the first place. The attempt to fix what we have declared is wrong, to set things up as we wish, and to believe we alone can ensure our success assumes an ability, even a right, that we do not have. It is fear's insistence on seeing the truth it wants rather than the truth that is. We have authorized ourselves as gods of our own world, pretending that we know how it should be arranged and have the ability to arrange it so. We would compel reality to bow to our demands. This is the basis for all our disillusionment as we go through life with wild dreams and expectations of how, as George Bernard Shaw (2001) said, the world should "devote itself to making me happy." This fifth component thought is a powerful tool in the arsenal of control.

All of these together create the sense that we are separate from where we need to be, having an experience other than the one we should be having. They therefore compel us to resist the reality we are in and try to create a different one. Yes, this is our attempt to reach wholeness and fulfillment, but always by keeping ourselves separate from it. We assume fulfillment is not available here and now. By resisting what is here and now, we perpetually postpone fulfillment, working toward a time in the future when we can finally "arrive." This keeps us forgetting who we truly are, locked in an experience of always "becoming," never "being." And this is how resistance creates suffering. This is why resistance *is* suffering—it creates the separation that keeps us from our good. It is what sets us up to live a life of constant yearning, driven by the hope of getting "there." Ultimately it wears us down, exhausting us, depleting our reserves. Whether we are chasing money, fame, love, or security of any sort, all defenses, and the resistance we use to enact them, backfire.

As we bring these thoughts out from hiding into the light of day, we see that they, too, are arbitrary projections—that they are "made up." It is we who decided to declare something was wrong, that we alone must fix it, etc. Blowing the whistle on their deception, we may withdraw such projections, no longer believing them to be real or even helpful. Perception shifts and the picture of control we hoped to achieve loses its luster. We unhook ourselves from our investment in it and simply let it go. With this, we no longer have to face the fear of what is wrong or the fear of not being able to ensure the outcome we wish. Instead, we see these projections forming and simply step back before they do.

AN EXERCISE FOR RELEASING RESISTANCE

We can create a formal exercise for this. If we were to achieve a complete insight into how they are operating within, the five component thoughts of control would lose their meaning. Our projections, based on these thoughts, would be seen as purely arbitrary and would dissolve by themselves. But having become such an automatic habit, these thoughts can be hard to lift out from the background. We can assist in this by evoking the resistance they inspire. That is, we can see the projections by their effects (the resistance). And how do we evoke this resistance? By "saying the opposite" of our five thoughts, challenging their assumption of control. This challenge not only helps us see the projections but, once seen, enables us to let them go, releasing all resistance as we do.

Our practice for releasing resistance starts with noticing the five component thoughts of control at work within us, trying to seduce us into action at any given moment. Then we practice pulling back from them as we repeat their opposite:

- "Nothing is wrong."
- "I don't have to change or fix anything."
- "I don't have to 'make sure' I get a certain outcome."
- "It's not up to me alone; I don't have to be responsible for the outcome."[10]
- "I can't get enough control to force reality to be my way."

Other variations might include

- "There's nowhere I have to go and nothing I have to do."
- "Everything is truly okay just as it is."
- "I am safe right now."
- "I don't have to fight to make things the way I want."
- "I can rest and let things unfold as they will."
- "I can tolerate this discomfort or unpleasant situation."
- "I am 'big enough' to absorb what's happening."
- "I don't have to get anywhere, accomplish anything, or make things different in any way."
- "I don't have to settle things or get them under control right away."
- "I can float with the anxiety, as if I have no ground under my feet" (cf. Chodron, 2002).
- "I may be here in this experience of tension or anxiety for a long time" (cf. the Alchemist).
- "I can enter fully into the sensation of the tension in this moment" (cf. the Witness).[11]

As we practice this exercise, we want to make sure we are actually seeing one or more of the five component thoughts of control. Only then can we effectively pit them against their opposites, appreciating that they really are arbitrary creations we have made up. As you recite the corrective words, imagine what it would be like if they were actually true. It won't do to just repeat these words in an automatic, unthinking way. We still have to face the fear of considering what they genuinely mean. Find your own wording to bring the ideas to life and keep them fresh.

When you are experiencing anxiety, when you feel pressured to fulfill some obligation, when you find yourself worrying, straining, or feeling unsettled, seeing these hidden thoughts in a deep way makes it possible to step back from them and release the resistance that is catching you.

AN EXERCISE FOR RELEASING THE RESISTANCE TO RESISTANCE

But here again, we can find ourselves trying too hard, using this exercise to secretly work for control over anxiety, trying to force the outcome we want. If that is the case, we have the following exercise for releasing the resistance to resistance, achieving the same meta-awareness of the problem of control at an even deeper level.

After repeating, "Nothing is wrong," "I don't have to fix anything," "I don't have to make sure I get anywhere or change anything," etc., we want to then add some version of the following:

- "I don't have to make sure I succeed with this exercise."
- "It's okay if I don't get free of tension or anxiety with this exercise."
- "There's nothing wrong if I don't or can't see that there is nothing wrong."
- "I don't have to fight to make this exercise turn out well. I can rest."
- "When I think I have to make it all work out, I actually create the problem."
- "I don't have to do anything but relax."

- "It's okay if I don't relax."
- "I don't have to make sure I let go of making sure I let go."
- "I don't have to make sure I get any experience at all."
- "I don't have to do anything. And I don't have to make sure I realize that."
- "I don't have to do a particular something, and I don't have to not do it."
- "I am free to do that something and free not to."

If one is simply too stuck to let go of the resistance to resistance with this exercise, we still have an answer: "Nothing is wrong with being stuck; I don't have to fix that problem." This will mean giving up trying to do the exercises altogether for the time being. As we said, this can indeed be scary . . . a true confrontation with the possibility of having to live with fear. After a lifetime of trying to get control over it, we are now being asked to let go of our most powerful habit. But remember that anxiety always passes and we are only being skillful in applying our strategies for seeing that it is not real, even if we are not ready to see it at a particular moment. In the meantime, we can use whatever is available to us to make ourselves comfortable, including distraction, some form of fulfillment or fun, performance of an abreaction of the pressure as in Gestalt therapy, etc. It may even be helpful to do something that provides a sense of control—not to buy into the belief that control is necessary but simply to release the resistance of trying too hard to let go of it. This is not a prescription for avoiding fear but a means to restore balance so we can get back to our practice with ease and flow at a later point. Most of all, we want to avoid the mistake of trying even harder to use the exercises as given. Instead, we wait and do whatever works to release the fixation. Eventually our "brainlock" will relax and we will remember ourselves once again, seeing that the fear was but a made-up projection.

THE ULTIMATE PRACTICE FOR RELEASING RESISTANCE

And still, there is one more way to release resistance, the most advanced practice possible. This approach bypasses the thoughts that entangle us in the resistance to resistance altogether. Remember, if the

Doorway of the Mind isn't available to us, we want to try the Doorway of the Body, the Doorway of the Spirit, or both. And that is what we will do now.

Along with the thoughts "Something is wrong," "I must fix it," etc., there is a *feeling* that occurs when we start to take control. This is the physical and spiritual movement of resistance, the contraction that comes from trying too hard. We experience this feeling as a tension, an interruption in flow. [12] If still caught after trying the exercises above, we may release the knot of resistance by relaxing this tension. Noticing the feeling of tension permits an inside view of the source of resistance, the initial stirrings of the impulse to control. And because we are working at the root level (the core defense), we can relax out of the process before it starts. So to release resistance, as well as resistance to resistance, we may simply concentrate on the feeling of tension it creates and then relax out of it. The tension is our cue that we are trying too hard. We notice the movement of it, like a hand inside rising up to form a claw that is ready to grasp, or a fist that is ready to hit, or a palm that is ready to push away. And in noticing it, we simply "do the opposite" and pull it back. Having deconstructed anxiety down to its very beginning, there is nothing further we need to do. We clearly see the button that, if pushed, would build the hologram of our projections, and we leave it untouched. [13]

This is vastly different from telling someone to "just relax." If they are not aware of the potential for trying too hard, if they do not see that it is a form of resistance, they will hear "just relax" as an invitation to *try* (too hard) to relax, reinforcing the problem once again. But when we notice and then relax out of such tension, we uproot the problem at its source. We uproot not only the resistance but "the resistance to the resistance" and thereby pull the rug out from under the whole thing. We have exposed the source and seen through its ultimate trick: using control to let go of control. When we notice the tension of trying too hard, we can't end up trying too hard; if we did, we would notice the tension of it!

We feel this tension primarily in the Nexus point. As we pull back and relax, we become highly tuned to the movement of the Nexus point. We begin to notice that every time we want to exercise control, to somehow change our experience, there is a subtle movement that contracts the Nexus point. When it combines with a thought about what the movement means, it starts the projection process, funneling the undifferentiated state of Oneness into manifest form. As we relax the tension, we let the projection sink back down into the realm of pure potential. We withdraw the meaning we assigned it, declaring there was something wrong that needed to be fixed, before the projection fully takes form. We rest in the place "before" projection, in a stillness and peace in the Nexus point that is perfectly balanced. There is no movement, no pulsing contraction. Just a deeply fulfilling balance. The final test of whether our path is true is whether it releases all tension, bringing this state of quietude and fulfillment. Only from there can we take appropriate action for change.

To summarize then: When we resist, we contract the Nexus point from its expanded state of undifferentiated Oneness. As with a prism dividing white light into separate discrete colors, or a Play-Doh machine squeezing out different forms from a non-distinct mass of clay, the world of manifestation thus appears. When we release resistance, we relax the Nexus point, stepping back and letting that world disappear. Withdrawing our attention from it, we stop projecting the perception of it. Instead of believing we are shadows on Plato's cave wall, we discover who we truly are . . . sitting by the fire and witnessing the whole scene. When well-established here, we can choose our next step without the influence of fear, moving toward wholeness, harmony, and flow.

This strategy makes it possible to release fear in a continuous way. We simply notice and let go of the stream of temptations to exercise control, to resist. We have tapped into the mechanism of projection, sending out the movie of our moment-by-moment experience. With our hands on the controls of the projector, we may stop the movie any time we wish, replacing it with one that works better or simply resting behind the scenes.

It is the ubiquity of fear that gives us the opportunity to practice continuously. Any time we are in action—trying to win control, reaching for goals, making progress, keeping to our agenda, etc.—we want to check the impulse to jump in and instead, first, relax. We can also be mindful of the thoughts that tell us something is wrong, in need of a fix, and so forth. Our goal is to rest in Oneness, identifying it as our true home, and choosing how we move toward fulfillment from there.

Letting go of resistance and the resistance to resistance resolves all five core fears. It dismantles the core defense and therefore all other defenses (chief and secondary) as well. It dissolves the projection of a separate self that can harbor a core fear and chief defense, for it is this separate self that chooses to resist, trying to secure its fulfillment in fear-based ways. Without a controlling self, there is no world to control, only the experience of Oneness where opposites are reconciled, conflict is resolved, and all the problems of separation are healed. This is when, as the great Zen master Dogen said, "body and mind both drop away." Or when, as Don Juan said to Carlos Castaneda, we "stop the world" (1991). Or when, in the language of Buddhism, we discover the "no self" that experiences an intimate unity with all things.

TECHNICAL TIPS FOR MASTERING THE PRACTICE

We now have a gold standard for measuring our success in releasing resistance: we know that we are free of resistance only if we *feel* relaxed. Our job is to encourage an increasing sensitivity to whatever blocks this feeling.[14] We want to become intimately familiar with the subtle push, the pressure and drive, of trying too hard, grabbing at the results we seek. It's a matter of fine-tuning our awareness of the feeling of trying too hard—and then *relaxing*. We catch ourselves trying too hard in a way that creates tension and then step back. Again, it feels like relaxation, like relief (from fear or whatever emotion was masking the fear). We can know that if we haven't found a genuine relaxation, there must still be a resistance operating behind the scenes. This is how we let go of control and escape the trap of trying too hard.

When we relax the tension of resistance, we are actually performing each of our earlier exercises in an instant. By releasing control, we are automatically confronted with the possibility that we will have to sit in the scene of our core fear forever, as in the Alchemist. It can therefore be helpful to flash back to that scene, remembering the freedom and fulfillment we found there. Similarly, in order to relax out of tension, we must let the physical sensations of it float freely, without trying to change them, just as in the Witness. Further, since resistance uses movement to effect its purpose, when we relax out of it, we actively refuse to "move" (mentally, physically, and spiritually) when tempted to take control—just as with the Warrior's Stance. We rest in the Nexus point, resolute and immovable, and remember the freedom this brings. Finally, whether consciously or not, we rehearse the thoughts of the "resisting resistance" exercises as we relax, reminding ourselves, "Nothing is wrong," "There's nothing I have to fix," "There's nowhere I have to go," etc.

Again, we want to practice *living in* the Nexus point, staying our mind there at the seat of the true self, resting in Oneness more and more. Ultimately, we want to keep our attention there continuously, moving from our "center."[15] Of course, this takes great commitment and plenty of patience. Our investment in projection has been practiced for a lifetime and doesn't give up easily. And above all, we don't want to add fear to the project by becoming anxious or guilty if we forget. We are looking for overall progress rather than the status of the moment. If we forget, the only appropriate response is to return to our practice as soon as we remember. But it's also important to understand that, in the end, it's really just a matter of choice. Only our projections will convince us that it's "difficult" to let them (our projections) go. And so we use the feeling of tension as a reminder to return again and again. If the tensions are subtle and hard to detect, we can help ourselves, as before, by holding our breath for a moment, perhaps squeezing down on the diaphragm a bit. This concentrates the tension in the Nexus point, making it easier to place our awareness on it. And as with the Witness, we can heighten the sensation by repeating the word "feel" several times. If we get caught in trying too hard, we consider giving up our practice altogether. While this takes courage, we remember it simply won't work to "try" our way out of the problem. But as we accept our lack of control, we feel the release of tension we were looking for and allow our attention to gently rest in the Nexus point once again.

At the most advanced level, we see our tension as neutral, not attaching any meaning to it. We let it float without resistance, softening around it, allowing it to be just as it is. Without resistance, our experience of it transforms. Because we have withdrawn the projection of it as something negative, it reveals itself to be just "energy." Seen in its most elemental form, this energy becomes interesting, even fascinating. It is the living experience of Oneness made manifest in form. It testifies to the extraordinary fact of consciousness . . . that it *is*, that it is alive and able to register such energy. Standing as witness, we watch, as if in slow motion, our projections taking shape as perception. We can almost see the lines of this perception being drawn in a uniform field of energy, giving rise to a particular "thing" or mood or experience. Or if we prefer, we simply rest in the undifferentiated peace of Oneness.

If the idea of staying in the Nexus point continuously brings up a concern that we will be too detached from the world, then know this too is a fear to be worked through. It is a fear of letting go of the investment in our projections. But entering and remaining in the Nexus point is our key to release from suffering, our path to freedom and fulfillment. In no way does this create unhealthy detachment or a laissez-faire outlook. We are simply standing in the place where we are free to choose our way. If detachment is called for, we will experience relaxation from too much trying. If involvement in the world is most helpful, we will do so without tension and in the most effective way possible. So yes, we want to return to this place and ultimately remain there, noticing and letting go of resistance at deeper and deeper levels.

Here's a way to foster this goal. As you practice any one of the previous exercises, pay attention to the moment when you decide it's time to finish and return to your familiar projections. Before you do return, ask yourself what it would be like to stay in the exercise forever. We had a taste of this with the Alchemist. The decision to finish an exercise is a decision to take fear's hand once again. What if, instead, we stayed "in" the exercise while going about our day? This is perfectly possible. We might do the same things as usual but without resistance. Consider what this would mean. Without the identity of a separate self that must exercise control, we step back from the consensual agreement to push, fight, judge, attack, and defend our way through life. We watch such impulses as arbitrary projections that don't help us reach fulfillment after all. Without the idea of a separated self, our definition of fulfillment moves away from our private interests and on toward the whole. Again, we may conduct ourselves as before but now without fear and tension, choosing our activities consciously, no longer driven by a need to obtain control. And remember, if we are connected by a morphogenetic field, as we release our identification with the separate self, we help others do the same, entering the Nexus point to find fulfillment in a collective Oneness.

NOTES

1. The separate self cannot exist if it is not exercising control; pushing against reality gives it its sense of separation. At the same time, control cannot exist if it is not being employed by "someone," a separate self. We may say that the two co-arise.

2. We have said that resistance is the action component of a defense, and control is the aim of all defenses.

3. Reinhold Niebuhr's "Serenity Prayer" makes the same distinction between trying and trying too hard: "Grant me the serenity to accept the things I cannot change, the courage to change the things that I can, and the wisdom to know the difference." This is our path, too, working to make positive change but not from a place of anxious need. Rather, we adopt a serenity that first is willing to let go of an insistence on change. Only then are we in a clear position to make change, free of fear's investment in a particular outcome.

4. This term captures the essence of an important part of the Buddha's teaching. When he was still Siddhartha Gautama, meditating by a riverbank and practicing extreme asceticism, he heard a music teacher giving a lesson on a boat floating by. The teacher told his student, "If you tighten the strings of the instrument too much, they will snap. If you leave them too slack, they will not play music." Siddhartha realized the truth of this "middle way" and gave up his asceticism while still working on his mind, this time with a gentle but firm holding of awareness. He credited this as key to his eventual enlightenment.

5. One such koan goes like this: "Enlightenment is unattainable; how will you attain it?" Here the ideals of striving and non-striving are pitted squarely against each other.

6. It may take a while before the knot of resistance releases and you can safely go back to the exercise. You'll know it's safe when your mind has let go of its grip and stopped thinking about the problem altogether. On the other hand, it may only take a moment if you become truly willing to give up the practice. This will bring an immediate feeling of relaxation. Then instead of rushing back into the exercise with the risk of trying too hard again, you can gently place your attention on this feeling of relaxation in the Nexus point and let it rest there without effort. This is the place the exercises are designed to arrive at anyhow.

7. We have seen this principle before. Any time there is interference with our exercises, it is always some form of our chief defense at work preventing us from facing and moving through the fear it is protecting.

8. Of course there are plenty of variations on these five thoughts, including "I have to get back to a state of being that I used to have," "I must get free from

where I am and arrive at where I want," "I have to fight to get what I want," "It's up to me," "I have to," "I want," "I don't want," etc.

9. It's helpful to realize our ideas of what is wrong are ultimately based on the five core fears: "Something is wrong if I don't have perfect love, if I don't know who I really am (identity), if I don't have enough value (meaning), if I don't have enough purpose," and "Something is wrong if I am not physically well and safe." This is really another way of saying the core fears are responsible for everything we are upset by, i.e., everything that is "wrong." This also explains our (ubiquitous) need to judge, a crucial part of the dynamic of control. We judge not just to praise or cast aspersions on others but to make sense of our world, to see that the meanings we have assigned to things all work together in a coherent way. Judgment is an attempt to get control by making sure that nothing is unaccounted for, that nothing can take us by surprise or leave us uncertain. It is the defense of trying to organize our accounting of things, protecting us from an unsettling vulnerability when we don't understand something. Consider, for example, our automatic response to a magic trick. We immediately ask, "How'd they do that?" And any time we find something mysterious, we insist, "There must be a logical explanation."

10. Once again it bears repeating: we are not abdicating responsibility, becoming complacent, or sitting back without taking appropriate action for change. We are simply releasing the resistance that would have us try too hard to make a change, freeing us to see clearly the most effective change possible in the moment.

11. It is because we are working with the deepest level of insight, the basic elements of the core defense, that this kind of thought replacement is possible. If someone hasn't first uncovered the many layers of fear and defense we have worked with to get to this point, the competing thoughts of resistance will prevent our new thoughts from penetrating through. As before, we must dig up the true root of a problem if we are to make effective change.

12. The words "feeling" and "tension" here are not meant to describe an emotion but only the physical and spiritual elements of resistance. As we have seen, any negative emotion includes the contraction of resistance, but it only becomes an emotion when it combines the physical, spiritual, and mental elements. When we assign a cognitive meaning to a particular physical and spiritual tension, we give a name to (and therefore bring to life) the emotion we feel.

13. It can be helpful to join this approach with our other two exercises for releasing resistance above, thereby combining mind, body, and spirit. We repeat the phrases in those exercises, realizing that "nothing is wrong, there is nothing to fix, etc.," while relaxing out of resistance. This is a powerful combination, but remember not to use the phrases to try too hard.

14. Until we develop this sensitivity, we won't notice many of the subtle tensions we carry because we are so used to them. As we continue our practice, this sensitivity comes spontaneously, enabling deeper and deeper release along the way.

15. This is similar to tai chi's goal of moving always from the tian tien.

15

"VISION QUESTING"

The Pursuit of Fulfillment

The greatest tragedy in life is to die with your music still in you.

—Anonymous

Now well established on the path to freedom from fear, we may at last open the doors of fulfillment. We have seen our core fear clearly and exposed the chief defense it was hiding under all along. And we have become adept at doing the opposite of the chief defense. This is the simple formula we rely on to deconstruct the anxiety at the root of all suffering. We use this formula to face our fears, practicing the Alchemist, the Witness, or the Warrior's Stance. For when we face fear, resistance dissolves and that which we were resisting is seen to be illusory. We may also use the Doorway of the Mind to release resistance (and the resistance to resistance) by rehearsing the opposite of its component thoughts. Or with the doorways of the Body and the Spirit, we may simply notice the tension of resistance and relax out of it. With this, the dancing images of our projections transform. We break free from the hypnosis of fear as well as its other deceptions and manipulations. Each time we step back from the projections of fear, we undo the very idea of separation, remembering the absolute truth of Oneness. The ceaseless search for security from fear gives way to the pursuit of a fulfillment that was our goal in the first place.

FIVE ASPECTS OF FULFILLMENT

Fulfillment comes with the resolution of the five core fears, no longer masking the transcendent experience we seek.[1] The five core fears, we may say, are transformed into the five aspects of fulfillment. Instead of projections about loss, they become opportunities for fulfillment. We seek:

1. Fulfillment in love—giving and receiving it.
2. Fulfillment in identity—knowing and being who we truly are.
3. Fulfillment in meaning—discovering the inherent value of our existence and of creation.
4. Fulfillment in purpose—expressing ourselves fully and contributing our talents, gifts, and passions.
5. Fulfillment in a peaceful acceptance of death—having lived life fully and feeling complete in the end.[2]

These, broadly described, are our five goals when pursuing fulfillment. They show up as spontaneous impulses that direct our life once core fears are resolved. They flow naturally when fear no longer blocks our path, allowing us to pursue the actions we might have taken all along if not for the undue influence of fear.

This doesn't mean, however, that we can predetermine what fulfillment should look like. Since fear obscures truth, we must always resolve it first before we can have a clear view of our next steps. Otherwise, we will fall back into the old habit of control, trying to secure a fulfillment we have prematurely decided should be ours. And of course, this will generate the fear of failing to do so. For instance, resolving the core fear of losing love does not automatically mean we will find the romantic partner of our dreams. It simply means that we resolve the fear of losing love. As with the Alchemist, the Witness, or any of our other exercises, fear is resolved when we are no longer afraid to lose that which we were defending. Only then are we able to see the truth of things. Only then can the most effective and appropriate path to fulfillment be appreciated. The great irony of using fear as a strategy for fulfillment is that it prevents us from seeing there are always many other options for fulfilling the need we were protecting so anxiously. For the fear of losing love, it may be that we find love through service to others, as Mother Teresa did so beautifully. Or we may find it in deep friendship, love for a child, or love from some spiritual source. We may also resolve the fear of losing love by becoming deeply peaceful with the idea of being alone. Or we may find love with a romantic partner. And even that will look very different from what we may have predetermined when looking through the lens of a fear-based need. Our ideas of romantic love have us projecting fantasies of "happily ever after" and never again encountering fear. But true fulfillment lies in working with where we are and transforming it, finding the freedom to be our authentic selves, giving and receiving love in ways that can work, with a meaning and purpose to help others do the same.

For another example, it's not for us to predetermine what forgiveness should look like. If we've had a difficult time with someone, we may plan a conversation asking for or giving forgiveness. But the other person may be too defended for this. If we are locked into the idea of such a conversation as our path to fulfillment, we will miss this point. The externals of a situation (projections) are not our concern; the forgiveness we seek is an internal affair. It comes from letting go of our own fears and defenses regardless of the other person's participation. Once achieved, this internal forgiveness may call for some external change, at least for us and possibly for the other person. But we can't know what that change should be in advance.

So universal prescriptions for fulfillment won't work. We must be deft in our pursuit, looking for how fulfillment wants to be expressed in the moment. Sometimes we discover it comes from being free to do that which we'd always wanted but were afraid to do. Sometimes it means living our life just as we have been living it, only now without fear and defensiveness.[3] Sometimes it means helping to change the world with action. Sometimes it means just resting after becoming exhausted by too much control. If that is the case, our rest is the most effective way to help others at that moment. Fear and defensiveness insist on one idea of what fulfillment should look like, creating a particular projection about how to reach our goal. As a defense, this will backfire. Instead of calling forth an experience of Oneness, it will create further separation. Without the blinders of fear and defense, however, we will discover a vast array of alternatives in any given situation. And no longer invested in one over the others, we will automatically recognize which would bring the greatest fulfillment.

VISION QUESTING: FINDING OUR "MIGHTY PURPOSE"

Fulfillment shows up spontaneously once the fears that were blocking it are resolved. But while our mastery of fear is incomplete, we can facilitate its arrival with a process I call Vision Questing. And because fear and fulfillment are inversely proportional, this process helps resolve further fear. When we find a vision for fulfillment, taking action to bring it into the world, we have a final and powerful method for resolving anxiety. Opening the Doorway of the Spirit, we find what George Bernard Shaw (2001) called "a mighty purpose":

> This is the true joy in life, the being used for a purpose recognized by yourself as a mighty one, the being a force of nature instead of a feverish selfish little clod of ailments and grievances complaining that the world will not devote itself to making me happy.
>
> I am of the opinion that my life belongs to the whole community and, as long as I live, it is my privilege to do for it whatever I can. I want to be thoroughly used up when I die, for the harder I work, the more I live.
>
> I rejoice in life for its own sake. Life is no brief candle to me. It is a sort of splendid torch I've got to hold up for a moment and I want to make it burn as brightly as possible before handing it on to future generations.

In Vision Questing, we design a "picture of fulfillment," a vision for our life so compelling that it transcends fear by engaging us in something we deem far more important. In so doing, it fully absorbs our attention, stealing it away from fear. When our vision is powerful enough, we can move straight through the anxiety that would otherwise stop us from pursuing our good. This is our third kind of "doing the opposite," placing our focus on something entirely unrelated to fear, showing that it doesn't have the power to force a response or even hold our attention.

Finding our picture of fulfillment resets our perspective to what really matters. The spirit expands and offers its transcendent view. Our ordinary state of consciousness, with its narrow focus on the separate self, releases its contraction, its petty and mean obsession with control, making sure it gets what it wants and avoids what it doesn't. The constant drone in the background, "How do I feel right now?" gives way to an interest in the greater whole. Achieving this perspective is inherently healing. It lifts us out of the pain of our limitations into a wide and expansive sense of self, of possibility. This is the ultimate prescription for anxiety. It is our natural state, as we see in children who express themselves freely and fully, readily aware of the goodness of life, open to a sense of the mysterious and the miraculous.

We want to remember this magnanimous point of view, to participate in a grander scheme once again. As Marianne Williamson (1996) says,

> Our deepest fear is not that we are inadequate. Our deepest fear is that we are powerful beyond measure. It is our light, not our darkness that most frightens us. We ask ourselves, who am I to be brilliant, gorgeous, talented, fabulous? Actually, who are you not to be? And as we let our own light shine, we unconsciously give other people permission to do the same. As we are liberated from our own fear, our presence automatically liberates others.

Our vision calls us to be "bigger" than our fear. Our "mighty purpose" fills us with a generosity of spirit that transcends limitation and returns us to wholeness. When we find our vision, fear gets lost in its overpowering vista. Once having loomed so large in our awareness, it disappears in the boundless landscape of Oneness with which we are now identified.

STARTING WITH PURPOSE

In the pursuit of vision, we could start with any of the five aspects of fulfillment. As with the core fears, they are so intimately connected that fulfilling one aspect leads to fulfillment of the others. For example, one might think their greatest fulfillment lies in finding love, and indeed, "Love casts out fear." But so does finding a deep meaning or profound certainty of who we truly are. And if we have a solid sense of our true identity, unafraid to be our authentic selves, we will naturally want to connect with others in some appropriate gesture of love. This might constitute our purpose . . . giving love as healing whenever the need arises. And it would certainly fill one's life with meaning. Imagine, too, the incredible power of a vision that could transcend the fear of death or provide a meaning that fills the existential void one has struggled with for a lifetime. How would that change our old experience of identity, love, or purpose? So again, we can start with any of the five aspects of fulfillment and, satisfying it completely, take care of the other four at the same time.

As it turns out, it is helpful to start with the fulfillment of purpose for several reasons. First, we are already talking about the purpose of finding a vision. This is a meta-purpose—the purpose of fulfilling our need for fulfillment itself. Furthermore, as we find our fulfillment on any of the five aspects, there is a natural impulse to share it with others.[4] This sharing usually wants to be expressed as a purpose, the drive to make our contribution to the betterment of others. It's almost an instinct; when we find something that helps us, we want to share it. This is the movement toward Oneness and connotes a sense of purpose or, we might say, a mission. Some will feel it as an empathic need to relieve suffering; others, as a drive to promote joy or beauty. We see a world in need of healing and it calls us to purpose.

It's also helpful to start with purpose because it gives us a clear direction on how to spend our time. The other four aspects of fulfillment are more abstract and don't prescribe action in as direct a way. When we find our purpose, we begin taking actions that promote love (again, out of the desire to share what we have found), create meaning, and express who we truly are. And a deep purpose that has affected others or made a difference in the world gives a transcendent sense of something that survives our physical death. The contribution one makes with their purpose, because it affects a larger whole, can take on a life of its own as others pick up the call and continue its beneficial effects after we are gone.[5]

Purpose is about *expressing* ourselves fully—expressing our authentic identity, expressing our love freely and fully, and expressing what is meaningful to us, unconcerned with the time limits imposed by death. And then it is about taking *actions*[6] that fulfill those expressions. In Vision Questing we develop plans for action compelling enough that their sheer "size," if you will, their potential for fulfillment, overwhelms any fear that might try to stop us. Such fears are then seen to be insignificant or even illusory as they become engulfed by the power of our purpose. They never get energized into being, never get projected as perception, when all our attention is fixed on our vision.[7]

One final reason to start with purpose is that by focusing on action, it takes our practice from the realm of abstraction, where we have simply released ourselves from fear, into actualization, where we manifest the potentials that have been hidden by fear. In the absence of such action, there must be a fear advising us against it, and we'll want to do any of our previous exercises for resolving that fear first.

EXERCISES FOR FINDING ONE'S VISION

How do we find our vision? How do we design our picture of fulfillment? Some of us know it readily and have never lost touch with it. Many have tucked it away to avoid the fear of being ridiculed, of having hopes dashed, or of being told their dreams are not important enough. For some, the learned repressions of a lifetime have kept them from even remembering the possibility of fulfillment. But the drive for fulfillment is fundamental and will not quit. It is still there, buried perhaps, but waiting. The following exercises, then, are meant to help grease the gears of such awareness, to invigorate a sense of the possible, and to reawaken our urge to build a better world. First, we will create the picture of our fulfillment, then discuss how we may resolve any fears that might keep it from coming to fruition.

Creating the Picture of Fulfillment

So we begin by simply asking, "What is my picture of fulfillment?" Some will have difficulty answering in a meaningful way, having become deeply inured to the idea long ago. They may try to comfort themselves with the thought that at least they are getting by in life without too many problems. This may be tolerable for the body and mind, but it will never satisfy the spirit. To help find our picture of fulfillment, then, we start by considering the question "What would be possible if I were completely free from the five core fears?" To yield more specific answers, we ask the following questions:

How has fear been limiting me when it comes to giving and/or receiving love? Some examples include holding yourself back from or clinging to love, rejecting others before they reject you, taking care of others but not allowing them to take care of you, hiding your passion, and so forth.

How has fear been limiting me when it comes to my identity? Examples here might include wearing a mask or persona, carrying feelings of low worth, hiding your true expression, putting on pretensions, changing your personality to fit in with the setting, and trying to convince yourself you don't need to be recognized for something that is important to you.

How has fear been limiting me when it comes to finding meaning? Perhaps you busy yourself, seek stimulation and distraction or avoid boredom or emptiness in unproductive ways (e.g., addictions of all sorts), fall into depression with the feeling that all is meaningless, or avoid taking action on what would be meaningful to you.

How has fear been limiting me when it comes to taking action on my purpose? You might resign yourself to being "too tired" at the end of the day, forget to ask whether your goals are truly fulfilling, design your goals more for control and safety than for fulfillment, or ignore your dissatisfaction with the circumstances of your life or the circumstances of the world. Some might say that the whole idea of making a difference is "unrealistic," that we must accept a more cynical view. This too is a defensive response to fear, as we will discover with our exercises, and it will never satisfy our need for fulfillment.

How has fear been limiting me to seeking security and survival (safety from sickness, pain, and death)?[8] Some people stay in a job or relationship they're not happy with, become highly "practical," obsess over orderliness, or preoccupy themselves with health issues or finances, this time for security. Others are overly cautious, preparing for problems long before they come into view. Still others defend against an awareness of mortality, trying to look and feel young rather than keeping pace with the realities (and privileges!) of aging.

Your answers to these questions will begin to reveal new opportunities for fulfillment now that you have the tools to transcend such limits. In designing a picture of fulfillment, we can also consider the following:

- What are my deep values—what causes, injustices, dreams, etc., are most important to me?
- What are my commitments (or at least, what commitments would I like to make)—what values have I decided (or would like to decide) to firmly act upon and how?

- What are my gifts and talents?
- What are my passions?
- What expertise do I have?
- What lessons have I learned from life experience that might be helpful to others?

Often our fulfillment comes from "using" that which we have acquired throughout our lifetime. The talents, passions, and insights we have cultivated become opportunities to make a unique contribution no one else can make, one that we are expert in and care deeply about. Other times, our vision might want to be completely unrelated to our past as we dare to act upon dreams we've always been too afraid to pursue. Of course, the age-old habit of our fears can still try to inhibit us. But if the project is fulfilling enough, the excitement it brings will overwhelm the anxiety that had us bury the dreams in the first place.

We now bring together our answers to the questions above, creating our picture of fulfillment with the following steps. This can be a work in progress, evolving as we evolve, so you'll want to write it down. Writing it down also concretizes the picture, beginning the process of bringing your vision from the realm of abstraction into the world of form. We will use this concrete picture in the next exercise to set actions for its fulfillment.

1. Start with anything you already know would be fulfilling based on the questions above. Remember, fulfillment is not necessarily about what makes us "happy" in the traditional sense (which is often more about control over and safety from anxiety) but about the five aspects of fulfillment described above. It usually also includes making a contribution to others or impacting your environment in a helpful way.
2. Ask yourself (or trusted friends) what others value in you, see as your gifts, etc. What contributions would they say you already make? In what ways do you already "shine"? Alternatively, you can ask if they see you holding back your potential in any way.
3. Think about what evoked your excitement as a child or young adult and how you might translate that into appropriate action today. If the repressions of a lifetime keep us from even imagining what would be fulfilling, it can be helpful to consider dreams

from a younger age before the burden of too many defenses took hold.

4. Look at what you've struggled with, what has really mattered to you, what you have cared about deeply or worked for most earnestly over the years. All of these, as we have seen, spin off from our core fear and chief defense. We've devoted a lifetime to following their strategy, discovering what does and doesn't work in our pursuit of fulfillment. We know, better than anyone else, the intricate steps of the dance with life when our particular core fear and chief defense set the rhythm. And so we have been uniquely groomed to help others with our experience. After all, this has formed our personality and built our lifestyle. And with our exercises, we now know the pitfalls to avoid and the paths to choose. We have amplified those characteristics in personality that support fulfillment and let go of those that backfire. Without the distortion of fear, we are free to choose wisely when acting upon our goals. Consider what you have come to know and do better than anyone else because of your life path. Appreciate that you have a knowledge base and experience about this that no one else has. Ask yourself if you feel called to somehow use all this to help others. Or perhaps you feel complete with that part of your life, finished with the lessons it taught you, and want to move on to other things. On the other hand, maybe you want to enjoy what fear and defense have always held you back from or simply rest in the fulfillment of the present . . . or all of the above!

5. Practice thinking, in exaggerated, seemingly unrealistic ways, about what would be fulfilling. It does take practice to loosen the gears of this kind of thinking from the old restraints of fear and defense. Don't let yourself be limited by practicality at this point. We are trying to access the fundamental drive for, and excitement about, fulfillment. If we introduce practicality before fully getting in touch with this drive, you can be sure there is fear and defense at work.[9] Allowing yourself to fantasize in a big and free way is essential at this point.

6. Talk to others about your vision for fulfillment and, again, do it in a full, even exaggerated, way. Hearing ourselves speak about it— our high purpose, who we really are, what really matters to us, our dreams for giving and receiving love—has a powerful impact

and can open up new insights. When we share our vision with others, with the full confidence of our conviction, it no longer remains a nice but abstract idea. It suddenly starts to become very "real."

7. Finally, you can use the Doorway of the Body to physically push through any fears that might keep you from acting on the above. In the end, living one's vision is a matter of action (even if internally), *"doing* the opposite" of what fear and defense held you back from before. A Gestalt-type catharsis (as described in chapters 2, 4, and 13) can be helpful here to blast through such resistance to action. The power generated by this puts one in touch with a greatly expanded sense of what is possible, beyond the limitations imposed by fear and defense.

"Death as an Advisor"

It bears repeating: fear and defense will try to hold us back from, or at least water down, our picture of fulfillment. Fulfillment is meant to be, well, fulfilling . . . and wildly so. Any lukewarm sense of love, meaning, purpose, or identity is limited in direct proportion to the amount of fear in the way. We may say we are too tired or too cynical to believe in the possibility of true fulfillment but those are some of the voices of fear we are talking about. Such thoughts may relieve a momentary fear of taking action but will leave us deeply unsatisfied in the long run. We all feel the call of vision. Only fear would say otherwise. Consider this beautiful little poem by Anais Nin:

> And then the day came,
> when the risk
> to remain tight
> in a bud
> was more painful
> than the risk
> it took
> to blossom.

So we want to bring all of ourselves to this endeavor, reaching for a vision that is "soul sized" (Houston, 1997). One way to help evoke the call to vision is, as Don Juan said to Carlos Castaneda (1991), to use death as an "advisor."

Death is the only wise advisor that we have. Whenever you feel, as you always do, that everything is going wrong and you're about to be annihilated, turn to your death and ask if that is so. Your death will tell you that you're wrong; that nothing really matters outside its touch. Your death will tell you, "I haven't touched you yet."

Without fear to distort our interpretation, this is actually a joyful pronouncement. Nothing really matters outside death's touch because it sets the end goal for our fulfillment in this lifetime. Death is only scary when it threatens to take away what we want. [10] But we have shifted our attention from the fear of losing our dreams to the excitement of realizing them. Again, from Anais Nin: "People living deeply have no fear of death." We want to find our fulfillment more than anything else, and we want to do so before we die! Using death as an advisor, we can ask ourselves, "What does fulfillment look like for me such that nothing would be left incomplete by the time I die?" We can find similar support in the Evening *Gatha* (prayer) recited by Zen students: "Let me respectfully remind you, life and death are of supreme importance. Time swiftly passes by and opportunity is lost. Each of us should strive to awaken. Awaken. Take heed. Do not squander your life."

Using death as an advisor in these ways, we transform it from a core fear into a tool for finding our fulfillment. At this point, death comes as a natural transition when the purposes of life in a body have been achieved.

And don't assume that your vision necessarily involves some big, grandiose scheme or a radical change in lifestyle. Of course these are possibilities—and we must be open to them—but once again, our job is not to predetermine anything. Most often, we find that our present circumstances provide plenty of fertile ground for self-expression and fulfillment. We usually also find there is a reason for our circumstances, that they are meant to be used. Again, our lifetime's work of wrestling with fear and defense has brought us to where we are and might become our best vehicle for expressing ourselves. Whether a radical change, a grand vision, or something much more modest, we are to work through any fear and defense that would keep us from accepting the truth of what best serves the cause of fulfillment.

So as you design your picture of fulfillment, remember you are reaching for that which is most important to you, your greatest longing, that which you have been striving for in every moment throughout your life. Now the time has arrived for action and we are no longer willing to postpone it any further. Our excitement about this is our best tool for realizing the vision. We don't want to let the by-products of fear keep us from the excitement we would naturally feel. We're working to bring back the same kind of fulfillment that children can have, eager to greet the day, following the flow of joy. We want to express ourselves fully, leaving nothing untapped. As Walt Whitman said, we want to "sound [our] barbaric yawp over the rooftops of the world!"

Remember, too, that we cannot seek fulfillment for ourselves alone. We now know that our experience is thoroughly tied up with those around us. This puts us in a position to effect real change in the world and promote the cause of healing. We make our life a work of art, expressing that which is "highest and finest in us" (M. Pressman, 2011). This is what Gandhi meant when he said, "My life is my message." Or what Whitman meant when he wrote, "The powerful play goes on, and you will contribute a verse" (1855). As we weave together all we have learned to this point, we want to make our life a thing of beauty, our contribution enriching, helping to advance the world. The more masterful over the forces of fear we are, the more we can help others to become so as well, freeing them to pursue their fulfillment along with us.

Setting Goals on a Timeline

To realize these high ideals, our next step is to set goals for action. As we do, we will discover what might get in the way of reaching those goals, knowing that it will always be some form of our core fear and chief defense. Our task then is to resolve such obstructions with the tools we now have, redirecting toward our goal as necessary.

It can be helpful to set these goals on a timeline. This helps bypass the problem of perpetually postponing our intentions (or any other defense against taking action). Obviously there's no point in creating a picture of fulfillment if we don't act on it. But in setting our goals on a timeline, we must be wise to the possibility of "trying too hard." The timeline is not meant to be a new source of fear, adding the pressure of "having to" meet deadlines. Any structure we create should not be a hidden form of control; we want to be willing to give up the structure at a moment's notice. But we don't want to harbor a subtle fear of structure either. This is a time to practice the "resisting resistance" exercises, finding the middle way between trying appropriately and trying too hard. We have a goal, and it is extremely important to us, but at the same time, we don't "have to" fulfill it—nothing is wrong and there's nothing we "have to" control. As we design a vision, we are reaching for our deepest fulfillment, an absolute truth and a mighty purpose. But using our awareness of the core fear and chief defense, we are wise to the trap of control and let go of any subtle fear of not reaching these goals.

We can set short- and long-term goals. Short-term goals give us something to start working on right away. Fulfillment lives in a continual state of flow so we don't want to wait to get started. Long-term goals can carry us for a lifetime, and we have created a picture of fulfillment that is meant to last that long. The combination of short- and long-term goals makes it possible to realize our ultimate vision by breaking it down into manageable steps. You decide on the steps and the length of time each requires, making sure the vision is fulfilled by the end of your life.[11] But once again, you don't want fear and defense to be your guide in this.

Setting goals on a timeline serves another purpose as well. When we invariably get thrown off course, unable to meet a particular deadline, we consider whether any fear and defense was at work and use our exercises to resolve it. Then, without the distorting lens of fear, we see how to redesign our plans and get back on track. Remembering that nothing is more important to us than fulfillment, we are determined to find our way back. Still, as always, we want to be flexible enough to change our plans, even changing the picture of fulfillment. As we evolve, so does the vision. Without a rigid defense of our original plans, we are happy to change them to comply with a living (and evolving) picture of fulfillment.

Making Public Commitments—The Gandhi Approach

Another way to help ensure we take action is to make our commitments public. Not only do we want to speak about our vision to others, we want to announce the specific plans for action we intend.[12] This may bring up a fear of not being able to get out of the commitment, the fear of letting others down or losing face. But we *want* to lock ourselves in this way! If fear comes up, we have our tools to sort it out. If our freedom from fear were complete, we wouldn't have to make commitments, create a timeline, or do anything to ensure our fulfillment. It would flow naturally as a spontaneous expression of who we are and what we value. But until then, fear and defense will always try to reassert their authority, and we need strategies to help us through this. Making public commitments to action, even if only to one other person, is an effective motivator to help us keep our commitments when challenged.

As we have said, moving from abstract ideals into action can be daunting. When the proposition is suddenly before us, resistance can be strong. It's a very different thing to have a good idea in our head alone, a plan, even a commitment, than it is to declare it to others. With no one holding us accountable, our best intentions can easily be swept away in the rush of other demands. Old habits (defenses) tempt us to avoid our fear and derail our purpose. Making public commitments is a powerful antidote to this problem.

And since our vision is meant to impact those around us, when we make such public announcements, we may find that others want to become involved. At that point, the vision can take on a life of its own, gathering momentum as more and more people spread the word and take up the torch. This is the ultimate way to lock ourselves in. We are the ones who gave voice to the vision in the first place, and others now look to us as its spokesperson. Again, this may bring up fear, but only if we feel a responsibility that is not ours, born of a defensive need for control that is not ours either. Instead we follow the flow of development taking us where it will. We do not force a particular direction since the vision is intended to evolve and change form continuously. We only act as its shepherd, keeping it safe from fear and defense, ensuring it serves the purpose of fulfillment.

Gandhi used the principle of making public commitments masterfully. When he decided to protest the law requiring Indians to buy British salt, he didn't simply make salt. He announced that he was undertaking a 240-mile march to the sea and made the announcement as public as possible. He gathered reporters and, as he began marching, people in villages along the way joined in. This of course increased the momentum of the movement, and word spread across the world. When he finally arrived at the ocean, he made a single pile of salt. Clearly this little bit of salt was not meaningful in itself. But as a symbol of civil disobedience, it was so powerful that others picked up the vision and soon Indians everywhere were making their own salt. With this, his vision was inaugurated on a national scale. In a very real sense, the moment Gandhi made the commitment to march, the goal was accomplished. It wasn't the walk itself, it wasn't the making of salt. It was the shift from idea to action that set the rest in motion.

So too are we transformed the moment we make a public commitment. We have moved out of our isolated, separate self, waiting on the outskirts of our life, to become engaged with the movement of the whole. Imagine you are having a hard time deciding whether or not to enroll in a class or take a vacation. The moment you make a public commitment, registering for the class or signing up for the trip, any anxious deliberation is relieved, replaced by the excitement of knowing an adventure is in store. This is the excitement of being in action, moving toward our good and actualizing fulfillment. We no longer feel as vulnerable to the fear of losing purpose, meaning, identity, or love. We can even feel a subtle "victory" over death, focusing on life and aliveness in the present rather than the possibility of what might go wrong in the future. Of course there may still be fear, the same fear that made the decision difficult in the first place. But it is now overwhelmed by the excitement of living our vision.

When we lock ourselves into a commitment, our fear transforms. Instead of filling our mind with all that might go wrong and how to escape it, we have resolved there's no turning back. Our attention is now directed toward getting the job done. John F. Kennedy, when a boy, was out for a walk with his friend. His mother told him to make sure he was home by dinnertime. They were on their way back when they came to a wall. It was too high to climb over. If they walked around it, they would have been late for dinner. So Kennedy took off his hat and threw it over the wall. This was his commitment to his friend that they were going to have to find a way over the wall . . . and so they did.

Two other examples from Gandhi's life demonstrate the power of involving others in your vision. Early in his career, just starting out as a new lawyer, he was thrown off a train for riding in the section reserved for British citizens. This inspired his first protest against the injustice of British rule in India. He put a notice in the local paper announcing a meeting about the problem. He also called the press to provide coverage of the event. Using his British papers as a symbol, he began burning them one by one in the presence of the police. The police warned him against this as a small crowd gathered to watch. He did it anyway. The police began beating him. He continued burning the papers nevertheless. They beat him until he fell to the ground but still he continued. At this point, the reporter who had showed up began feverishly taking notes for his article to be published the next day, inspired by Gandhi's commitment. Word spread quickly, and his movement was launched.

On another occasion, this time when his movement was in full force, Gandhi planned a speech that once again would decry the injustices of British rule in India. Publicizing the speech widely, he was not in the least surprised when the police came to arrest him for sedition. As they began taking him to jail, his wife followed. The officers told her that she was not under arrest, only her husband. She responded, "If you take my husband, you will have to take me too since I will speak in his place." Of course, when they began taking her with them, a third person came forth saying the same thing, and another and another until the police realized there would not be enough room in the jail cells for everyone. The speech went on as planned.

Martin Luther King Jr. also used this principle of making public commitments.[13] We told the story earlier of his agony one night when he couldn't sleep, anxious about threats to his life and his family's. He wrote in a letter to a friend that he wanted to "quit" the movement that night but could not, with so many depending on him for their civil rights. It was only when he accepted there was no way to move but forward that his fear left him. The moment he did, he felt a powerful sense of guidance from above, a sanctioning of his decision. Shortly thereafter, he gave his extraordinary speech on the mall in Washington, including these words: "Like anybody, I would like to live a long life— longevity has its place. But I'm not concerned about that now. I just want to do God's will . . . And so I'm happy tonight; I'm not worried about anything; I'm not fearing any man." This is the power of vision to wipe out fear. And it was his commitment to others that helped him get there.

Mother Teresa had a vision to help "the poorest of the poor." She left the comfort and security of her convent to go out on the streets of Calcutta despite dire warnings for her safety. Appalled at the sight of people dying abandoned and alone, she went to the first such person she saw, picked him up in her arms, and tended to his needs. He passed away shortly thereafter, looking into her eyes and thanking her for helping him to die with dignity instead of like "a dog in the streets." Mother Teresa often said that if not for him, she would never have been able to help the millions of others (through her own efforts and those of the Sisters of Charity) that came after. In taking that first step, she made her public commitment—putting "love in action," as she called it. Others began to take notice and join in her efforts. Eventually, word spread and her work gained wider and wider attention. People gathered around the force of her vision, making it their own, until it became the worldwide movement it is today.

Viktor Frankl, whom we also spoke of earlier, had a vision so powerful that it helped him survive the concentration camps of World War II. At the height of suffering, he observed certain inmates giving away their last bit of soup or bread. This, he noticed, seemed to give them a purpose for living that transcended their circumstances. While others in the camp were choosing to end their life, throwing themselves against the electric fence, these people found a reason to live. Frankl caught the fire of this idea and developed his own vision from it. He would write down his observations on scraps of toilet paper, hiding them under the floorboards when SS guards came by. Even though he was often tempted to end his life as well, he became determined to share what he had discovered should he be released. This was his commitment to others, giving him a lifeline to the outside world. The book that resulted, *Man's Search for Meaning* (2006), draws its exceptional force and influence from the power of his vision, so great that it could overcome the most extreme kind of despair.

In making public commitments, giving our life to something larger than ourselves, our experience of separation is vanquished. We get swept up in the movement of the whole. Even if not helping others in any overt way, we still make our impact by demonstrating what it is to live our vision, living for fulfillment rather than fear and defense. Our demonstration is our public declaration, just as it was for Gandhi when he said, "You must be the change you wish to see in the world." Here he makes the case even more poignantly:

> We but mirror the world. All the tendencies present in the outer world are to be found in the world of our body. If we could change

ourselves, the tendencies in the world would also change. As a man changes his own nature, so does the attitude of the world towards him. This is the divine mystery supreme. A wonderful thing it is and the source of our happiness. We need not wait to see what others do.

CASE HISTORIES

Vision often comes, as we have said, from our unique insight into the core fear and chief defense—our life experience. Here's one example: Jennifer was a fifty-two-year-old holistic nurse. She worked in the cardiology unit of a traditional hospital. During our time together, she uncovered a core fear of abandonment and a chief defense of being a nurturer—taking care of others in the hope of feeling the fulfillment of love herself. Of course her nurturing was a good thing, but she was emotionally exhausted from a lifetime of it, never having let herself receive in return. In discussing her history with romantic relationships, I inadvertently opened up a deep pocket of pain. Her relationships had always left her bitterly disappointed. She would give and give and, in the end, feel taken advantage of by a partner who couldn't or wouldn't reciprocate. Working with the Warrior's Stance, she began "doing the opposite" by not giving to others unless she was sure it was fulfilling rather than draining to do so. During this time, she discovered her vision. She came into session one day and pronounced tearfully, "My heart has been broken every which way but loose. I want to help heal broken hearts." She didn't quite realize the coincidence until I pointed it out . . . that she worked in a cardiology unit! With this, she understood why she had been drawn to that specialty, saying, "I guess I wanted to heal broken hearts from the start." After she had fully laid out her picture of fulfillment, I asked her to make a public commitment (to me) about what her first step would be. Looking at her timeline, she declared that she would seek permission from the hospital to incorporate a certain holistic healing technique in her work with patients. When I saw her the next week, she was positively glowing, the exhaustion of her defenses seemingly erased from her face. The administration had approved her request and she was already using the technique. This enabled her to talk to and connect with her patients in a new way. She was able to sit with them, listening to their emotional pain, sharing her own story as appropriate, and offering what she called "a healing of the heart."

Here is an example of someone whose vision was to express that which fear had suppressed. Jennifer, a thirty-five-year-old woman, went through a session of holotropic breathwork (see chapter 7). At the end of the session, participants were instructed to draw a mandala reflecting their experience. Given a piece of paper with a circle on it and some crayons to draw, she found her arm frozen, locked in a spasm and impossible to move. She wrestled with this for quite some time but eventually broke free of the paralysis and began drawing mandala after mandala, gorgeous pieces that covered the workshop floor. Describing her experience, she remembered a time when she was a young girl "coloring" in her bedroom. Her parents saw her talent and became afraid that she would want to pursue a career as an artist. They took away her crayons and told her in a stern voice she must become a secretary or nurse. Afraid to disobey, she locked the impulse to draw, we might say, in the muscles of her hand and arm. When given permission to draw again these many years later, she broke through the resistance as the fulfillment of her self-expression overpowered the anxiety of it. She incorporated her rediscovered passion into daily life after this experience, saying that it made her feel "whole again."

And here is a demonstration of someone whose vision was simply to live in a way free from the constraints of fear and defense. Rubin was fifty-six years old and a highly successful radiologist. When he first came to see me, he owned and operated six radiology centers and was busily planning more. We discovered his core fear was a loss of identity, developed at the hands of a severely critical father who would never praise him. In response, he built a chief defense of trying to establish his identity by being extremely productive. He was continually running, generating, accomplishing . . . producing. In addition to the radiology centers, he had a large family to take care of, including a wife, four children, two stepchildren, and other relatives he took in from time to time. He also had a menagerie of pets as well as a few prized sets of collectibles, both of which required a good deal of time and energy. After we worked together for a little while, he slowed down enough to discover that none of this was making him happy. He was burned out and irritable from too many demands, especially with the radiology centers. To add insult to injury, every time his father would visit, Rubin would still get criticized, being compared to his even more successful brother. He began to recognize that his strategy for securing an identity was backfiring and would never bring him the fulfillment he sought.

One session, after going through a deep transformation with the Alchemist, Rubin resolved his core fear and chief defense to find his vision. No longer obliged to seek his father's approval, he wanted to throw off all unnecessary responsibility and "just play my guitar and compost my garden." This was his metaphor for enjoying the moment, looking at it with fresh eyes to see what fulfillment would call him to do. He didn't want to build an empire after all, nor did he want a vision that would require him to be productive in a different way. Instead, he wanted to experience the simple joys of whatever the moment suggested. Over time, he sold his radiology practices, relieving himself of what he now saw as a burden. He realized he could make the same amount of money by hiring himself out as an independent contractor, reading films sent over the Internet while enjoying more time at home. We also worked on allowing his children to assume more responsibility for themselves so he wouldn't have to. This of course was helpful for all concerned. Eventually he sold his collectibles too, deciding they had served their purpose and were now creating "clutter." And he has indeed been playing his guitar, as well as taking vacations (which he never used to do), going to hear his favorite musicians perform, and exploring spontaneous ways to enjoy the moment.

The following story is a beautiful testimony to the idea of transforming one's fear into a vision. Before he found his vocation, Francis of Assisi had a true phobia of lepers. One day, while Francis was riding his horse, a leper appeared in the road, blocking his path. Filled with fear and a racing heart, Francis felt moved nevertheless to get off his horse and approach the leper. Standing before him, Francis kissed the leper. With this, his fear left him completely and he described a beatific experience, seeing the face of the "Beloved" in his mind. From that moment forward, he not only lost his fear of lepers but often went with his fellow monks to the leper colonies, washing the lepers, feeding them, and otherwise tending to their needs.

Earlier, I mentioned the story of Angela, a client who had dissociative identity disorder (formerly known as multiple personality disorder). In her first session, she declared over and over, "I want to be a success story." This vision motivated her through the extraordinary challenges of her recovery. After a triumphant conclusion, with all personalities fully integrated, she was excited to live a new life, free of the fears that had plagued her so. She found a new vision, asking if we could write her story together "so others could have hope." And so we did (see Fisher & Pressman, 2008). In addition, she had always been a spiritual person. One of her "alters" had even presented as a voice of great wisdom and guidance. Now integrated, this wisdom became part of her. Eventually she found the next part of her vision, feeling called to offer spiritual counseling sessions. I know many people who have benefited greatly from these sessions.

Another client, Steve, was only twenty-five when I met him. He came in for help with depression. Struggling with a loss of purpose, he felt himself being sucked into the "rat race," losing the aliveness of his youth. During our time together, I learned of his great passion for writing hip-hop lyrics. But in his depression, he felt no one would be interested in what he had to say. As we worked through his chief defense (shutting down to avoid the pain of disappointed expectations), he began, cautiously at first, showing me some of his lyrics. They were truly exceptional and I told him so. I also pointed out that they spoke directly to questions of deep purpose, the one thing he was struggling so hard with. This was the connector for him. He realized that if he were to revive his enthusiasm for life again, he was going to have to risk disappointment and share his lyrics with others. We then performed a session of the Witness, focusing on this fear. At the end of the exercise, he announced confidently, "If someone rejects me, I'll keep trying until someone else doesn't." He began calling local bands to perform his work and started looking for an agent. At our last session he stated, "I just have to do this, no matter how long it takes, no matter how many times I get rejected." Already fulfilled by virtue of being in action, Steve showed no more traces of his depression.

As we have said, it is natural to want to share what we have learned from our journeys. The fulfillment we have found from releasing the core fear and chief defense can inspire a vision of helping others do the same. The stories presented here of Martin Luther King Jr. and Mahatma Gandhi provide two important examples. Their visions of relieving oppression grew out of knowing what it was like to be oppressed. Harriet Tubman drew her tremendous strength, helping so many slaves to freedom, from her own painful experience of slavery. Emmeline Pankhurst was denied the educational opportunities given to her brothers because she was a girl. She grew up to lead the women's suffrage movement. And once Saint Francis of Assisi and Thoreau made their respective vows of poverty, they wanted to share their message of freedom from material possessions.

We'll end this section with one more story from Gandhi's life. Having realized the vision of a free India, Muslims and Hindus began fighting over who would run the newly independent country. The fighting became violent. Of course, Gandhi's vision was built on the principle of nonviolence and he focused his efforts on a peaceful resolution to the conflict. After trying all other measures, he announced that he would undertake a fast, vowing not to break it unless he could be assured the fighting had ceased. He was so fused with his vision that it had become his identity. He felt he could not live if it could not live.

This commitment to vision was powerful enough to change the minds of millions of people. Their love for Gandhi and what he represented was such that when he was close to death, they did, in fact, end the hostilities. Just at the point when Gandhi was being told the fighting had stopped, a Muslim man rushed into the room where he was lying. The man threw a bit of food at Gandhi demanding he eat. He said he did not want Gandhi's death on his hands. He was obviously torn between his love for the Mahatma and his hatred for the Hindus. Gandhi asked why he was so angry at the Hindus, and the man stated that his young son had been killed by a Hindu man. Gandhi offered a solution to his pain, a remarkable suggestion that came straight from his vision. He instructed the man to find a young boy about the same age as his son, someone whose parents had been killed in the violence, and to raise this boy as his own. But, Gandhi said, the man must make sure he was a Hindu boy, and that he be raised as a Hindu.

GUIDELINES FOR SHAPING ONE'S VISION

How to Make Decisions

As we enact our vision, we will continuously confront opportunities to make decisions from either fear or fulfillment. We want to keep our path true. There is a fail-safe rule for this: Whenever we have a decision to make, our job is to be perfectly willing to choose among the options involved and being perfectly willing *not* to choose any of them as well. This frees us from any secret investment, based on fear, in making one decision over another. When we are completely willing to take any course of action (including no action at all), there is no possibility that fear will distort our awareness and we will be free to see which decision best serves. This is the truth revealed by our third postulate.

So we make our commitments to action but at the same time are ready to change our course as necessary. Having resolved the five core fears, we know our decisions are free of the need to "make sure" things turn out the way we want. We realize we don't have that control anyway. This means we are willing to make a decision and abandon it at any moment. And therefore we are completely free to do what we do with pure intentions: we act out of love with no ulterior motive; we are authentic in who we are when making decisions; we create meaning out of a drive for fulfillment and not an existential despair; and we express what needs to be expressed with a high sense of purpose, no fear holding us back. This is how we make our life a work of art. In the same way that facing fear shows the truth hidden behind our defenses, this technique reveals what choice actually serves a situation best rather than what our defensive strategies would have us believe. This can save us from enormous trouble when making decisions, big and small. As we know, our life has been dramatically affected by decisions made unconsciously, directed by unresolved defenses.

We also use this principle to ride the line between avoiding our fears and trying too hard to face them. Asking ourselves, "Am I totally willing to take this action and totally willing not to?" we steer clear of both defenses. For example, if confronted with a decision to take some action now or wait until a later time, we become equally willing to do both. This resolves any potential problem with impatience on the one hand and avoidance on the other, being too eager or not eager enough. The same is true for any defense. If we are feeling "lazy," we must become just as willing to move as we are to sit. Someone with OCD is already willing to work (too) hard to finish a task but must become equally prepared to leave it unfinished. A defense of intellectualization must be balanced with a willingness to act on intuition, without figuring anything out first. A Zen master I knew, when he first became a monk, simply despised cocktail parties. Of course, his teacher's first direction was to send him to cocktail parties.

This principle for making decisions takes care of another potential problem as well. People with a fear of making a wrong decision can become paralyzed, never making any decision. The willingness to make a wrong decision just as much as a right one frees us to see where the truth lies. It shows that our fear of making a wrong decision is—no surprise—built on an illusion. It's not the particular decision we make but the act of making the decision that puts us in the game. This is what starts the flow. If we don't like the outcome of our decision, we use the information to redirect our course. But if we wait until we can make a "perfect" decision, we never get started. In fact, this is an important truth. There is no perfect decision . . . we discover our fulfillment only by virtue of being free from fear. It may look totally different than expected, and it will evolve and transform as we go. But when we are just as willing to follow one path as we are another, we let go of attachments to a particular view and open to a fulfillment that is always available.

Taoism describes three basic principles for "living in the Tao" (in the flow of things): naturalness, spontaneity, and ease (Flaws & Wolfe, 1985). The practice of being willing to face the fear of any option promotes all three of these. This technique is how we achieve balance. Of course it is another way of "doing the opposite." It is also an excellent addition to the practice of relaxing the tension of resistance. If we try too hard to let go of resistance, we want to become just as willing not to let it go. Only this will bring the relaxation we seek.

Living in the Moment

The willingness to make our plans and simultaneously relinquish them reminds us that fulfillment is lived in the moment. We let go of the orientation to past and future that marks our transit through time, an orientation born of fear. But, we may ask, isn't Vision Questing about working to create a better future? And doesn't that require an awareness of what was wrong in the past? These questions confuse vision as a path for fulfillment with fear as the strategy for securing that path. When we release all fear we naturally fall into the present moment. We no longer fear the future and have no thought of protecting it with our defenses. We simply enjoy our fulfillment here and now. But while we still participate in the projections of the world, we need a vision to unfold this experience of fulfillment in time and space. A *Course in Miracles* (Foundation for Inner Peace, 1975) describes it like a carpet: when we are fulfilled, the carpet is rolled up in the present moment. When we jump to thoughts of past and future, the carpet rolls out and the path to fulfillment seems to take time. While others live in the dream of past and future and we ourselves still forget, our vision points the way back to the present moment. So yes, we have work to do and a vision to engage, but we do so without defense. Completely willing to move in one direction or another and completely willing not to move at all, we simply notice the truth of the moment and follow its lead. This is the prescription for finding fulfillment in the moment.

The End of the Separate Self

There's no avoiding it: relationships are central to fulfillment and will almost certainly have a place in our vision. Without a fear of being alone, we are free to pursue connection. And again, because of our *inter*connection, it is natural to want to share our freedom with others . . . to help. Virtually every spiritual philosophy promotes the importance of service, compassion, and love. In the Tao Te Ching, Lao Tzu says, "To give without seeking reward / To help without thinking it is virtuous—therein lies the great virtue" (2003). St. Paul tells us, "And now these three remain: faith, hope, and love. But the greatest of these is love." The Bhakti yogi follows a path of devotion; the Sikh commits to selfless service; and the Zoroastrian commits to "good thoughts, good words, and good deeds." Fulfillment always includes an impulse to help, connect, or share with others. It is a simple expression of Oneness, the disappearance of our separate interests. A few stanzas later in the same verse, Lao Tzu says, "The highest virtue is to act without a sense of self / The highest kindness is to give without condition / The highest justice is to see without preference" (2003). We cannot be fulfilled while focusing on our private concerns. To do so is to cut ourselves off from the whole, to disavow the totality of ourselves, and to experience loss and deprivation as a result.

There is a story in the Hebraic tradition that describes a scene in hell. Everyone is seated around a banquet table covered with the most exquisite foods and as much as they could want. The problem is that each person has a spoon that is longer than their arm so no one is able to get anything into their mouth. In heaven we see the same scene, only here, everyone is feeding each other. Our greatest fulfillment is in the exchange of this kind of mutuality, the spontaneous flow of caring for each other as for oneself. Of course it is important to distinguish between authentic giving and a defense of needing to look like a "good person." We are not talking about a fear of looking ungenerous. It can be risky to think of oneself as a "helper"; doing so usually hides a defense of bolstering one's identity, bargaining for love and appreciation. As Lilla Watson, the aboriginal activist put it, "If you have come to help me, you are wasting your time. But if you have come because your liberation is tied up with mine, then let us work together." This is the virtue Lao Tzu spoke of, a spontaneous, effortless, and natural giving. It comes from a recognition that, as per the principle of Oneness, another's good is our own and vice versa.

And it is important as well to be aware of any hidden fear of receiving from another. Kahlil Gibran (1923) talks about "the charity of receiving"—that we actually give a kindness to another by receiving their gift. Elsewhere he says we should "give as in yonder valley the myrtle breathes its fragrance into space," that we should be as "the trees in [our] orchard . . . [that] give that they may live, for to withhold is to perish," concluding, "For in truth it is life that gives unto life—while you, who deem yourself a giver, are but a witness."

So as we pursue our vision, we want to look out for any defenses that would serve our own interests at the expense of the whole. Fear and defense all spring from an exclusive focus on "me" and "mine," an endless attempt to secure what the separated self wants. We seek a higher vision that fills us with meaning, identity, love, and purpose . . . a vision beyond the individual self and its preoccupation with survival. We want to become part of the whole and lose the anxiety that comes from too much thought about "self." When we stop using fear to protect our fulfillment, when we fully resolve all five core fears, we lose this sense of a separate self. There is no longer a need to control and arrange circumstances according to our private wishes. There is simply the natural "movement toward wholeness" (Grof, 1988), joining with others in a spontaneous and effortless fulfillment. Our job is only to get out of the way.

Creating the Field of Enlightenment

There is a phenomenon I call "creating the field of enlightenment." This field is the result when people build a new expectation of the possible. When enough people hold such an expectation, they project a reality that is picked up by others, reinforcing the field. It used to be thought that no one could run a four-minute mile. But when Roger Bannister did it, suddenly others could as well. Today it is common-place. We are seeing the same phenomenon in figure skating. Only a few years ago the idea of a quadruple jump was inconceivable. Now if the senior-level men don't have several in their program, they don't stand a chance of winning. Similarly, I remember participating in a firewalking workshop. I wondered in advance what the secret would be that would make it possible to defy the laws of physics. But the process, as it turned out, was simply a matter of generating the belief that walk-ing on hot coals was possible. From that point, all that was required was to see the facilitator walk across the coals. Suddenly, we all knew we could do it too. "Creating the field of enlightenment" is the hundredth monkey phenomenon we spoke of earlier. It is Sheldrake's morphoge-netic fields, Jung's collective unconscious, and Theosophy's "thought forms." We choose a projection coordinated with our vision and invite others to choose it too. The more people join in, the more we build a consensual reality. When it is combined with action, we lock in this reality, demonstrating that it is so by living it in mind, body, and spirit.

So to dramatically enhance your practice of Vision Questing, seek out your tribe. Find or create a community of people dedicated to living their vision. Build the expectation that you can achieve a *complete* reso-lution of the core fears, living without defensiveness and following your fulfillment. Create a field of enlightenment together! Make your public commitments and support each other in working through anything that might interfere with keeping them. Let it be a group that understands fulfillment is found in the moment and that the act of engaging with vision is the key to that fulfillment. Let your commitment be that each one finds the love, meaning, purpose, identity, and freedom from the fear of death that such fulfillment brings. As more and more people join together in this commitment, the field of enlightenment grows, creating an ever-more-powerful sphere of influence, tipping the balance of ex-pectation for what is possible in our world.

NOTES

1. Remember, even though everyone has a single core fear, predominant over the rest, we all have some of each of the five core fears. Yes, resolving one's predominant core fear will spontaneously resolve the other four core fears that derive from it. But it is helpful to talk about resolving all five core fears as a way to ensure the complete resolution of our predominant core fear.

2. This can include a spiritual fulfillment that for some means death is not the end.

3. A famous Buddhist saying speaks to this possibility: "What did you do before Enlightenment?" "Chopped wood, carried water." "And what did you do after Enlightenment?" "Chopped wood, carried water."

4. If we don't feel this impulse, we want to look for a wish we may be harboring (based on fear) to defend our "secret," keeping it to ourselves for personal gain.

5. Still there will be times when we need to start our approach with something other than purpose. Someone facing a terminal illness, for example, may want to focus on resolving their fear of death (imagine the sense of meaning and the shift in identity that can come when one truly loses the fear of death!) while someone who has resolved a core fear of abandonment or loss of meaning or identity may need to start on a path to fulfilling those needs.

6. Even if the action is to rest, as described above.

7. This is not an invitation to repress any fears that may remain. This point is critical. We don't want to "try too hard" to fill ourselves up with a sense of purpose, or pretend we are "above it all." Our vision must be genuinely compelling, spontaneously drawing our attention to it and away from fear. We can test ourselves in this by bringing to mind what we were afraid of, even trying to exaggerate the sense of danger. If our transformation is real, we will simply see through such attempts, recognizing that fear is only *ever* a projection. An example of an incomplete transformation is the high we can experience at a motivational program. We can truly get in touch with the possibility of fulfillment, but any fears and defenses that have not been worked through will quickly reassert themselves, allowing no real or lasting change.

8. Of course all of these questions are deeply related, as are the core fears they speak to. A fear of abandonment may inhibit the expression of our purpose. Without a fulfilling sense of purpose, we don't feel like our authentic selves. This can strip away the meaning of life, to which we may respond by distracting ourselves from the reality of death. And so on.

9. Here are some examples: "I can't act on my fulfillment because others will think poorly of me," "I can't act on my fulfillment because I have to take care of something else first," and "I can't act on my fulfillment because it's too

selfish" (and remember, our fulfillment positively impacts the whole even if we are not directly doing something for others).

10. If someone has a fear of what happens after death, it's still the same problem, imagining the afterlife will block our fulfillment, threatening us with one or more of the five core fears. Our exercises have exposed this interpretation as a distortion of fear, overlaying arbitrary ideas we have chosen on top of the objective situation. How, for example, can hellfire burn if we have no body? Even if we did have a body, the only thing we might be afraid of is its death . . . something we have already "lived through." (Remember too, our fear of pain is really the fear that such pain might lead to death, as in our example of the bear in chapter 2. And as with the Alchemist or the Witness, we would completely adapt to such pain in the course of time and the infinity of space.)

11. This is a bit of a ruse, a device for actualizing our plans. Of course we don't know when we will die, so the exercise requires making our best guess. If we should die before the completion of our vision, it's really not a problem for the following reasons. The vision is not simply an end goal. It is more fundamentally about fulfillment in each moment. Being engaged in our vision, working toward its final realization, gives us that fulfillment from the very start. Furthermore, because of our interconnection with others, our fulfillment in the moment fosters theirs, as we have discussed. And this was the goal of our vision after all—to find our fulfillment and help others do so as well. So the act of embarking on a Vision Quest brings a fulfillment in the moment that, in a real sense, constitutes the fulfillment of the vision as a whole. Finally, as we will discover in the next section, when we make public commitments, others can take up the cause of our vision and see it to fruition if we are not able to.

12. And if we have created a timeline, we can lock ourselves in further by announcing the date by which we intend to complete those plans.

13. King modeled much of his work on Gandhi's principle of nonviolent noncooperation, while Gandhi in turn modeled his own thinking on Thoreau's ideas of civil disobedience.

EPILOGUE

The three postulates have been our guide on this journey. They have given us the goal of an absolute truth, the understanding that fear is the obstacle to this truth, and the prescription to deconstruct anxiety for the return to truth. Until we recognize that fear is the great illusionist, we will continue to engage in a war with reality, believing it is necessary to secure our fulfillment. And the strategy will backfire each time.

But we are only at war with a projection, a distortion of reality overlaid upon the original nature of things. With this revelation, we understand the whole of human suffering, the intricacies of unconscious conflict, and the complexities of our relationships in one great stroke. It is the dance of fear and defense, the hapless and futile attempt to find fulfillment by achieving control. Now we know we have a choice. We have deconstructed anxiety and seen that fear is a deceit. The projection has lost its ability to captivate us. As we bow out of the dance, the mirage of fear disperses. We set our sights on a new vision, projecting a world that reflects the fulfillment of Oneness.

The fear-defense dynamic makes the world go 'round. Any group, from a couple to a family to the whole of humanity, has its own "personality." It therefore has its own core fear and chief defense. The personality of the group projects its fear onto the whole just as individual personalities do. The group sees what it wants to see and believes what it wants to believe. It imposes these beliefs upon "what is" and upon other groups as well in the endless attempt at control. This is the driving force behind all of human history, evolution, economics, politics . . . any aspect of human life. It is what crusades and holy wars are made of. It is what governmental regulation and social conditioning are built upon. And these structures will continue to create suffering until we take our stand against fear. Imagine how marriages, families, and other relationships would be transformed if the people involved worked through their own anxieties. Imagine how social or political factionism would change with the recognition that our goals can never be met at the expense of others. Imagine how world leaders would negotiate differently, free from the defensive need to control and manipulate.

The only way to make real change, whether on an individual or global basis, is to resolve our fear. When we work at the level of the core fear, perception transforms at the source and we find dramatically new and sweeping solutions to our problems as a whole. We no longer get mired in an inexhaustible array of separate problems, addressing each one individually. We make change at the fundamental level from which all such problems spring forth. And if we don't work at that level, resolving one problem simply makes room for another to take its place; the root has been left intact and will creep up in other ways. Real change can only happen at the level of the core fear and chief defense because that is where our struggles begin.

The challenge of the postulates is that we must take responsibility for any fear distorting our perception. Otherwise, we will aggress on reality and each other in an attempt to gain control over imaginary projections. One person attempts to control another and triggers a defensive response. Both become caught in a mutual projection of anxiety and suffering. The same is true for societies and nations. Fear begets fear. Defense evokes counter-defense. Personally and collectively, our first task in any situation is to work through our fear *before* acting upon it with our defenses. When we do, we let go of the hopeless effort to bend circumstances to our will. We take our place in the natural flow of things, surrendering a control we never really had. Instead of seeing what we wish to see, we open to reality-as-it-is. Only then can we make a true appraisal of a situation. And such an appraisal will inevitably point us to new solutions for how best to serve the interests of all involved.

Each time we take responsibility for our own fear, we dissolve a little bit more of the shared projection that causes our suffering. Our work on ourselves cannot help but make reverberations in the whole. When we demonstrate the possibility of a new projection, one built on freedom and fulfillment, others see the potential for themselves and join us in it. And when enough of us contribute to this collective vision, it gathers a momentum that changes the balance of power. Fear diminishes and fulfillment increases in direct proportion, spreading its mantle over wider and wider circles. Individuals, groups, societies, and nations surrender their separate interests, no longer hypnotized by an obsession with control. The blinders of self-preoccupation begin to fall away as we recognize our interdependence. A natural spirit of cooperation emerges, each contributing their energies, talents, and resources to a common good. And the dream of separation gives way at last to the living experience of Oneness and fulfillment. This is how we create real change. This is how we build a world that works.

REFERENCES

Aly, A., & Green, L. (2010). Fear, anxiety and the state of terror. *Studies in Conflict & Terrorism*, 33(3), 268–81.

American Psychiatric Association. (2013). *Diagnostic and Statistical Manual of Mental Disorders* (5th ed.: DSM-5). Washington, DC: author.

Bach, R. (2001). *Illusions: The Adventures of a Reluctant Messiah*. Eastbourne, UK: Gardners Books.

Barasch, M., & Hirshberg, C. (1995). *Remarkable Recovery: What Extraordinary Healings Tell Us About Getting Well and Staying Well*. New York: Riverhead.

Becker, E. (1976). *The Denial of Death*. London: Macmillan.

Blake, W. (1977). *Songs of Innocence and Experience: Shewing the Two Contrary States of the Human Soul*. Oxford: Oxford University Press.

Brach, T. (2004). *Radical Acceptance: Embracing Your Life with the Heart of a Buddha*. New York: Bantam Books.

Burns, D. (1999). *Feeling Good: The New Mood Therapy*. New York: Harper.

———. (2007). *When Panic Attacks: The New, Drug-Free Anxiety Therapy That Can Change Your Life*. New York: Harmony Books.

Campbell, J. (1991). *The Power of Myth*. New York: Anchor Books.

Camus, A. (1993). *The Stranger*. New York: Knopf.

Capra, F. (1983). *The Tao of Physics*. Boulder, CO: Shambhala.

Castaneda, C. (1985). *The Teachings of Don Juan: A Yaqui Way of Knowledge*. New York: Washington Square Press.

———. (1991). *Journey to Ixtlan: The Lessons of Don Juan*. New York: Washington Square Press.

Chodron, P. (2002). *When Things Fall Apart*. Boulder, CO: Shambhala.

———. (2012). *Taking the Leap: Freeing Ourselves from Old Habits and Fears*. Boulder, CO: Shambhala.

Chopra, D. (2005). *The Book of Secrets: Unlocking the Hidden Dimensions of Your Life*. New York: Harmony Books.

———. (2015). *Quantum Healing: Exploring the Frontiers of Mind/Body Medicine*. New York: Bantam Books.

Clark, T. (2011). It's not the job market. *Slate Magazine*. https://slate.com/culture/2011/01/american-anxiety-the-three-real-reasons-why-we-are-more-stressed-than-ever-before.html.

Clinton, C. (2005). *Harriet Tubman: The Road to Freedom*. New York: Back Bay Books.

Coan, J., Schaefer, H., & Davidson, R. (2006). Lending a hand: Social regulation of the neural response to threat. *Psychological Science*, 17(12), 1032–39.

Crouch, B. (2018). *Dark Matter: A Novel*. New York: Broadway Books.

Csikszentmihalyi, M. (2008). *Flow: The Psychology of Optimal Experience*. New York: Harper Perennial.

Desbordes, L. T., Negi, T. W. W., Pace, B. A., Wallace, C. L., Raison, C. L., & Schwartz, E. L. (2012). Effects of mindful-attention and compassion meditation training on amygdala response to emotional stimuli in an ordinary, non-meditative state. *Frontiers in Human Neuroscience*, 6, 1–15. doi:10.3389/fnhum.2012.00292.

Dias, B., Banerjee, S., Goodman, J., & Ressler, K. (2013). Towards new approaches to disorders of fear and anxiety. *Current Opinion in Neurobiology*, 23, 346–52.

Dickinson, E. (2005). *The Poems of Emily Dickinson*. Edited by R. W. Franklin. Cambridge, MA: Belknap Press.

Dozois, D. J., Frewen, P. A., & Covin, R. (2006). Cognitive theories. In *Comprehensive Handbook of Personality and Psychopathology*. Edited by J. C. Thomas, D. L. Segal, & M. Hersen, 173–91. Hoboken, NJ: John Wiley & Sons.

Eck, D. (1998). *Darsan: Seeing the Divine Image in India*. 3rd ed. New York: Columbia University Press.

Elkins, D., Hedstrom, L. J., Hughes, L. L., Leaf, J. A., & Saunders, C. (1988). Toward a humanistic-phenomenological spirituality: Definition, description, and measurement. *Journal of Humanistic Psychology*, 28, 5–18.

English, J. (1985). *Different Doorway: Adventures of a Caesarean Born*. Mt. Shasta, CA: Earth Heart.

Fisher, A., & Pressman, T. (2008). *The Bicycle Repair Shop: A True Story of Recovery from Multiple Personality Disorder, As Told by Patient and Therapist*. Raleigh, NC: Lulu Press.

Flaws, B., & Wolfe, H. L. (1985). *Prince Wen Hui's Cook: Chinese Dietary Therapy*. Taos, NM: Paradigm Publications.

Foa, E. (2001). *Stop Obsessing: How to Overcome your Obsessions and Compulsions*. New York: Bantam Books.

Foa, E. et al. (2012). *Exposure and Response (Ritual) Prevention for Obsessive-Compulsive Disorder*. Oxford: Oxford University Press.

Foundation for Inner Peace. *A Course in Miracles*. (1975). New York: author.

Frankl, V. (2006). *Man's Search for Meaning*. New York: Beacon Press.

Freud, S. (1913). *On Beginning the Treatment (Further Recommendations on the Technique of Psycho-analysis, I)*. In *Standard Edition of the Complete Psychological Works of Sigmund Freud*. Edited by J. Trachey, 12:123.

Gibran, K. (1923). *The Prophet*. New York: Alfred A. Knopf.

Goldin, P. R., & Gross, J. J. (2010). Effects of mindfulness-based stress reduction (MBSR) on emotion regulation in social anxiety disorder. *Emotion*, 10, 83–91.

Grof, S. (1980). *Beyond the Brain: Birth, Death and Transcendence in Psychotherapy*. New York: State University of New York Press.

———. (1988). *The Adventure of Self-Discovery: Dimensions of Consciousness and New Perspectives in Psychotherapy and Inner Exploration*. Albany: State University of New York Press.

———. (1996). *Realms of the Human Unconscious*. London: Souvenir Press.

———. (2012). *Healing Our Deepest Wounds: The Holotropic Paradigm Shift*. Pagosa Springs, CO: Stream of Experience Productions.

Grof, S., & Halifax, J. (1977). *The Human Encounter with Death*. New York: Dutton.

Grupe, D. W., & Nitschke, J. B. (2013). Uncertainty and anticipation in anxiety: An integrated neurobiological and psychological perspective. *Nature Reviews in Neuroscience*, 14, 488–501.

Hanson, R. (2009). *Buddha's Brain: The Practical Neuroscience of Happiness, Love and Wisdom*. Boulder, CO: New Harbinger Publications.

———. (2013). *Hardwiring Happiness: The New Brain Science of Contentment, Calm, and Confidence*. New York: Harmony Books.

Hecht, D. (2013). The neural basis of optimism and pessimism. *Experimental Neurobiology*, 22, 173–99.

Hofmann, S. G., & Smits, J. A. (2008). Cognitive-behavioral therapy for adult anxiety disorders: A meta-analysis of randomized placebo-controlled trials. *Journal of Clinical Psychiatry*, 69(4), 621–32.

Horney, K. (1991). *Neurosis and Human Growth: The Struggle Towards Self-Realization.* New York: W. W. Norton & Company. (Orig. pub. 1950.)

Houston, J. (1997). *The Possible Human.* New York: TarcherPerigee.

Hugo, V. (2012). *Les Misérables.* Blacksburg, VA: Wilder Publications.

Hyman, B., & Pedrick, C. (2001). *The OCD Workbook: Your Guide to Breaking Free from Obsessive-Compulsive Disorder.* Oakland, CA: New Harbinger Publications.

James, W. (1890). *The Principles of Psychology.* New York: Henry Holt.

———. (1982). *The Varieties of Religious Experience.* New York: Viking Penguin. (Orig. pub. 1902.)

Jerath, R., Barnes, V. A., Dillard-Wright, D., Jerath, S., & Hamilton, B. (2012). Dynamic change of awareness during meditation techniques: Neural and physiological correlates. *Frontiers in Human Science*, 6, 1–4.

Johnson, S. (2011). *Hold Me Tight: Your Guide to the Most Successful Approach to Building Loving Relationships.* London: Piatkus Books.

Jones, S., & Krippner, S. (2016). *The Shamanic Powers of Rolling Thunder.* Rochester, VT: Bear & Company.

Jung, C. G. (1981). *The Archetypes and the Collective Unconscious.* Edited by G. Adler & R. F. C. Hull. Princeton, NJ: Princeton University Press.

Kabat-Zinn, J. (2005). *Wherever You Go, There You Are.* New York: Hachette Books.

———. (2013). *Full Catastrophe Living: Using the Wisdom of Your Body and Mind to Face Stress, Pain and Illness.* New York: Bantam Books.

Karris, M., & Caldwell, B. E. (2015). Integrating emotionally focused therapy, self-compassion, and compassion-focused therapy to assist shame-prone couples who have experienced trauma. *Family Journal*, 23(4), 346–57.

Kellogg, J., Mac Rae, M., Bonny, H., & DiLeo, F. (1977). The use of the mandala in psychological evaluation and treatment. *American Journal of Art Therapy*, 16.

Keyes, K., Jr. (1984). *The Hundredth Monkey.* Harrisonburg, VA: Vision Books.

Kornfield, J. (1993). *A Path with Heart: A Guide Through the Perils and Promises of Spiritual Life.* New York: Bantam Books.

———. (2014). *A Lamp in the Darkness: Illuminating the Path Through Difficult Times.* Louisville, CO: Sounds True Publishing.

Krause, L. (2013). *A Universe from Nothing: Why There Is Something Rather Than Nothing.* New York: Atria Books.

Krippner, S. (1992). *Spiritual Dimensions of Healing.* Stratford, NH: Irvington Publishers.

Lao Tzu. (2003). *Tao Te Ching.* Translated by J. Star. New York: Tarcher.

Laszlo, E. (2016). *What Is Reality? The New Map of Cosmos and Consciousness.* New York: Select Books.

LeDoux, J. E. (1996). *The Emotional Brain: The Mysterious Underpinnings of Emotional Life.* New York: Simon & Schuster.

Levine, S. (1978). *A Gradual Awakening.* New York: Anchor Books.

Levine, S., & Levine, O. (1989). *Who Dies? An Investigation Into Conscious Living and Conscious Dying.* New York: Anchor Books.

Lowen, A. (1967). *The Betrayal of the Body.* New York: Harper & Row.

———. (1994). *Bioenergetics: The Revolutionary Therapy That Uses the Language of the Body to Heal the Problems of the Mind.* London: Penguin/Arkana.

Maslow, A. (2014). *Toward a Psychology of Being.* Plano, TX: Sublime Books.

Massumi, B. (2005). Fear (The spectrum said). *Positions*, 13(1), 31–48. https://doi.org/10.1215/10679847-13-1-31.

Nolen-Hoeksema, S. (2000). The role of rumination in depressive disorders and mixed anxiety/depressive symptoms. *Journal of Abnormal Psychology*, 109, 504–11.

Orsillo, S. M., Roemer, L., & Segal, Z. (2011). *The Mindful Way Through Anxiety: Break Free from Chronic Worry and Reclaim Your Life.* New York: Guilford Press.

Oschner, K. N., Ray, R. R., Hughes, B., McRae, K., Cooper, J. C., Weber, J., Gabrieli, J. D. E., & Gross, J. J. (2009). Bottom-up and top-down processes in emotion generation. *Association for Psychological Science*, 20, 1322–31.

Otto, M. W., & Hoffmann, S. G., eds. (2010). *Avoiding Treatment Failures in the Anxiety Disorders*. New York: Springer.

Park, C. L. (2010). Making sense of the meaning literature: An integrative review of meaning making and its effects on adjustment to stressful life events. *Psychological Bulletin*, 136, 257–301.

Pert, C. (1999). *The Science Behind Mind-Body Medicine*. New York: Simon & Schuster.

Peters, M. L., Flink, I. K., Boersma, K., & Linton, S. J. (2010). Manipulating optimism: Can imagining a best possible self be used to increase positive future expectancies? *Journal of Positive Psychology*, 5, 204–11.

Pittman, C. M., & Karle, E. M. (2015). *Rewire Your Anxious Brain: How to Use the Neuroscience of Fear to End Anxiety, Panic, and Worry*. Oakland, CA: New Harbinger Publications.

Plato. (1997). *Plato: The Complete Works*. Edited by J. Cooper & D. S. Hutchinson. Indianapolis, IN: Hackett Publishing.

Porter, G., & Norris, P. (1985). *Why Me? Harnessing the Healing Power of the Human Spirit*. New York: Stillpoint Publishing.

Pressman, M. (1999). *Enter the Supermind*. Pittsburgh, PA: CeShore Publishing.

———. (2011). *Living in the Supermind*. Scottsdale, AZ: Inkwell Books.

Pressman, T. (1988). In pursuit of the goal of science through a synthesis of phenomenology and lucid dreaming. *Lucidity Letter*, 5(1), 1–6.

———. (1989). In pursuit of the goal of science through a synthesis of systems theory and the Eastern mode of inquiry. *Proceedings of the International Society for the Systems Sciences*, 1, 279–95.

———. (1992). The therapeutic potential of non-ordinary states of consciousness as explored in the work of Stanislav Grof. *Journal of Humanistic Psychology*, 32(3), 8–24.

———. (1999). *Radical Joy: Awakening Your Potential for True Fulfillment*. New York: Kensington Books.

Rank, O. (1952). *The Trauma of Birth*. New York: Robert Brunner. (Orig. pub. 1923.)

———. (1958). *The Idea of the Holy: An Inquiry into the Non-Rational Factor in the Idea of the Divine and Its Relation to the Rational*. London: Oxford University Press. (Orig. pub. 1917.)

Reich, W. (1949). *Character Analysis*. New York: Farrar, Straus & Giroux.

Rodegast, P., & Stanton, J. (1987). *Emmanuel's Book: A Manual for Living Comfortably in the Cosmos*. New York: Bantam Books.

Rossi, E. L. (1986). Altered states of consciousness in everyday life: The ultradian rhythms. In *Handbook of States of Consciousness*. Edited by B. B. Wolman & M. Ullman, 97–132. New York: Van Nostrand Reinhold.

St. John of the Cross. (2003). *The Dark Night of the Soul*. Mineola, NY: Dover Publications.

Sartre, J. (1958). *No Exit*. New York: Vintage Books.

Satprem. (1981). *The Mind of the Cells*. New York: Institute for Evolutionary Research.

Schachter, S., & Singer, J. (1962). Cognitive, social, and physiological determinants of emotional state. *Psychological Review*, 69, 379–99. doi:10.1037/h0046234.

Segall, M. H., Campbell, D. T., & Herskovits, M. J. (1963). Cultural differences in the perception of geometric illusions. *Science*, 139(3556), 769–71.

Seligman, M. (2012). *Flourish: A Visionary New Understanding of Happiness and Well-Being*. New York: Atria Books.

Sharaf, M. (1994). *Fury on Earth: A Biography of Wilhelm Reich*. Boston, MA: DaCapo Press.

Sharot, T. (2011). The optimism bias. *Current Biology*, 21, R942.

Shaw, G. B. (2001). *Man and Superman*. London: Penguin Classics.

Sheldrake, R. (2009). *Morphic Resonance: The Nature of Formative Causation*. Rochester, NY: Park Street Press.

Siegel, D. (2007). *The Mindful Brain: Reflection and Attunement in the Cultivation of Well-Being.* New York: W. W. Norton & Company.

Solomon, S., & Greenberg, J. (2015). *The Worm at the Core: On the Role of Death in Life.* New York: Random House.

Teasdale, J., Segal, Z., Kabat-Zinn, J., & Williams, M. (2007). *The Mindful Way Through Depression.* New York: Guilford Press.

Thoreau, H. D. (1971). *Thoreau: Walden and Other Writings.* Edited by J. W. Krutch. New York: Bantam Books.

Upledger, J. (1983). *Craniosacral Therapy.* Seattle, WA: Eastland Press.

Walsh, R., & Shapiro, L. (2006). The meeting of meditative disciplines and Western psychology: A mutually enriching dialogue. *American Psychologist,* 61, 227–39.

Whitman, W. (1855). *Leaves of Grass.* Oxford: Oxford University Press.

Wilber, K. (1980). *The Atman Project.* Wheaton, IL: Theosophical Publishing House.

Wilkinson, P. O., & Goodyer, I. M. (2008). The effects of cognitive-behaviour therapy on mood-related ruminative response style in depressed adolescents. *Child and Adolescent Psychiatry and Mental Health,* 2, 3–13.

Williamson, M. (1996). *Return to Love: Reflections on the Principles of a Course in Miracles.* New York: Harper One.

———. (2017). *Tears to Triumph: Spiritual Healing for the Modern Plagues of Anxiety and Depression.* New York: Harper One.

Wilson, R. (2009). *Don't Panic: Taking Control of Anxiety Attacks.* 3rd ed. New York: Harper Perennial.

Wolitzky-Taylor, K. B., Horowitz, J. D., Power, M. B., & Telch, M. J. (2008). Psychological approaches in the treatment of specific phobias: A meta-analysis. *Clinical Psychology Review,* 28, 1021–37.

Wolpert, S. (2008). Study offers new insights into teenagers and anxiety disorders. *UCLA Newsroom.* http://newsroom.ucla.edu/releases/study-offers-new-insights-into-55905.

Wulff, D. (1991). *Psychology of Religion: Classic and Contemporary Views.* New York: John Wiley & Sons.

Young, S. (2016). *The Science of Enlightenment: How Meditation Works.* Boulder, CO: Sounds True Publishing.

Zeidan, F., Martucci, K. T., Kraft, R. A., McHaffie, J. G., & Coghill, R. C. (2013). Neural correlates of mindfulness meditation-related anxiety relief. *Social Cognitive and Affective Neuroscience,* 9(6). doi:10.1093/scan/nst041.

INDEX